Leadership in Nonprofit Organizations

*To the thousands of unsung heroes who
lead nonprofit organizations*

Leadership in Nonprofit Organizations

Barry Dym
Harry Hutson
WorkWise Research and Consulting

SAGE Publications
Thousand Oaks ▪ London ▪ New Delhi

For information:

Sage Publications, Inc.
2455 Teller Road
Thousand Oaks, California 91320
E-mail: order@sagepub.com

Sage Publications Ltd.
1 Oliver's Yard
55 City Road
London EC1Y 1SP
United Kingdom

Sage Publications India Pvt. Ltd.
B-42, Panchsheel Enclave
Post Box 4109
New Delhi 110 017 India

Printed in the United States of America

Library of Congress Cataloging-in-Publication Data

Dym, Barry, 1942-
Leadership in nonprofit organizations / Barry Dym, Harry Hutson.
    p. cm.
Includes bibliographical references and index.
ISBN 0-7619-2924-X (Paper) — ISBN 1-4129-1446-9 (Cloth)
  1. Nonprofit organizations-Management. 2. Leadership. I. Hutson, Harry. II. Title.
HD62.6.D96 2005
658.4′092—dc22   2004021887

This book is printed on acid-free paper.

05   06   07   08   09   10   9   8   7   6   5   4   3   2   1

Acquisitions Editor:	Al Bruckner
Editorial Assistant:	MaryAnn Vail
Production Editor:	Diane S. Foster
Copy Editor:	Jo Gates, Publication Services
Typesetter:	C&M Digitals (P) Ltd.
Proofreader:	Scott Oney
Indexer:	Molly Hall
Cover Designer:	Michelle Lee Kenny

Contents

Acknowledgments

O ur research consisted of two types of interview approaches. The first and most important involved interviews with leaders and those who surrounded them—board members, peers, and direct reports. This is the method used for "360-degree feedback," and it provides a much more comprehensive view than single interviews with leaders. However, we also conducted many individual interviews. Since both authors work in the field as executive coaches and organization development consultants, we also called upon our knowledge of the leaders we have worked with over months and years.

We would like to thank the many nonprofit—and some corporate—leaders who have generously shared their insights with us during the creation of this book. It goes without saying that, without them, there would be no book. They include Sarah Alvord, J. J. Bartlett, Suzin Bartley, Shani Bechofer, John Bell, Howard Blackman, Bill Bradford, Judy Brain, Pat Brandes, Lee Buckman, Andrew Bundy, Linda Butler, Jonathan Cannon, Caroline Cassin, Winn Churchill, Elaine Cohen, Herbert Cohen, Katherine D'Amato, Rick Daniels, Daniel Derman, Jerry Doherty, Faye Donahue, Deborah Dumaine, Caroline Edwards, Josh Elkin, Shulamith Elster, Michael Epstein, Neil Epstein, Karen Feller, Cheryl Finkel, Jossie Fossas, Naava Frank, Nancy Fuller, Abraham Fuks, Bink Garrison, William Gately, John Glenshaw, Amy Goot, Paul Grogan, Anne Harrington, Debbie Harris, Ed Harwitz, Bruce Hauptman, Bonnie Hausman, Lenny Hausman, Bea Mah Holland, Rob Hollister, Robert Hunter, Lindalyn Kakadeles, Peter Karoff, Marianne Kane, Jonathan Katz, Brian Kaye, Barbara Kohn, Bob Krim, Rene Landers, John Laupheimer, Mary Kay Leonard, Robert Lewis, Gerry Martinson, Judy McBride, Molly Mead, Brenda Miele, Jack Miller, Joseph O'Connell, Tom O'Donnell, Kathy O'Loughlin, Carolyn Oppenheim, Kathryn Plazak, David Portman, Bruce Powell, Majorie Radlo, Jack Radlo, Curt Rawley, Gail Reeh, Carman Rivera, Debbra Robbins, David Rockefeller, Mia Roberts, Serita Rogers, B. J. Rudman, Jessie Saacke, Lynn Schade, Jay Schechter, Alan Shapiro, Tina Scheinbein, Pamela Stall, Roz Stein, Dorethy Stoneman, Vincent Strully, Joseph Weil, James Wessler, Susan Weintraub, Nancy Young, and Rebecca Young.

Then there are colleagues and friends who lent us their experience, scholarship, and wisdom during the book's creation or over a number of years. Among them, we want to thank Suzin Bartley, Pat Brandes, Kenneth Dym, Al Fitz, Steve Jenks, David Kantor, Richard Lerner, Elaine Millam, Shiela Moore, Bruce Powell, Alan Shapiro, Michael Sonduck, Dorothy Stoneman, and David Treadway.

Thanks to Tamar Hausman and Josh Golin for their wonderful help with the research.

A special thanks to Richard Lerner for reviewing the book in both its early and late stages, offering both encouragement and astute criticism—and connecting us with Sage Publications in the first place.

Al Bruckner of Sage welcomed our book when it needed a home and guided it through the complications of editing and publishing.

The person with whom I, Barry Dym, most share life, love, joy, and ideas is Fran Jacobs—herself a wonderful leader at Tufts University—and I would like to thank her for lending both her ideas and her support for this book. Then there are my children, Jessica Dym Bartlett and Gabriel Dym, who have already become leaders in both their personal and professional lives. It warms and thrills a father's heart to observe the way they take responsibility and forge new directions for themselves and others.

And I, Harry Hutson, want to thank my wife, Sally, for her love—and her courage. Our children, Emily and Matthew, now in their twenties, are making the world better in their own ways. So must we all.

The contributions of the following reviewers are gratefully acknowledged:

Richard M. Lerner
Bergstrom Chair in Applied Developmental Science
Director, Institute for Applied Research in Youth Development
Tufts University

Patricia H. Deyton
Consultant to Nonprofit Leaders
Harvard University
Simmons School of Management

Mary Tschirhart
Senior Research Associate, Campbell Public Affairs Institute
Maxwell School of Citizenship and Public Affairs
Syracuse University

1

Introduction

This is a book about exemplary leadership, which, in any society, is a precious resource that must be identified, nurtured, and celebrated. Good leadership can be found in both corporate and nonprofit organizations, though its corporate forms are generally taken as our culture's ideal—widely researched, broadly revered, and, as we see it, routinely misapplied to nonprofit organizations.

We began our thinking and research with a simple concern: Nonprofit leaders rarely get their due. In classrooms, government funding agencies, and charitable foundations, in their own boardrooms, and throughout the vast literature on leadership, they are regularly required to lead like their corporate colleagues—or as the popular imagery about corporate leadership would require them to lead. The distinctness and complexities of their own worlds tend to be ignored. We intended to take up the mantle in their defense—to study them, to learn from them, and where deserved, to praise them.

Along the way, we discovered that our original intent had led us in unforeseen directions. We discovered a great variety among nonprofit leaders, as befits the great variety of challenges they face and circumstances in which they find themselves. It soon became clear that it made no more sense to try to identify or impose the finest, one-size-fits-all leadership style in the nonprofit world than it had in the corporate world. Rather the fit between leaders and their organizations seemed the key to effective leadership. Many different leaders and leadership styles were required for many different kinds of organizations. The difference between corporate and nonprofit leadership ceased to be our focus. Drawing a clear boundary around "nonprofit leadership" served as a launch point and not a destination.

As we unpacked and elaborated the idea of fit, we observed how effective organizations had aligned the character, skills, values, and personal objectives of leaders with the character, resources, culture, and objectives of their organizations, and how the qualities of leaders and their organizations were aligned

1

with the communities or markets they served. When organizations were aligned in this way, they hummed with productivity, collaboration, and satisfaction. So we came to see alignment as the fundamental task, the fundamental measure of effective leadership.

The Journey

The ideas in this book emerged gradually, through a circuitous and sometimes difficult journey. The journey itself has been instructive to us, and we want to introduce the book by inviting readers to join us. In our careers as organization development consultants (both of us) and psychotherapists (Barry Dym), we have worked with many leaders in both the corporate and nonprofit worlds. The leaders we have come to know vary enormously. Some are executive directors of large nonprofits or CEOs of major corporations; others head small grassroots or high-tech startup organizations. We have worked with family-owned businesses and public-private partnerships. Some of the leaders we know wear corporate attire and speak in crisp, crafted sentences honed at Ivy League colleges and business schools. Others speak in the tones and vernacular of ethnic or professional communities. Still others speak and act with the sense of noblesse oblige and the sonorous tones of feudal lords. Some, having founded their own organization, work with a passionate fury—almost unaware of their appearance and sometimes barely aware of the people around them. Others trust their minions to do the bulk of the work, and spend time with family or charitable causes, or keep their golf game in good repair. Leaders are short and tall, smart and not so smart. They are men and women. They are from black, white, Latino, Irish, Jewish, Chinese, Italian, and many other cultural backgrounds that help shape the ways they think and behave, the dreams, the fears, the ambitions, and the inhibitions that define their character and their actions.

Often this variety seemed a matter of fact—the way things are—but just as often the variety struck us as interesting, challenging, and the stuff of creative tensions. At the very least, the variety among leaders needs to be supported, affirmed, and utilized. We are a nation defined by our diversity, invigorated and ennobled by the waves of new and different people who come to coexist and contribute. As Americans, we dislike and mistrust efforts to ignore differences or to merge people into a single standard in which one type of person is said to be better than others. We appreciate the jazz of life—free-form within form.

In our consulting travels, on the other hand, we couldn't help but notice a certain homogenizing process with respect to leadership. More and more of the books we read insisted on a single best way to lead. Organizations followed suit, developing programs to identify and train young leaders in the "correct" approach. The archetypal leader they celebrated was something of a bold manager or an entrepreneur with a solid grounding in modern management techniques, as taught in MBA programs. Foundations, management consultants, and non-profit boards almost all seemed to accept this MBA-like prescription, and insisted that nonprofit leaders either fit themselves to the mold or make way for those who could.

This homogenizing process seemed to us an enormous waste. It left out many talented people and potential leaders. It squeezed other leaders into a mold that made use of only some of their talents, and often made them so uncomfortable—trying to be people they were not—that they were rarely at their best. And it replicated itself through leadership training programs in which people are measured against the right way to lead rather than encouraged to build outward from their innate character and strengths.

Like the multicultural/diversity consultants who emerged in force during the 1990s, we tried to communicate the importance of being inclusive, of nurturing a variety of leaders and leadership styles. In parallel with the diversity consultants, we generally received token responsiveness and programmatic rejection. Usually we did not speak as complete outsiders; we would already be working with senior executives in large corporations, and we had their ear. They would agree that there are many different ways to lead, that diversity in method and point of view could be creative, that it might also be ethical, and that it might even be good for business; but they did not let it influence how they selected, trained, promoted, or rewarded organizational leaders at the highest levels.

We were satisfied neither that we were making adequate headway on behalf of our clients nor that we had done our homework. We wanted to be able to point to other models of leadership that were both successful and deeply different. So we turned away from the corporate world to make our case.

Two consulting experiences spurred us on. One took place during a two-year consulting experience with a large urban newspaper in the Midwest. Call it the *Standard Tribune* (ST).[1] Recently purchased by a still larger and more prestigious newspaper, the ST was being pressured to modernize its operations. Like most newspapers, the ST had long been a family-owned, paternalistic organization, with virtual lifetime employment guarantees and a stable network of employees who were in place as much for who they knew as for how well they could do their job. It was not a contemporary, hard-driving meritocracy disciplined by market forces. During difficulties, for example, the publisher would simply contribute his own money to tide them over until good financial times returned.

To spearhead the ST's modernization, the parent company introduced a new publisher, one who had earned his spurs at the parent company as a disciple of Six Sigma improvement processes. He could take on a department or a companywide process and make it leaner, faster, and more efficient. He was a smart, determined, no-nonsense kind of guy who got things done. While he went through the motions of consulting others and talked a language of collaboration, he would make up his mind and hand out assignments to others whose job was to execute his orders. Having introduced a strategy to guide the ST's future, he was frustrated that departmental managers and other influential leaders were not implementing it with alacrity. So he decided it was time to clarify the nature of good leadership and achieve greater conformance to specifications.

Of course there was no question that leadership would need to be molded to the publisher's image. The organization was embarked on a long and arduous change process. But there were other effective leaders at ST, many of whom did not resemble the publisher at all. The chief operating officer, for example, tended to be a terrific individual problem solver and sole practitioner who had gathered around him a bevy of young people who could be deployed like SWAT teams to rescue or upgrade any department. The vice president for human resources was an extraordinarily personable woman, who had earned her spurs as an adviser to leaders and, because she was so trusted, as a source of information. She knew the pulse of the organization. She was not, at heart, a manager, but she was immensely valuable for the perspective and advice she lent to situations. The senior vice president for finance was probably the most effective manager, who worked almost entirely through her trusted senior team. She empowered others and facilitated their efforts by providing resources and clearing away obstacles. Perhaps more tellingly, the newspaper had lost several opportunities to integrate internet-related businesses—once due to the absence of an internet-style leader; another time, due to the absence of entrepreneurial leaders able to build a new initiative from scratch.

The publisher was blind to the idea of building on each of his executives' strengths and identifying others with strengths that might be particularly relevant to the fast-changing world of media and communications. Of equal importance, he was shy and uncomfortable in groups, and he did not know how to build or to trust a leadership team composed of his senior people, a team in which each person's strengths and limitations were optimized by the whole. Instead, he wanted each person to have the "right" skills. So he called for a series of executive meetings to define an ST model of leadership and instructed the Human Resources Department to hire only people who fit the model.

Barry was on the team charged with designing the process, and he argued for a multitude of ST leadership models with the emphasis on their learning to work together in a collaborative and complementary manner. He described the different skills brought by different leaders and the missed opportunities due to a lack of entrepreneurial leadership. And he specifically noted that the publisher's proposed model would probably either exclude three of his most valued senior managers or require them to turn themselves into pretzels, trying to succeed in styles that did not suit either their character or the relationship they had built with their own staffs. And he lost the argument.

While this kind of replication of self—what works for me should work for everyone, everywhere—is familiar and understandable, it does not leverage organizational resources. If, for example, the publisher had had the courage to surround himself with different kinds of leaders, with people who complemented rather than mimicked his set of skills and his style, then he would have increased the executive capability of his organization.

The idea that there is one kind or a best kind of leadership, so prevalent in the popular literature,[2] in which there exist formulas for leadership success, is offensive to us on a number of levels. First, our experience tells us that it does not make sense. We have led, worked in, and consulted to innumerable organizations, in which many types of leaders worked effectively. Second, as a cultural norm, a single leadership ideal is reminiscent of the melting pot idea, the notion that many diverse cultures that make up our country would eventually merge into a single, American culture. What the purveyors of this idea meant is that we would all become White Anglo-Saxon Protestants, and that non-WASP culture would eventually fade away or be relegated to ethnic neighborhoods and rural backwaters. The melting pot ideal is, at heart, a nativist ideology, one that favors culturally dominant groups and dismisses the contributions of minority groups. Third, the belief in one correct leadership style is personally offensive to us because it marginalizes many of the people we find most compelling, talented, and effective.

In another situation, this time a nonprofit, we observed this homogenizing impulse close up. The organization had been funded largely by a grant from a foundation, which, in turn, was the instrument of a wildly successful businessman. He and his program officers tried to convert the very experienced and talented nonprofit leaders into corporate managers. They did so both explicitly and implicitly, by demanding a kind of extensive strategic planning and program assessment that required the leaders to behave like managers of large-scale corporations. The leaders were dependent on the foundation and so turned themselves inside-out trying to behave in ways that were unnatural to them. Much that was best about them—the ways they inspired staff, taught, brought out energy and ideas in staff, and reached out to potential clients—grew dull and ineffectual as they attended to the program officers.

There is nothing dramatically unique about this foundation-nonprofit relationship. Foundations, boards of directors composed of wealthy donors from the professional and corporate worlds, and government agencies routinely tone down and systematize nonprofit leaders, trying to squeeze them into the archetypal leadership style. This process has a parallel in the corporate world, in which venture capitalists and their boards generally assume they will have to replace the early-stage entrepreneurs before the next stages of financing. Their belief is that these passionate entrepreneurs are useful in the very beginning for their ideas and frantic energy but have to be replaced by effective managers who know how to put in systems—the infrastructure that sustains—and people capable of scaling up the organization. Often enough, the baby goes out with the bathwater. Instead of building on the imagination and passion of the founder by complementing her with good managers, they eject her and weaken the organization's founding spirit, mission, and momentum.

These two experiences were not isolated. They reflected what we were seeing in corporations, in nonprofit organizations, and in the books and articles we were reading.

We began our research with a review of the literature, imagining that this would yield sufficient material to write a few papers portraying the distinctive qualities of nonprofit leaders. But the literature on nonprofit leadership, while growing (see the journal *Nonprofit Management and Leadership*), is still pretty thin. Generally, it follows the corporate leadership literature in being primarily prescriptive, not descriptive. It tells more about how to lead and much less about how leaders actually go about their business. It seemed to us that prescription before description is putting the cart before the horse.

Interviews with nonprofit leaders proved instructive in explaining why this is so. Several confidently proclaimed that corporate and nonprofit leadership were the same. Nonprofits had to be profitable, as well, they claimed. What did this mean? we asked. There is no profit in nonprofits. Did they mean that nonprofits had to be efficient, well organized, accountable to their stakeholders, fiscally responsible, and, at times, competitive? Yes, they said. This reasoning makes good sense, but not the wholesale importation of corporate, free-market language and concepts—the ascendant vocabulary in our culture. After hearing this language so often from board members and funding sources, nonprofit leaders were speaking it. Some had lost their distinctive vocabularies of mission, ethics, community, advocacy, and hope.

The general search for insight into nonprofit literature led us to an important early realization: The majority of people working in nonprofits, both as employees and volunteers, are women.[3] While there is little in the way of a distinctive literature on how this preponderance of women helped to shape nonprofit leadership, there is a burgeoning literature on women's leadership in general. The research and writing about women is essentially divided into two camps: the popular writers, journalists, consultants, and feminists, who see women's leadership style as distinctive (Helgesen, 1995; Blumen-Lipman, 1996; Gilligan, 1982); and social scientists, who do not (Eagly, Karau, & Makhijani, 1995). Authors in both camps are almost exclusively women.

This schism makes intuitive sense. Researchers argue that when placed in the same circumstances, men and women operated in similar ways. When large organizations have prescribed certain modes of behavior, women who rise will have mastered those behaviors. In fact, women who rose in male-dominated organizations—the vast majority of corporations and a substantial proportion of the large nonprofits—behaved in ways associated with men: hierarchical, competitive, and the like. Those who built their own organization or who rose in women-dominated organizations, however, fit the descriptions of the popular writers. They were more democratic and less hierarchical, more nurturing to younger employees, more collaborative, and the like. Moreover, there is a generational difference. Younger women, whose way was paved by feminists in their mothers' generation, tended to behave more like men. Older women tended to build leadership styles based on older cultural norms, working around formal hierarchies and making extensive use of networks.

In the end, then, the literature on women's leadership confirmed a basic premise: that leadership varies according to the needs, norms, and objectives of the organizational and community culture in which it arises. What was disappointing, though, was that both camps were at such pains to compare women with men that they tended to ignore the rich diversity of leadership among women.

Here and there in this literature were references to minority women. Although writings about them are scarce, it is immediately clear that they developed styles to fit their circumstances. African American women who participated in the Civil Rights struggles of the sixties and seventies, for example, were not yet permitted to assume leadership positions in mainline, multiracial institutions (Elazer, 1995; Woocher, 1991). Lacking organizational position, they made things happen through informal networks and developed leadership styles analogous to the way they organized for church activities.

At the same time that we were looking into the research on women's leadership, Barry was consulting to a Jewish nonprofit organization dedicated to launching new day schools. Leadership was a key area of inquiry: the grassroots leaders who launched the schools, the professionals who took over the boards after these entrepreneurial beginnings, and the professional educators who ran the schools. Since these schools were launched to preserve Jewish tradition (Dym, 2003), the question arose, is there a distinctly Jewish way to lead?

Leadership in the Jewish community, for example, almost always has its eyes on both local needs and those of the world community (Elazer, 1995; Woocher, 1991).[4] And Jews have been a peripatetic group, moving from land to land to escape oppression and to find the freedom to practice their religion in their own way. Because of this nomadic tradition, Jewish nonprofit leaders, from community-based organizations to religious schools, see themselves as serving a dual function: running their organizations and providing for their people, in essence, a government in exile. Here, then, is another illustration of variety and the importance of context.

At this point, we were primarily interested in identifying the variety of effective leaders and arguing that excluding many of them was a waste of an extremely valuable resource as well as a culturally insensitive and ethically dubious practice. This celebration of diversity could be a valuable contribution to the leadership literature. It would fit well into many of the current conversations, particularly those about multiculturalism. Any help we might offer in broadening the idea of good leadership, which, in turn, might increase the dignity and strengthen the voice of less powerful communities, would be worth the effort.

But we grew wary about celebrating leadership diversity either for its own sake or just to strengthen the idea of multiculturalism, which many people dismiss either indirectly through tepid support or directly through an expressed distaste for political correctness. The fate of multiculturalism in American organizations that are led by mainstream stakeholders is often sad. We see this in diversity workshops that seem compelling at the time but are rarely followed up with structural or programmatic change. However, it is also true that multiculturalism misconceived as valuing differences for their own sake can turn into a dogma of its own.

So in asking ourselves how to conceive of and affirm diversity in a way that is oriented to both the coherence and quality of organizations, we were led to the notion of "fit." Simply put, fit means placing the right person in the right place at the right time. Thought of this way, good leadership requires different people for different ends in different circumstances and at different times.

Think of the high percentage of organizations that are successfully launched by entrepreneurs, people who passionately believe in the possibility and value of their efforts, who are not discouraged by setbacks, and who sometimes override what others see as realistic. They frequently work overwhelming hours for long periods of time. They tend not to trust others, nor to delegate well, even while commanding great loyalty. Yet entrepreneurial leaders, in their mad dash to the prize, may let important matters fall between the cracks. If they don't delegate well, and if in turn they limit their organization's capacity for growth, they demonstrate lack of fit. More managerial types may then be required to move the organization along—either by themselves or in complementary relation to the entrepreneurs. At later stages in an organization's life, this managerial capacity is often a better fit.

To state the obvious, an organization focused on violence against women that works through shelters—an organization like the one we explore in our central case study in Chapter 2—needs a woman as a leader. The clients and the staff, many of whom were themselves victims of violence by men, are mistrustful of men. If such an organization is located in and serves a primarily Spanish-speaking population, then a Latina will have a distinct edge in understanding the cultural aspects of the problems, the responses and needs of clients, and the political buttons to push in the community. So it is for many other organizations that serve distinctive stakeholder communities. The leader of an information technology company needs to have sufficient technical knowledge and experience to gain credibility with employees, investors, and customers.

The more we thought about the importance of fit, the more we began to identify variables involved: the skills, character, and values of the leader or leaders; the organization's objectives and strategies, as well as its structure, processes, history, and internal culture; and the larger context or market, including the potential for fund raising or paying clients, the regulatory situation, the surrounding community, and the current economic climate in communities, states, and nations.

Fit bridges leadership variety and complexity of circumstance. We had come to believe that having the right person in the right spot at the right time is a better predictor of leadership success than any particular qualities of individual leaders. During the startup phase, an entrepreneurial style generally works best. Excellent managers—principals in large school systems, for example—often find themselves adrift in the startup's absence of rules, clear-cut roles, and organizational structure. They regularly fail as leaders in new organizations but succeed when brought in after stability has been achieved. Family-business leaders, having been promoted over more seasoned professionals, often blunder; yet, during crises, with their family pride, security, and community standing on the line, they hold on with such tenacity that they seem the only leader who could have succeeded under the circumstances. Katherine Graham, who took over from her father and later from her husband, brought the *Washington Post* through just such a crisis brought on by a striking printer's union.

In the wrong circumstances, even great leaders will fail. Churchill's frustrations and frequent ineptitude during peacetime illustrates this point. Both Dostoyevsky (2002) and Mark Twain (2002) wrote powerful stories about angels and saints returning to earth centuries after they had spoken to loving crowds, preaching, again, as they always had, only to be rejected by the now-skeptical crowds who gathered around.

The idea of fit, however, conjures up a relatively simple and, perhaps, mechanical image: placing one object into another. The process of leadership is dynamic. It is a process "whereby an individual influences a group of individuals to achieve a common goal" (Northouse, 2001). And it is a complex process involving the leader, the organization, and the community or markets that utilize the organization's services. "Alignment" seemed more apt than "fit" to describe the complexity of this process.

Alignment

The more we observed effective leadership in action, the more convinced we were that leaders become effective by aligning themselves with all available resources in the service of the organization's mission, objectives, and strategies. In other words, the leader's character, skills, style, values, and personal objectives have to mesh with comparable qualities in the organization she leads: its processes, structures, values, and culture; the way it develops and utilizes its staff; the way it interacts with its community; and, perhaps most important, the way it pursues its strategies for success in the communities and markets it serves.

The image of alignment, of many moving parts working together to create something as a whole, worked better for us. Leadership can be conceived less as the work of a single individual person, and more as the unfolding of a system; less as a pattern strictly defined by following, and more as a mobilization of organizational or community resources to achieve collective ends. The process by which this happens can vary immensely. When people and their interests, affections, and information are working well together, when good decisions are made and executed efficiently, then we can say the organization is aligned in support of its objectives. Leaders that play effective roles in this complex process can be said to be good leaders.

When there is alignment of leader, organization, and community or market, we observed, it brings out the best in everyone. Leaders give clear instructions, and employees know what is expected of them and are provided the proper resources with which to accomplish their jobs. They can succeed. When they do, they receive positive feedback, which encourages them to work harder and do better. Managers and their staffs feel supported not only by clarity, feedback, and resources but also by the processes and programs that link people and resources. Programs are suited to their skills and to their ideas about what constitutes success. Information is provided to help them do their jobs. And, as each does her job in concert with others, the organization hums.

But the emphasis on alignment has its own downside, as well—"too much" alignment can threaten variety. We had been in too many organizations where leadership called for everyone to "get on the bus" or find another place to work, where, in the name of alignment, ideologues and autocrats tried to get everybody to think alike and to act in programmed ways. Leaders like this were successful in the short run, but they ended by creating rigidity, narrow focus—ignorance, really—and an inability to adapt to the constant changes in their communities and markets.

We observed that alignment, in the best sense, was a temporary arrangement and a temporary experience for leaders and their staffs. Organizations adapt to changes—internal and external, social, technical, intellectual, and ethical—and they move in and out of alignment. They can be set for success one moment and still be thrown into confusion or instability by the introduction of new demands by clients, new markets, and new technologies. When successful organizations work their way out of their confusion, they realign themselves. They change the way they think and behave, and the way individuals, departments, programs, and processes relate to one another. And the new alignment tends to be a synthesis of its traditional way of conducting itself and some of the ways it has adapted to change.

This dialectical process is, in fact, a better description of alignment than one that resembled the infamous Cartesian clock, in which all the parts work perfectly together but within a closed and controlled universe. The challenge of leadership, from a dynamic perspective, is to acknowledge, affirm, and facilitate the ongoing process of alignment, change, and realignment.

Even when we added the adaptive and dynamic qualities of alignment, however, we worried that the end operational goal might still seem to make everything and everyone the same. Each time the organization realigns itself, it could return to a clockwork precision. And we noted that many managerial types of leaders, brought in to remedy the confusion and excesses of entre- preneurs and their startup organizations, do, in fact, achieve an order that becomes rigid and stultifying.

So we raised this question: How does leadership align organizations in a way that is inherently dynamic? To answer this question, we began with another: Does alignment mean making the parts all the same? Our answer is no. In fact, alignment more often means bringing together different, comple- mentary qualities and organizational structures.

One of the most basic complementarities in leadership and organizations— the partnership between a visionary or entrepreneurial leader and a well- organized operating manager, or the chief executive officer and the chief operational officer—illustrates this point.

Teams are built on complementarities, as well: people with different skills, each one necessary but not sufficient, joined together in the right combination for the task at hand. And, of course, teams work at all levels of organizations, from boards of directors and senior management teams to departmental teams to program teams and project teams, some full-time and some part-time teams. All of them depend on the dynamic and complementary interaction of their members. Effective teams are aligned teams. They do not consist of iden- tical parts, but the alignment of different parts makes them purr.

Beyond individual partnerships and the synergies of teams, there are com- plementary processes. Sometimes, there are people and teams in organizations whose role it is to design innovative products or service methods that are inherently disruptive to organizations—their purpose is in fact to disrupt out- moded methods. But there are also people and teams whose role it is to take those innovations and implement them in ways that eventually lead to very orderly functioning. These two types of individuals and teams complement one another. They must work together; when they do, they are aligned.

An important role of field-based staff members is to bring in clients and ideas that do not exactly fit with the organization's current capabilities or its current ideas about how to do things. Program directors who need clients are likely to modify their programs to accommodate new clients or to accommodate ideas that will bring in new clients. In unaligned systems, these directors will reject what the field people bring in, or the field people will cease their efforts to recruit new clients because "they just aren't out there." In an aligned system, the two groups work in tandem; they are aligned.

Organizations and their communities can be aligned through both similarities and complementarities. For example, organizations can be a corrective to a neighborhood deficiency, such as housing, food, or political representation. At the same time, organizations can be "of" the people they serve, sharing their values, goals, and ethnic or racial origins.

Leaders and organizations can complement one another. A fast-paced, entrepreneurial organization and leader can benefit from a prudent, more careful board of directors—so long as they each appreciate what the other brings and do not try to make the other into their own image. Similarly, a long-standing executive director, who has developed very stable, effective service programs, may benefit from a board at the top or program directors below who insist on risk-taking to meet foreseeable challenges in the future.

As we thought over this more complex idea of alignment through balances of similarities and complementarities, we still thought it a little too cozy. Often, creativity and the urge to change only emerge out of friction. A new leader is brought in who does not quite fit with the organization. She may come out of the corporate world and into a nonprofit role, for example, and introduce financial disciplines that make program directors uneasy. If some friction, a little conflict, and a great deal of negotiation lead to positive changes in both leader and organization, this process too is the process of alignment.

Yet even this idea of alignment seemed to be missing something. In our interviews, we began to hear stories that filled in the blank. One leader said she hadn't a clue what leadership meant (Gerry Martinson, Big Sisters of Massachusetts, research interview). She never set out to be a leader. Things needed to be done, so she did them. When they were too much for her, she asked others to help. When they were all working together, when things were "flowing," then, she supposed, leadership was happening and, if pressed, she would say she was the leader. Her employees told a similar story. "You should see us when we're really working together," they said. "Gerry gets us going but we take over. Then it's hard to tell if anyone is leading. We're all just doing it."

What was missing was the experience—some would say the phenomenology—of leadership. So we asked leaders not only how they understood and carried out their leadership function but how they felt when they were doing it, how they felt when things were going well and when they were not. And the more we learned about the experience of leadership—from all concerned—the more it sounded like what athletes and athletic teams mean when they say they are "in the zone," an utterly unselfconscious process in which all the parts come together and just flow.

Excellence in leadership surely requires talent and character. But these come in many forms, and each form works best when there is a fit between the leader and the circumstances in which he or she must lead. This fit, because it involves so many moving parts, is best thought of as alignment. Good alignment optimizes the opportunity for leader and organization to enter the zone of effectiveness and flow.

So, at last, we come to the idea of leadership as alignment, and alignment as a complex system of interrelationships including cycles of sameness and difference, convergence and divergence, and hoped-for moments when everything works together.

Notes

1. We have changed the names and enough of the detail to protect the privacy of this organization but have preserved enough detail to be true to the activities witnessed.

2. The attempt to define the best form of leadership may be seen in the work of our best known and best respected leadership pundits, among them Tom Peters, Warren Bennis, James McGregor Burns, and John Kotter.

3. See Odendahl and O'Neill (1994) and articles by Ronald Shaiko (1996, 1997). Shaiko maintains that 75 percent of the nonprofit labor workforce is female, compared with 50 percent of the total workforce. Some 50 percent of women in the sector occupy "professional and managerial" positions compared with 21 percent in the government sector and less than 10 percent in the business sector. He cites various characteristics of organizations as predictors for whether women or men will serve in the top spot. Women are more likely to serve as executive directors of smaller, newer, less wealthy nonprofits headquartered outside the Washington beltway. Conversely, men are more likely to occupy the top spot if the organization is larger, older, wealthier, and inside the Washington beltway and close to the center of government power (Shaiko, 1997).

4. On minority women leaders, there are several helpful articles and a few books. We found two by Nancy Naples particularly informative: *Grassroots Warriors: Activist Mothering, Community Work, and the War on Poverty* (Naples, 1998b) and *Community Activism and Feminist Politics* (Naples, 1998a). Also see Barnett (1993).

References

Barnett, B. M. (1993). Invisible Southern Black women leaders in the Civil Rights movement: The triple constraints of gender, race, and class. *Gender & Society, 7*(2), 162–182.

Blumen-Lipman, J. (1996). *The connective edge: Leading in an interdependent world.* San Francisco: Jossey-Bass.

Dostoyevsky, F. (2002). *The brothers Karamazov: A novel in four parts with epilogue.* (R. Pevear & L. Volokhonsky, Trans.). New York: Farrar, Strauss and Giroux.

Dym, B. (2003). *Leadership transition in a Jewish day school: A guide to managing the transition to a new head of school* [Monograph]. Boston: Partnership for Excellence in Jewish Education.

Eagly, A., Karau, S., & Makhijani, M. (1995). Gender and the effectiveness of leaders: A meta analysis. *Psychological Bulletin, 111,* 3–22.

Elazer, D. J. (1995). *Community and polity: The organizational dynamics of American Jewry.* Philadelphia: The Jewish Publication Society.

Gilligan, C. (1982). *In a different voice: Psychological theory and women's development.* Cambridge, MA: Harvard University Press.

Helgesen, S. (1995). *The female advantage: Women's ways of leadership.* New York: Doubleday-Currency.

Naples, N. (1998a). *Community activism and feminist politics.* New York: Routledge.

Naples, N. (1998b). *Grassroots warriors: Activist mothering, community work, and the war on poverty.* New York: Routledge.

Northouse, P. G. (2001). *Leadership: Theory and practice* (2nd ed.). Thousand Oaks, CA: Sage.

Odendahl, T., & O'Neill, M. (Eds.). (1994). *Women and power in the nonprofit sector.* San Francisco: Jossey-Bass.

Shaiko, R. G. (1996). Female participation in public interest nonprofit governance: Yet another glass ceiling? *Nonprofit and Voluntary Sector Quarterly, 25*(3), 302–320.

Shaiko, R. G. (1997). Female participation in association governance and political representation: Women as executive directors, board members, lobbyists, and PAC directors. *Nonprofit Management and Leadership, 8*(2), 121–139.

Twain, M. (2002). *The mysterious stranger and other stories.* New York: Signet Classic.

Woocher, J. S. (1991). The democratization of the American Jewish polity. In D. J. Elazer (Ed.), *Authority, power, and leadership in the Jewish polity: Cases and issues* (pp. 167–185). Lanham, MD: University Press of America.

2

Casa Myrna Vazquez

C asa Myrna Vazquez is an organization that provides services to victims of domestic violence. Its story illustrates how leadership works as a process of alignment.

By any measure, Casa Myrna is a well-run organization, focused on clearly defined outcomes and managed through clear lines of accountability. Its executive director, Shiela Moore, demonstrates the qualities of leadership lionized by the contemporary literature on the subject. She is smart, courageous, decisive, innovative, and able, maybe even eager, to take calculated risks. She forms teams, delegates readily, and gives her staff room to both shine and learn from errors. She is, in short, that combination of entrepreneurial and professional leadership that our society reveres.

Meeting Shiela Moore

Barry first met Shiela Moore in a small meeting with two other executive directors, Gerry Martinson, the passionate leader of Boston's Big Sister Association, and Catherine D'Amato, who has helped triple the Greater Boston Food Bank. Martinson and D'Amato are powerful, articulate women who talked eloquently about the unending challenges of nonprofit leadership. For much of the meeting, Moore was quiet, almost unassuming. Throughout the meeting, she listened carefully and generously, and commented sparely, almost diffidently. Yet, in the days that followed, Barry found himself thinking about the marriage of candor and conviction that colored everything she said, and he wanted to learn more about her leadership of Casa Myrna.

A few days later, Barry called Moore to say he was writing a book about nonprofit leadership and wanted to interview her. He explained that he wanted to understand her leadership in context—not only how she saw herself but how others, including staff and board members, understood what made her effective. Some executives are threatened by this sort of 360-degree interviewing process, but not Moore, who readily agreed. Barry suggested they meet first to get comfortable with each other, and then meet with others. "That's fine with me," she said in that soft voice that seems to characterize her public persona. Then she surprised Barry by inviting him to meet her first with a group of senior staff and board members, as if to say, "This is the Casa Myrna leadership, not me."

On the telephone, Barry assured Moore that all the interviews could be confidential. Privacy would be preserved. He was not an investigative reporter looking for dirt. Moore surprised him again by saying that nothing needed to be confidential. There was nothing to hide. In fact, she would like to see the staff of Casa Myrna rewarded for all of its hard work. This was another surprise. For a woman who seemed shy in person, she was willing, even eager, to let the world into her organization and into her own life.

Background

Casa Myrna was founded in Boston in 1977 as a single shelter for victims of domestic violence. It is currently Massachusetts's largest provider of such services, helping more than 15,000 women, children, and families each year. To put this in perspective, it represents close to 60 percent of Boston's long-term domestic violence shelter beds and 19 percent of those available in the state.

Casa Myrna offers residential programs, both emergency and longer-term transitional living, for more than 350 women and children, as well as mental health, legal advocacy, and economic literacy programs for 800 women. It operates *Safelink,* a hotline that responds to over 30,000 calls per year, over half of which are requests for immediate help or emergency shelter. *Safelink* provides a 24-hour live response in 140 languages that links callers to more than 40 community-based domestic violence programs statewide.

Shiela Moore assumed Casa Myrna's executive directorship in 1997. Under her stewardship, the organization has expanded existing programs and developed innovative approaches to the treatment and prevention of domestic violence, while raising revenues and improving operational capacity to make the programmatic growth possible. In 1999 alone, its overall income grew by 19 percent, its nongovernment income grew by 26 percent, and its assets grew by 11 percent, while its mortgage debt decreased by 13 percent. By 2001, Shiela had led an internal change process that dramatically increased the organization's operating capacity by installing information and financial systems and transforming both the management process and the culture. Before Moore, Casa Myrna had been freewheeling and grassroots; under her stewardship, Casa Myrna became professional.

Beyond the expansion of its traditional shelter and hotline programs, Casa Myrna has been innovative in other ways. For example, Casa Myrna introduced a Mothers and Sons program, including a separate shelter, based on the understanding that, as they said in promoting the program, "intervention with boys who have witnessed domestic violence may be the best form of primary prevention of adult domestic violence." Young men had almost always been excluded from shelters. This followed from the belief that battered women and small children most need safety. But the Casa Myrna staff insisted this practice not only prevents intervention with these boys but also inhibits mothers of teenage boys from making use of the services. So they responded with this pioneering program.

Casa Myrna's rapid recent growth has been fueled by its widening public profile, its partnerships with other agencies such as the Dorchester Domestic Violence Court, and its superb financial management. It has become a national and international player, consulted by UNICEF and organizations in Israel and Japan to help develop culturally competent strategies to address domestic violence in their countries. Shiela Moore has helped shape state policies through countless speeches and panels; participation in Jane Doe, the statewide coalition of domestic violence and sexual assault service providers; and membership on Governor Mitt Romney's transition team.

Casa Myrna is now 27 years old. Its success has been accomplished thanks to countless contributors and several capable leaders. But in the late 1990s, as is true of many grassroots organizations, its early success had begun to flag. It was in fiscal trouble and its management and decision-making capabilities were ad hoc and amateurish. Shiela Moore changed Casa Myrna. Let's see how she did it and what kind of leadership she exercised.

Origins: First Alignment

Casa Myrna began in 1977 to serve the unmet needs of battered and sexually abused women, both as a shelter and as a provider of educational, therapeutic, legal, and a potpourri of other services. Most believe that it was formed to serve Latina women in Boston's South End, then a very poor area, but some argue that it was meant to serve a more general population of women of color. Either way, there was a gap, Casa Myrna filled it, and it grew steadily from the beginning.

From the day it opened, Casa Myrna tried to make the structure and processes of its organization fit its values and its mission—to help women heal and build a sense of community in a violent, hierarchical, male-dominated world. There was a passionate wish not to reproduce traditional power structures. Instead, Casa Myrna would be egalitarian and inclusive. Many if not most of its staff and leadership had themselves been survivors of sexual and physical abuse. The experience of victimization was seen as almost a prerequisite for staff membership. How else could one empathize with and serve these battered women with proper respect?

For a long time, and by design, there was no executive director. Casa Myrna was organized as a collective. Informally there were leaders, the program directors, but if asked, they would deny their power and insist that power was in the collective. At most, they would say they could merely influence the actions of others. The program directors led indirectly, pushing the generation of ideas, programs, decisions, and other vital organizational activities back into the group. They led by empowering the group, by being "servants before leaders," in the words of Robert Greenleaf (1977). Yet it is fair to say they ignored one of *Servant Leadership*'s dictums: "Everything begins with the initiative of an individual" (Greenleaf, 1977, p. 14). Their capacity to lead, to suggest ideas, and to make things happen was highly dependent on the agreement of both staff and clients. Under this model clients were included as much as possible in their own treatment.

During Casa Myrna's early years, everything had to be discussed and deliberated with as many people as possible contributing. Dialogue would go on for hours and hours, often without resolution, only to be resumed the next day or the next week. Yet these seemingly endless and argumentative conversations served purposes well beyond information sharing and decision making, for it was in just such communication that the staff found a sense of connection and nurture. It was reassuring to know that discussion could get hot without violence, and that emotionally charged issues could be explored without someone either walking out or clamming up at crucial moments. This had not been part of the women's experience in their partnerships with men or in male-oriented organizations. In this way, the collective formed a cocoon-like environment, in which both staff and clients could feel safe and intimate, prerequisites to healing and the ability to get back on one's feet.

The staff at Casa Myrna mistrusted hierarchy, which they saw as an essential component of the male world. They saw hierarchy as the domination of some people by others, usually men dominating women. So no one at the collective was permitted to get too high and mighty or too strong. Even distinctive roles, like director, and areas of expertise, like financial management, were suspect because they implied hierarchical standing. So roles were kept undifferentiated; generalists, not specialists, were esteemed; program people, who dealt directly with the battered women, were more highly valued than those with administrative—or management—responsibilities.

Everything was personal at Casa Myrna. There was little separation between business and relationships. "We answered hotlines in our homes," said one of the early program directors, and "we talked about work at home, about home at work." Feedback about work was feedback more about character than skill. Everything was about relationships and healing. "This was not employment," says Debra Robbins, "it was a calling. . . ." It was a lifestyle as well.

They learned as they went, with virtually no formal training. Training was suspect for its tendency to teach traditional values and to reinforce the status quo. Thus, in the traditional view, professional meant high and well, while a client or patient carried baggage of being low, needy, and unhealthy. Furthermore, most training was seen as impersonal and at odds with intimacy, which was at the heart of their notions about healing.

However distant Casa Myrna's original organizational and leadership style was from the traditional and current models with which we are familiar, it did grow and thrive. In this first phase of its history, Casa Myrna's founders' and leaders' emphasis on collectivism, connection, and egalitarianism, and their creation of a marked boundary between the organization and the surrounding community, worked well. Women healed, and the organization grew in its ability to serve more and more women.

If the primary task of leaders is to align themselves with the organization and the communities they serve, Casa Myrna's leaders succeeded. Surely, their own life experience, and the character and values it formed, lined up well with Casa Myrna's mission. So did their skills of empathy and collective team building. And their objective of serving others with similar experiences while continuing their own healing process was well served. These precise qualities of leadership were crafted, through trial and error, into an organizational form, whose strategy, structure, processes, and resources fit in a seamless way. Given the needs of clients for sanctuary and the undeveloped consciousness of the larger public concerning domestic violence, the cloistered organizational form fit well into the larger society.

PREDICTABLE DEVELOPMENTAL DIFFICULTIES
FOR GRASSROOTS ORGANIZATIONS

Typically, organizations move through a number of developmental passages. Probably the most defining is the passage from grassroots or entrepreneurial to professionally managed. Before describing Casa Myrna's distinctive route, we would like to say a few words about the more familiar-looking course of successful grassroots and entrepreneurial organizations.

The transition from entrepreneurial leadership to professional management can be understood as an initiation ritual marking the passage from youth to maturity. The passage is demanding and often painful, involving conflict, confusion, and loss—as well as an extraordinary leap forward in organizational capacity. But even if it skips a generation, as it often does in family businesses, the passage is unavoidable for organizations that grow beyond the capacity of one person to oversee, in detail, the entire operation.

The founders of grassroots organizations and the organizations they build represent the seedbed of America's civil society and economy. Everything begins with these practical visionaries, with their willingness to take responsibility for almost everything that happens, to take frequent calculated risks, and to persevere in the face of great odds and almost constant pressure. Entrepreneurs are leaders by virtue of their actions, drive, purposefulness, and apparent certainty—qualities that inspire trust in others.

At the same time, entrepreneurs have been known to be inconsistent, untrusting, impulsive, and controlling. Visionary leadership sometimes turns into grandiosity. Certainty masks uncertainty. The willingness to accept responsibility for all that happens and to be in charge becomes arrogance and obstinacy that eventually isolate the entrepreneur from the information and people who had been the lifeblood of the organization.

The organizations they form generally mirror the entrepreneur's personality: energetic, informal, innovative, driven, and independent. Profit seems to take a backseat to growth. Planning tends to be ad hoc. Budgets and financial controls are almost absent. Training takes place on the job. Roles and responsibilities are defined by the tasks at hand, often shifting and overlapping one another. When small, informality enables the entrepreneurial organization to be agile and adaptive to market demands. One crucial exception to the informality, however, makes all the difference: the entrepreneur is in charge. Although informal, these organizations are not fully participative. Power and prestige flow directly from relationships with the leader. Long-term, this inhibits the development and retention of strong managers and the capacity for autonomous action when, for example, the leader must devote much of her activity to positioning the organization in the external world.

In contrast to entrepreneurs, managers, as a type, tend to be consistent, cautious, detail-oriented, and generally conservative in their personal style. Yet, managers can be farseeing in their own way. Long-term planning, for instance, is a central management activity, as is development of able managers to guarantee the organization's future. There is an emphasis on budgetary performance and quality controls, with course corrections for variances. Managers create more formal organizations, in which goals, structures, operational processes, roles, and responsibilities are explicitly articulated, implemented, and monitored.

There is a point in every growing organization's life when ad hoc planning and determined, centralized leadership are no longer adequate to the complex tasks at hand, but there is not yet a full commitment to change. Such a moment is ripe for a developmental crisis. The processes that characterize professional management—careful planning, clearly defined roles and responsibilities, the monitoring of budgets, the tracking of performance and quality, and the delegation of major responsibilities—are unappreciated or even resisted by the founders. As customer demands increase (signs of success), the capacity to meet them decreases. Chaos reigns: The organization's atmosphere is one of reactivity and firefighting, confusion and anxiety about organizational direction, and inconsistent follow-through on projects and plans. There are too few hours in the day and even fewer good managers. Everyone in any responsible position tries to take every job into her own hands, trusting only herself or a few others, while no one seems to know what anyone else is doing. All of this undermines the entrepreneur's confidence and her credibility with others.

Some entrepreneurs, even as they flounder, struggle to create an infrastructure that will help them meet the challenge of growth. They put in information systems, introduce improvement programs, clarify roles and responsibilities, begin to manage their budgets, and think about long-term planning. Their problem is a lack of the skills necessary to make these systems work, or a lack of the ability to depend on them when they do. Time management is an additional hurdle. The demands of the present seem to conspire against their own long-term interest. Just as they build the infrastructure, they undermine it, relying on guts and determination, intuition, and even harder work. It doesn't quite work, and they renew their efforts. Back and forth they go, oscillating in a fruitless effort to escape their predicament. Morale drops. Skepticism about the capacity of the entrepreneur to lead through this crisis grows. This is the fulcrum on which the developmental crisis turns. Predictably, the transition is only completed by the introduction of a new, more professionally oriented leader.

Lost Alignment, and Positioning Casa Myrna for a New Alignment

Casa Myrna was not an exception to the developmental rule. Its strengths were the strengths of entrepreneurs. They were risk-taking visionaries, imagining and forming a new, antiestablishment form of therapy for battered women, in which the problem and therefore the healing process were defined as social and societal, not a matter of individual pathology and cure. To realize their vision, the founders created a new type of organization—collective, egalitarian, and intensely interpersonal. In the process, they worked long hours and suffered through hard times and tough criticism from the medical establishment, from skepticism to scorn. They persevered, with the passion of religious converts, because they were convinced they were right.

As with individual entrepreneurial leaders, Casa Myrna's founding leaders were impulsive, trying all kinds of programs without adequate information on which to base decisions. The very passion and certainty that helped them persevere closed them to the ideas and interventions of outsiders and caused them to override opposition from collective members with differing opinions.

In other words, many of the very qualities that defined and supported their initial conception got in the way of continuing growth. They were soon strapped for funds. For a while, they failed to develop sustaining financial partners from among foundations and individual donors. Decisions often did not hold; people would leave the room after conversations with vastly different ideas about what had been decided. As a result, uncertainty reigned.

As the organization and its programs grew, the need for clear management and expanded funding increased in importance. New leaders were brought in and given more traditional executive responsibilities and authority, but they were not fully empowered. Their mandate, at least in part, was to preserve the Casa Myrna way. They were often caught between trying to be loyal to the feminist collective and trying to solve problems presented by clients, funding agencies, and new board members who were oriented toward professional management methods. The tension of this kind of situation was immense, causing debilitating staff and leadership turnover.

FORAYS INTO A NEW ALIGNMENT

During the late 1980s a series of leaders was brought in, each of whom tried to bridge the gap between the spirit of the original Casa Myrna and the needs of professional management. Teresa Wade, a young woman from the financial services industry, became the board chair. She began to challenge the rubber-stamp quality of the board, the leadership of the current executive director, and the organization's financial practice. Her challenges clashed with the organization's culture, she made little progress, and she soon left.

As executive directors, Mercedes Thompson, Kim Cofield, and Michelle Drum all tried, perhaps with increasing success, to impose order in the form of clearer lines of responsibility onto the Casa Myrna organization. But each of these directors also struggled with the board of directors and eventually left. By the early 1990s an outside evaluator would have found that Casa Myrna, though filled with well-meaning and talented staff people operating in an increasingly appreciative community, was very much in disarray.

During this period, Kim Cofield hired Josefina Fossas as financial officer. Fossas was an MBA with 16 years of experience in the private sector, at RCA and a bank. She was hired to systematize Casa Myrna's financial systems, improve relations with outside funders, and help the organization get out of debt.

Fossas says that Casa Myrna "was the toughest environment I ever worked in." On one hand, she loved it. "Everyone cared," she recalls. "It was their lives ... Everyone was very passionate ... It was grassroots, mission driven, and multicultural—although almost everyone spoke Spanish." On the other hand, the staff was almost uniformly unsympathetic with her efforts to bring order to financial and other reporting systems. At the time, Casa Myrna's offices were in a basement. There was one "dying" computer. "They operated in a crisis style," Fossas recounts, "with little planning, less time on paperwork, and no systems in place." This made billings to the government very hard. Accounts were in such disarray that she couldn't put together a simple financial statement. When Fossas began to establish simple rules, such as insisting on accurate time sheets, she encountered little support from the program directors and outright hostility from many of the staff people. The harder she tried, the more resistance she seemed to engender, and this pushed her to the brink of leaving.

Several changes kept her at Casa Myrna. Making Fossas a part of the management team and retaining her services in the face of opposition represented a major step in the transition between the old and new Casa Myrna styles. She is very professional and competent. On the other hand, she is bilingual, compassionate, and very immediate; she is someone who would have fit easily into the intense conversations that had always characterized Casa Myrna.

What changed? First, Carmen Rivera, a very compelling, straightforward, and experienced woman who had held major management positions in New York City, agreed to chair the board. Rivera persuaded Fossas, who is also Puerto Rican, to stay. Then, Fleet Bank agreed to a one-year line of credit for $100,000, which eased the atmosphere of crisis. By the time Shiela Moore became executive director, Casa Myrna was out of the financial woods. The deficit had been reduced from $185,000 to $12,500. Then a strategic planning process got under way, providing hope for a clearer and more orderly future.

In 1992, the United Way and the Boston Foundation stepped in to help. They appreciated the importance of Casa Myrna's work. They also believed that it was not being done efficiently and that the organization might implode without a clear plan and rigorous reorganization aligned to the plan. Together, the two foundations funded a strategic planning process called "Common Ground." With the help of a professional consultant, Judy Freiwirth, they embarked on a planning process that formed an almost perfect bridge between Casa Myrna's past and future. The process sought opinions of Casa Myrna's stakeholders: people within Casa Myrna, outsiders from the domestic violence movement, members of the community at large, and potential donors from financial institutions. Everyone was consulted during a three-year process that eventually created tremendous buy-in. This was a process with enough conversation, argument, and reconciliation to fit the founders' sense of community, equality, and healing. It tore down walls between factions that had been built up in the preceding years. It was also very systematic, and it concluded with a clear idea about Casa Myrna's direction. It offered a rough idea about the type of professional management and organizational processes it would take to realize the newly clarified strategic directions.

The proposed future of rapid growth required the development of an infrastructure of informational systems and financial management. This meant highly differentiated roles and executives with the authority to bring decisions to realization. This, in turn, would require not just a new leader but a new kind of leadership to work effectively with foundations and government agencies.

In fact, it is possible to see the change in Casa Myrna's leadership and alignment to plan as being driven by forces outside of the organization. In a very real sense, the stimulus for a new alignment came from the community as represented by the foundations, the professional consultants, and the new board members. Similarly, a changing marketplace will send signals to a business that a new strategy is required to serve the interests of customers. If Casa Myrna wanted to fund itself for future growth, it had to align itself with funding sources. Thus, the foundations represented the changing values, objectives, culture, resources, and skills of the surrounding culture.

Combined with the strategic planning process, the most significant internal change during this period was Carmen Rivera's ascension to board chair. Both the United Way of Massachusetts Bay and the Boston Foundation had pressed for more professional processes at Casa Myrna. Along with two other accomplished professional women, Rivera had joined the board in 1992. Within a year, she was asked to be its chair, and she proceeded to dedicate almost 20 hours a week to the organization for the next two years. Rivera had come out of a background of political and community organizing, in particular for Puerto Rican statehood. She had worked in a high-level post for David Dinkins when he was in the Borough of New York City administration. Rivera is a principled, disciplined, and dedicated person, who, for the two years she was at Casa Myrna, was its main leader. Carmen Rivera was the person who paved the way for the organizational transition that Shiela Moore then led.

At first, the board and staff were not happy with Rivera's leadership, a common response to those brought in from outside of Casa Myrna's inner circles. This was an organization that tried to protect its culture and values. Rivera was dedicated to Casa Myrna's mission and to its potential to develop and promote women as leaders, but she did not like its collectivist processes. She began by reshaping the board of directors so that it could oversee the organizational transition she was convinced was required and could support a new and different kind of executive director. Rivera had been brought on by Clark Taylor, "a wonderful man" and a steadying force for many years on the board. She added Andrew Bundy, another man, who became Casa Myrna's most eloquent spokesperson in the Boston community.

Carmen Rivera was a near-perfect interim leader. She was a Latina who had extremely good community-based credentials. This made a difference to the staff. She was equally credible with the professional community, including the foundations, government funders, and other community groups with whom Casa Myrna would form partnerships. Her insistence on finding a savvy, professional leader for Casa Myrna was an essential part of the transition. Her own burning interest was leadership development among women of color, and she saw Casa Myrna as a wonderful incubator for that kind of leadership. In effect, she had a double agenda in identifying and mentoring Jossie Fossas, Shiela Moore, and others: both to help Casa Myrna and to increase the pool of competent women leaders whose work would spread to other local and national venues. Finally, she wanted very little for herself. Soon after Shiela Moore was in place, Rivera resigned. As she put it, Shiela Moore was "the right person" for the job, and her own job was done.

BRINGING SHIELA MOORE ON BOARD

An interim executive director (ED), Michelle Drum, had been appointed. Michelle was white, nurturing, and tough, and very well respected by the staff. She fit the ideal of program director-as-leader. Though she was white, she was a French immigrant who understood issues of oppression and alienation and was acceptable to Hispanic and black staff. According to Fossas, "everyone wanted her to shift from interim to permanent ED." Andrew Bundy, then a new board member, called Drum a "fabulous administrator."

After the first effort to find a new ED failed, Drum threw her hat into the ring, with considerable support. But Shiela Moore was also a candidate of the new board's search committee, under Rivera. Moore had many more management skills, and Rivera believed that this was what Casa Myrna needed at that point in its life. This was 1997.

Carmen Rivera was the person who most clearly pushed for Moore's selection as Casa Myrna's executive director. She describes Moore as "soft-spoken, deliberate, and visionary. She won't knock people over with charisma. She's mature, honest, and has integrity. With Moore, there's very little hype." Instead, she "rolls up her sleeves with conviction, and a clear sense of where she's going, and she will get the job done."

Rivera said Moore "knows how to take an idea and develop it—all the pieces it takes: the networking, talking to people, going after the money, creating organizational processes and teams . . . She's not shy."

Shiela Moore was not from the battered women's movement, however, a fact that raised more than eyebrows among the Casa Myrna staff and (old) board. Rivera thought what the organization needed was "organizational savvy" of the sort Moore learned from Jackie Jenkins Scott, the head of Dimmock Health Center (in Jamaica Plain). According to Rivera, Scott is a "real businesswoman with real political savvy." According to Rivera, Moore "has a good entrepreneurial sense. She's strong in management in that she'll work with a team. She knows her strengths and where she needs help, and she pulls people together. She says she's not process-oriented but not anti-process.

She will pull people together, then either abide by their decision or end discussion and make the decision. She has the *gana,* the will to make decisions."

When Moore came on board, "the organization needed shaking up," Rivera continued. There was a tremendous amount of staff and leadership turnover. Moore came in, rapidly assessed the situation, accepted the strategic plan that had been developed prior to her arrival, and developed her approach to achieving the plan. This provided a very clear direction for others. "With Shiela," according to Rivera, "you're on the train with her or you're either out or marginalized."

At first, Moore was mistrusted because she was seen as corporate, and, according to one colleague, her "straightforward African American way" of dealing with conflict seemed in contrast to the Hispanic culture. So, early on, there was conflict and skepticism about Moore. Still, Moore fit the strategic planning's emphasis on multiculturalism and a move away from a primary focus on Hispanic culture toward a broader client base. And, of equal importance, Moore learned. She came around on values, accepting the shared reproductive health and feminist values that had been the hallmark of the Casa Myrna culture. This included a greater acceptance of collaborative decision making than Moore had been accustomed to. In other words, she not only shaped but was shaped by the organization's expectations, values, and needs.

The first thing Moore did, according to Andrew Bundy, was to tell Michelle Drum that she valued her and needed her, both for the transition period and in general. Michelle stayed on until she left for maternity leave, and she felt well-treated by Moore.

Another of Moore's early objectives was to win Jossie Fossas over. Fossas had already begun to bring the financial systems into order. She was also a strategic thinker. For example, she had successfully argued that funding had to be diversified. Casa Myrna had been 70 to 80 percent government funded, and she began the move to increase funding from donations and service to 50 percent.

So Moore invited Fossas on a walk, then another and another, until they walked every day and joined a health club together. Moore was explicit: "We are going to be very close." They talked constantly about Casa Myrna, and how to put it on a more systematic basis. Soon Fossas was a convert, and she and Moore formed a team. "I could tell people they needed to speak better English. Moore could not—that was the beauty of our teamwork."

Moore knew she needed Fossas to put Casa Myrna on a financially sound basis. But Fossas felt she was a big winner in the exchange. "A lot of what I am today is due to Shiela. She challenged me, coached me, and gave me latitude to fall on my face. She was big on buy-in to her program but very receptive to what I had to say." Today, Fossas is a successful independent consultant and a dedicated Casa Myrna board member.

Still another early move: Shiela took the strategic plan as her mandate, even though it was done before she came, and she ran with it. We know how unusual that is. Most new leaders seem to feel the need to put their mark on the organization and often fail to assess its strengths while making changes for their own sake.

We should add that there was a great fit between Moore and the plan. At Dimmock, she had a history of taking on substantial initiatives. There was a "happy congruence," says Andrew Bundy, between Moore's own approach of focusing on increasing the capacity of organizations and the plan's aggressive goals.

Some Personal History

Indeed Moore took the baton from Rivera—partly leading in tandem with her, partly following and taking over—in keeping with who she is as a person. Moore's story demonstrates how success can be achieved when a leader's character and values, not just her skills, are aligned with the organization and community.

Moore's early experience and upbringing contain themes of both community activism and betterment, along with a fierce, contained individualism and ambition that she learned from her mother. Before Moore, Casa Myrna embraced collective values and eschewed individuality and initiative. Moore would build on the old Casa Myrna and now make it work. And most tellingly, Casa Myrna would evolve toward a different clinical idea of the victims of violence, thus achieving a more complete alignment than before.

Moore was born in rural Georgia to teenage parents. The family moved to Columbus, Ohio, and when Moore was 13, her parents divorced. Her mother soon remarried and moved to Cleveland, taking Moore with her. In Cleveland, her mother found work at Stouffer's Frozen Foods, where she worked her way up to be a top buyer.

Her mother was both mentor and model, and Moore's first organization was her extended family. Mother "taught me to be independent, to depend only on myself." This was definitely not the Casa Myrna ethic. And her mother believed in education; she insisted on Oberlin for her, instead of a local college with her high school friends. Moore's mother modeled uses of authority, as a leader in the family and at her work, which established a base of confidence for Moore: "I didn't realize I wasn't the smartest kid in the world until I got to Oberlin."

Her aunt, a hospital administrator focused on policy development, was another mentor, and they were very close. Moore applied to a hospital administration program at Xavier after college. Moore was the only African American and also the youngest in the program. The fact that it was a Jesuit school with its emphasis on ethics also had an influence on her. She felt the need to struggle with ethical issues in the workplace. Further, from her aunt and her training at Xavier, Moore acquired a kind of respectful formality, including what was appropriate attire at work. This would be another part of the change Moore would bring to Casa Myrna culture.

Yet in Moore's background there are the precursors of the community values she adheres to and the cross-fertilization she seeks in Casa Myrna. Every summer as a child, Moore spent with her grandmother in a small Georgia town. Each evening they would visit each relative. Later she realized that the visits were more than social. "We were checking on them, on their health, how they felt, making sure they weren't alone." Also, Moore would clean the houses of elderly neighbors. This is a version of "it takes a village"—not to raise a child but to look out for the welfare of everyone. "That was a place where I felt loved. I'm very rooted there, rooted in being part of a community that is larger than me."

In Cleveland, Moore grew up in an African American neighborhood when Carl Stokes was mayor. She was proud of her tradition and felt supported by the community feeling. The community tracked its college prep courses—everyone was expected to do well. This "nurtured me," Moore says.

"People care" at Casa Myrna, Moore says, and "they would work for free if they could afford it. This is a community. In domestic violence, it's a pretty cloistered community and in fact, they've tried to keep others out, but that's not realistic. I've opposed that, but the dynamics of being cloistered and taking care of each other and letting others and other ideas in has been important to what we've done. So I've tried to break down barriers, such as letting boys into programs and adding men onto our staff and our board."

This is her understanding of the value of both individualism and the community and the value in its blend for Casa Myrna. In Moore's view, progress in institutional funding—and individual healing—can be enabled when abused women stand up, individually and not just as part of a community of abused women, and begin influencing society at large.

The way in which she is personally aligned with the past and future of Casa Myrna and the full societal context for battered and abused women is what made Shiela Moore the right person at the right time.

Leading Organizational Change and Alignment

Carmen Rivera agrees: Shiela Moore was a good fit. That is, she was aligned to the organization's mission, vision, and directions as laid out in the strategic plan. The role was a natural extension of the one she played at Dimmock, building on her skill in managing large projects, satisfying her own need for advancements, and working well with her own values supporting social justice and feminism. The big question was whether her strong preference for orderly processes, respectful interaction, and focused work could help transform the Casa Myrna culture.

When Moore started work, she felt people were doing a good but not great job. They were working hard but not very smart, and they were inadequately professional and accountable. Infrastructure was poorly integrated with operations. Program and administrative personnel hardly knew each other and did not collaborate. Further, there was not enough recognition in the larger community to bring people in and attract funding. Finally, the board needed development and new members.

According to Moore, the strategic plan to conduct more service and to be bigger lacked a compelling vision of how to get there. "I gave the vision life. If we were going to add programs, we were going to need money. So I went to the Boston Foundation and told Anna Faith Jones that Casa Myrna and the Boston Foundation's goals were in alignment and won a $100,000 capacity-building grant." Here Moore was aligning the organization's strategy internally while aligning it to the larger community.

They built a steering committee whose job it was to manage the change process and gain adherents. "We put up huge graphs to show where we were, where we are now, where our goals are." And "everyone understood." There would be no question about shared meanings and their importance for shared effort at Casa Myrna.

Operations

Operationally, Moore knew that she had a big job to do. There was inadequate support for the programs in funding, data, management, and financial accountability. She approached this systematically, as she says, "just finding good people and paying attention to parts of the organization that were broken." She focused on finance and grants management, in particular.

As a primary illustration, Fossas was a disempowered financial officer. As we recall, the original culture eschewed hierarchy, role differentiation, and capitalist society. So when Fossas came to Casa Myrna, she had a terrible time doing her job without reasonable financial records, much less getting people to be accountable with their record keeping. The program people, who ruled and who represented the core and symbolic center of Casa Myrna, were contemptuous of the "help." They simply talked over Fossas and didn't respond to her requests. Moore recalls that "these were very articulate and, to be honest, loud women."

Moore "set out to change that paradigm" in a few ways. She befriended Fossas and won her confidence. Then she supported her, and insisted that Fossas's "rules" be followed. In effect, this meant that all the program directors had to listen to Fossas's. Fossas had her role; they had theirs. This represented several big shifts: first, clearly differentiating roles; second, respecting administrative people; third, systematizing administrative processes; and fourth, rational decision making based on facts and data.

In the past, decisions had been made through extensive conversation but with little reference to solid information. The therapists who had ruled the roost made psychological issues paramount. Now decisions could be data driven, taking into account program and also larger organizational needs. And in the process of getting to know Fossas so well, Moore also came to understand the finances in detail.

At staff meetings, Moore intentionally and forcefully insisted that people listen respectfully to one another, keep voices to professional levels, and listen to nonprogram people. As Moore puts it, "We were abusive to each other: yelling, screaming, taking out the frustration from our work on each other." At its heart, the Casa Myrna culture was more about victimization, survival, crisis management, and blaming the perpetrators than problem solving. Moore insisted that the "blame game" be stopped. She indicated that their job was to deal with crises in people's lives, but that the organization could not operate on a crisis-management basis.

According to Fossas, "Shiela depersonalized the situation, made it more professional. She let go a couple of central people who could not get with the new program of respectfulness, accountability, and problem solving. Don't forget that the others were perfectly respectful in the old mode, which required them to argue in an egalitarian mode for what they believed. The manifestation of respect was being shifted from beneath them."

In a way, then, Moore brought the organization's mission of opposing abuse and healing its wounds into Casa Myrna. Outside and inside could be consistent.

What Moore could not accomplish at staff meetings, she did in one-on-one encounters. One key staff member, for example, continually sounded off. Moore took her on and after a couple of months of regular meetings a potentially oppositional person was very much in her camp. Moore also modeled the culture change she wanted down to little details, including formal dress, which on occasion she insisted upon.

Moore put Casa Myrna on a performance basis. Each department and program was required to set goals that fit the overall strategy and commit to plans to meet their goals. Advancement was contingent on achieving results against stated plans. Michelle, the interim ED, was made director of operations, a post she held very skillfully until she left after having a baby. Her replacement was a man who could develop their management information systems. Although hiring a man violated tradition and created anxieties, it worked out and became a significant shift to opening Casa Myrna to a larger group of ideas and people. The culmination of this move to incorporate ideas from the outside was a $300,000 grant Moore got from Massachusetts to include teenage boys in the programs; that relieved mothers from having to choose between shelter and their sons.

Employees at odds with the evolving culture, which was characterized as accountable, collaborative, not egotistical, problem-solving, tough, hard-working, dedicated, and respectful, generally left by themselves. They got the message. A few were asked to leave. With time, training, and the hiring of new people who fit, all internal operations were aligned to the strategic plan.

To new people, she said, "More than likely, you have more skill than the person you have replaced. We are raising the bar. We expect a great deal from you." To her managers, she said, "Problems can't be fixed by others. It's our responsibility—each one of us."

Over and over, she would insist at meetings that people take responsibility, blame no one, and sit there and keep working on problems until new, better solutions were found. Executive and other team meetings turned into tough problem-solving sessions that challenged participants but also satisfied them. It brought out their best.

Moore's personal style during these meetings was very much like the one Barry had encountered at the small meeting of executive directors. She is generally quiet. Many take her quiet manner as shyness. "I am comfortable with silence," she says. "I wait for people to come to good solutions, not necessarily mine but ones I recognize as effective and I can live with and promote. I hire people who are smarter than I am and expect them to produce." By and large, she lets them do their thing and does not micromanage.

Her staff calls this "management by consensus." Generally speaking, leadership is practiced in this form. Even when Moore is unsure about the quality of problem solving, she will generally assent and let people learn from their own mistakes. At times, however, Moore is clear that the team decisions are off-target. At such times, Moore is not at all above pushing or insisting on her own solution. She says herself that she is a tough boss. "I'm patient but have little tolerance for those who don't really get it. I don't often fire them, but they see the way the wind is blowing and leave of their own accord." When Moore does fire, it is generally strategic, not just to replace a person, but to send a message to the entire organization.

As she says, "I'm not happy to fire someone, but I've never been afraid to do it. When I was 23 and in my first job as assistant director of health care, I had to fire the head of nursing, who was a very poor manager and bad-mouthing the administration."

What bothers her most? "Not paying attention to doing things with care, not delivering. In the end, I'm a work-product person . . . I expect people to work hard, to get grants in on time, to keep me informed."

Advocacy

Moore loves advocacy. When she was leaving Dimmock, she told its executive director and a mentor, Jackie Jenkins Scott, "I want to be an ambassador for something I believe in." She was tired of managed care, of faceless bureaucracy.

At Casa Myrna, she was exhilarated by fighting the good fight, and she was challenged by the prospect of bringing in funders herself. So she set out to tell the Casa Myrna story with a quiet but ferocious energy. She wrote articles, including an op-ed piece in the *Boston Globe* that caught the public's attention. She attended and talked at public forums, each building on the others, until she and Casa Myrna became or appeared to become a major player in the domestic violence field. After a few years, Casa Myrna has become "the most respected domestic violence organization in New England."

Experience

By the time Moore came to Casa Myrna, she had become a very confident manager. She maps out and implements her plans with a good deal of certainty and intentionality. "I know when to be quiet, when to act up, when to praise, and when to criticize. The people closest to me use the word 'strategic' to describe my style, and I think they're accurate. I'm always thinking."

Her rapid early success built on itself. "It feels like, once you've had success, people want to be around you and you exude an air that it's going to happen. It looks like confidence to others. But to me, it's more expectations. It's almost faith. You just believe. There is something around me, looking out for me and us, and I expect good things to happen."

LEADERSHIP AS ALIGNMENT

Moore brought herself, the organization, and the community into alignment. As a person, she combines social purpose and professional rigor. Her personal priorities are consistency of action and purpose, and she affirms individual ambition. The organization under Moore's leadership has developed clear roles and structure, carefully managed processes and infrastructure, clear strategic directions, and a culture of mutual respect in service of healing and social justice. The larger community was satisfied in its demand for more and better service to battered women, and increased professionalism and accountability. As a result, foundations and government agencies are better represented, and more resources have been made available.

NONALIGNMENT, FRICTION, AND
THE DYNAMICS OF CREATIVE LEADERSHIP

While there were many ways in which Shiela Moore lined up well with Casa Myrna—most powerfully with its readiness for a developmental shift—it is also the ways that she did not fit that contributed to her success. Any leader who fits too well eventually grows complacent or breeds a staff that grows complacent. There is a need for friction and difference that creates the urgency for change. Moore's quieter personal and more systematic professional style was somewhat at odds with Casa Myrna's traditional culture. Casa Myrna's passionate, mission-driven culture was at odds with the more systematic ways of managed care, in which Moore had previously worked. The need to resolve these differences created a more dynamic relationship between leader and organization. In this way, the movement toward alignment became a creative act, not an effort to consolidate the status quo.

LEADERSHIP AS RELATIONSHIP

Moore created the move toward alignment through relationships. She had the full support and endorsement of the board, and she built strong relation-ships with Michelle Drum, the popular interim ED, and Jossie Fossas. Then she made a series of hiring and firing moves that brought each key person into her camp. They believed in her and were dedicated to her. The culture she created was not so different from the one she knew in Georgia, as a child, in which people looked out for each other. The basis for relationships of the original Casa Myrna—intense, constant, argumentative, cloistered engagement—was replaced with respectful, professional caretaking, open to the larger world.

CREATING VIRTUOUS CYCLES

Moore knew that the creation of professional behavior in a few key places would have a ripple effect. Supporting Fossas, for example, created account-ability from program directors. When program directors "got on the train" with Fossas, they also communicated the need for accountability to their staffs, for setting goals, developing strategies within each program to realize goals, reporting on progress, and making course corrections. Those who could not or would not get on the train were exposed and pressured, in which case they got on board or left. Then they were replaced with better managers more in tune with the new style. These new managers then supported executive committee members in ways that were impossible before, by helping to provide data, write grants, and so forth, thus making the executive committee's decision making more effective. And so it went, with each change pushing on another in an upward spiral—or virtuous cycle—all choreographed by Shiela Moore, with her graphs, inspirational talks, and continual mentoring of key people.

LEADERSHIP AND READINESS FOR CHANGE

If leadership concerns itself with change—helping an organization or a community move toward its goals—then effective leadership depends, in part, on the organization's readiness to change. An organization is ready, for example, when its staff is receptive to the directions mapped by its strategy. Because of its long and inclusive planning process, just prior to Moore's arrival, Casa Myrna was ready to move in a more professional direction. She had support from above and below for that direction and relatively little resistance to change. Organizations are also ready to change when they are unstable, uncertain, and seeking a strong hand. This, too, was true of Casa Myrna, as it careened among several leaders, changing funding sources and community demands, and in its high staff turnover. Moore could provide the steady hand that was reassuring in times of uncertainty, and this increased her credibility when the steady hand led to change. Finally, organizations are ready for major changes when strong forces, some obvious, some not clearly identified, are already moving toward change. In such cases, leaders need only identify those forces and push them from behind, as a judo expert might do in martial arts. Again, Moore found such forces: in the changing board, in the new strategic plan, and in the eagerness of the funding community to help—if Casa Myrna became more professional.

SEEDS OF DISRUPTION, CHANGE, AND THE NEED FOR NEW ALIGNMENT

According to one critic, the Casa Myrna organization is much smoother, with more teamwork, less gossip, and greater efficiency, but a "little dry." There could be a need to reinject some of the passion that informed Casa Myrna's origins. During her first couple of years, Moore invited new thinking and big ideas. Then, with the need for programmatic focus and discipline, intellectual exploration temporarily decreased, with some important issues left undeveloped.

It may be that a more staid mentality is replacing the excitement of the original organization and of the early years under Shiela Moore's tenure. There are voices that say so, and these are voices that may get louder and may call for reform and renewal. It is likely enough that Moore, who is alert to the need for continuous improvement and change, will listen. And it is likely that she and the organization will continue to change together, so that a new alignment is reached without the need for new leadership. But many good, even innovative leaders do not achieve such realignment. They grow dedicated to their own ideas, to the organization they have built or rebuilt, to what they often refer to as "my baby." If this happens to Moore, we can expect an interim period, perhaps with a few executive directors until the right one is found, with high staff turnover and with an uneasy relationship to the larger community. . . . As we shall see, alignment is a dynamic process that demands wakefulness and agility.

Reference

Greenleaf, R. K. (1977). *Servant leadership: A journey into the nature of legitimate power and greatness.* Ramsey, NJ: Paulist Press.

3

Theoretical Alignment

O ur understanding of leadership as a process of alignment draws from many disparate theories of leadership. We can identify a dominant cultural narrative of leadership, that is, an informal, often implicit consensus on how leaders should lead, but there is no comprehensive, commonly held formal theory of leadership. Instead, there are many, various, sometimes conflicting theories. Some focus on the archetypal character traits of leaders. Others emphasize the ways in which leaders interact with followers. Still others concern themselves with the circumstances that bring out leadership or that demand different kinds of leadership. Each theory has its explanatory virtues. Each seems cogent. When immersed in reading any one of them, it seems entirely accurate. Yet, by itself, each is incomplete.

Reading through leadership theories, one is reminded of Wallace Stevens's (1965, p. 92) poem, "Thirteen Ways of Looking at a Blackbird," and its exploration of multiple perceptions.

> I do not know which to prefer.
>
> The beauty of inflections
>
> Or the beauty of innuendoes.
>
> The blackbird whistling
>
> Or just after.

Trying to pull together the variety of theories into a single theory of leadership has pitfalls. Two contemporary books, by Northouse (2001) and Rost (1991), summarize and categorize the many and divergent theories that are currently influential. Their descriptive efforts have provided a great service to the study of leadership. But their efforts to create meta-theories—really meta-definitions—end up being so abstract that they miss the liveliness and muscularity of the particular theories. Northouse, for example, says, "Leadership is a process by which an individual influences a group of individuals to achieve common goals" (Northouse, 2001, p. 4).

The question we asked is this: Could there be an overarching conceptual framework that brings the theories together, or at least describes how the theories relate to one another, that maintains the vividness and distinctness of each? Alignment theory makes this integration possible. It brings together the psychological approaches to leadership that focus on character and style with those that emphasize the more active interpersonal aspects of leadership, then places both within the context of organizational systems and community systems. Alignment theory represents a meta-theory that preserves the power of these individual views and emphasizes the way that they interact with one another.

Since our work draws from many other theories of leadership, which we don't want to make abstract, we want to sketch the major theories and to indicate how ours relates to each. So what follows in this chapter is a brief survey of ways to understand leadership's inflections and innuendoes—we describe eight—with a view toward shedding a general light on our theory of alignment and on the specific, concrete life of Casa Myrna Vazquez. Our own sketches owe much to excellent compendiums created by both Rost and Northouse.

Trait Theory

Trait theory identifies the characteristics that distinguish leaders from others. This approach has a long history; no matter how many times it is challenged, it continues to surface and often dominate the field. Trait theory was given its classic formulation by Abraham Zaleznik (1977) and may be seen in the current romance with charismatic and visionary leadership, exemplified in the writing of Bennis and Nanus (1985) and Nadler and Tushman (1989, pp. 135–139). There is no mystery why trait theory is so compelling. It is simple and straightforward, following the dictates of common sense, and it joins person, role, function, and character. Perhaps most important, trait theory lends itself to good storytelling. Throughout history, the stories of great men (trait theory is often called "great man theory") have been told and retold to admiring crowds in speeches, novels, plays, and newspaper articles.

According to empirical research, the observations of management consultants, and the memoirs of CEOs themselves, leaders are said to be intelligent, self-confident, persistent, and sociable. They communicate well, and they have great drive and originality. They accept responsibility for their decisions. While they urgently advocate change, they are patient and strong enough to tolerate delays and ambiguous situations. They are masterful strategists, who are able to structure situations and rally people to achieve their objectives. Finally, they are said to have integrity, which is what makes them credible with their followers.

There is little doubt that leaders, like Scott Fitzgerald's upper class, are "different than you and me." There may well be some more-or-less universal qualities, such as the ability to influence others and to identify with the people who are led. But the qualities emphasized in the literature are partial and perhaps serve better as a portrait of white male leadership than of all leadership. These lists, for example, do not focus on nurture, or the ability to bring out the best in others, or the quality of embodying the story and struggle of a particular people. Furthermore, the theory implicitly suggests that selecting the right leader will solve any organizational problem, ignoring questions of fit, alignment, support, and resources.

We would agree that the character of the leader—skills, personality, and values—are key elements of leadership, particularly when aligned with the organization, cause, or culture, but they are only part of the leadership puzzle.

Shiela Moore of Casa Myrna fits very well with the conventional trait theorists. She is very intelligent, and she has seen herself in this light since elementary school. This adds to the quiet confidence she exudes. While not abundantly creative, she has spearheaded important innovations, such as the program for mothers and their teenage sons. Her courage stands out. She is a constant advocate for her cause and her organization, speaking to larger and larger audiences. She is patient with her employees—for a while—yet very clear in what she demands. She structures work so that her employees can succeed if they have what it takes. If not, by mutual agreement, they will recede and Shiela will select others. She is both a tactician and a strategist to the bone, priding herself on the intentionality of her leadership, in matters small and large. Finally, as all who know her say, she has an unshakable integrity.

Moore conforms to the trait theorist's description (expanded beyond the typical list for great white males), but her success has to do with much more. Furthermore, while exemplary, she is part of a cadre of extraordinarily talented nonprofit leaders.

Style

Today, people frequently discuss leadership style, which shifts the emphasis from character, which is internal and, to a large extent, inborn, to behavior, which is external and learnable. Some leaders, for example, initiate action, and formulate plans that others carry out. Others gather information and mediate among subordinates. Some are charismatic and inspiring, others cautious, intentional, and methodical. Some tend to coach and encourage; others bark out orders and emphasize accountability in subordinates. Currently, the servant leadership (Greenleaf, 1977) style, which emphasizes the support and empowerment of others, tends to share the stage, however quietly, with the great man style.[1]

Surely behavioral style and a distinctive voice are key components of what we think of as leadership. The emphasis on behavior brings leadership outside the leader's skin so that it is observable, changeable, and subject to influence by others. It is one thing to say that a person is strong or determined, but it is much more graphic and testable to describe how that person acts with strength and determination in a particular context. Style is more contextual than trait theory.

The distinction between character traits and behavioral style has immense implications for the way we relate to leadership. If leadership is inherent, for example, then the emphasis is on selection: Find the best person and let her do her thing. If leadership is behavioral, then it can be modified by circumstance and by training. In this light, organizations can breed leaders—the basis for leadership training programs. Bringing the two ideas together, leadership development programs identify those with the right traits, then mold them by providing appropriate experience, resources, and training.

When we say that a leader is aligned with her organization, we can see how her style fits, and how it calls forth or fails to call forth effective behavior on the part of followers. Style means behavior—behavior is interactive, reinforcing behavior in others and being reinforced by others. We can imagine an organization as having a leadership style. A style that did not fit would not be supported or reinforced, and a style that fit would be reinforced.

Where an emphasis on traits leads to the selection of leaders based on constant criteria, style leads the selection and training of leaders in the direction of alignment.

Shiela Moore's leadership style sometimes looks like that of a servant leader. She listens a good deal. She is comfortable with silence, and she waits until others express their opinions before contributing her own. Once the organization is aligned, she is happy for others to make the decisions they will carry out, while she provides resources and removes obstacles. If people head in directions she can't countenance, however, she will intervene. Early in her tenure, in order to align strategy and clarify what kinds of people acting in what kinds of ways would fit with the new Casa Myrna style, she would listen carefully but take much stronger stands.

Her leadership depends a good deal on her character and the confidence she has to listen, delegate, and let others take credit, but it is also situational. It shifts according to the needs of her organization, her staff as a whole, and individual staff members and clients.

Situational Leadership

Ken Blanchard has popularized the situational approach in such best sellers as *Leadership and the One Minute Manager* (Blanchard, Zigarmi, & Zigarmi, 1985).

Its premise is that different situations demand different kinds of leadership. To be effective in this style, leaders must be flexible; they must adapt their styles to the challenges presented by a variety of different situations.

In Blanchard's view, leaders need to match their actions to the competence, commitment, and independence of subordinates, according to a developmental continuum consisting of four leadership styles. New situations, where employees have not yet got their feet under themselves, mostly require directive behavior on the leader's part. At the next stage, leaders can move to a dual emphasis on direction and support—like a firm but appreciative coach. Then, as employees grow more knowledgeable, competent, and confident, leaders would do well to emphasize supportive behaviors. The fourth stage requires minimum direction and support—employees have developed the capacity for independent decision making and action. Now the leader can delegate extensively and concern herself with broad strategic directions.

The situational leadership approach is compelling primarily because it tells what to do when, and it implies that many can do it. In contrast to trait theory, which suggests you have it or you don't, one can learn to be a better situational leader. So conceiving leadership in this situational manner is attractive to human resource departments, who can build training sessions around it.

From our perspective, situational leadership leads us in the direction of developmental systems theory. It suggests that the relationship between leaders and followers evolves over time and varies according to context. Blanchard's definition of situations is narrow, however, and other situations bear on the appropriate leadership style. Different stages in organizational life, for example, demand different kinds of leadership—entrepreneurial or managerial, to name two. Furthermore, different stages in the life and career of the leader influence how she will be able to match up with different organizational situations. There are also cultural, ethnic, or racial contexts that can make specific demands, as well as strategic objectives. A strategy of rapid growth requires a different leadership style, for instance, than a strategy of slow and sustained growth.

Shiela Moore moved through phases that resemble Blanchard's four quadrants. At first, she herself bought into the strategy that had emerged from the planning process prior to her arrival at Casa Myrna, and she helped give it shape. Then she was directive and supportive to those who had the talent and who bought into the organizational culture she was trying to build. As people got on board and new people arrived, and professionalism took root, Moore increasingly backed off. She delegated broadly and focused on issues of policy, strategy, and funding in the larger community.

From another perspective, Shiela Moore entered Casa Myrna as it struggled to move from a grassroots to a professionally managed organization. She was the ideal leader for that kind of situation, respecting the creativity of organizational beginnings yet deeply committed to and experienced in the management of more mature organizations. Had she been asked to lead Casa Myrna several years earlier, she would have refused; if she had accepted, she probably would have failed. The situation would not have been right for her character and style. She could not have aligned herself to the organization, nor would she have had the credibility born of organizational match to align the domestic violence programs with Casa Myrna's strategic plan.

Contingency Theory

Contingency theory, associated with Fred Fiedler (1967), brings us closer to the central ideas of alignment. It is based on the belief that leadership effectiveness depends on the quality of match between leadership style and the context. Fiedler focuses on three factors that mediate the match. The first, leader-member relations, describes the degree of attraction, confidence, and loyalty followers feel for their leaders and the general atmosphere created by these feelings. The second, task structure, concerns the clarity of task definition. The third, position power, describes the leader's authority and emphasizes the power to reward and punish followers. Together, these mediating factors predict how "favorable" the situation is.

Contingency theory almost takes the leader out of leadership, because it measures effectiveness according to impact, atmosphere, and formal position. It focuses on the situation even more than situational approaches. Leadership selection here begins with an analysis of the situation and almost assumes that individuals who understand it can succeed within it. While this seems like a good place to begin—search firms, for example, do essentially begin here—it ignores the fact that the character and behavioral styles of leaders may vary according to context but also have considerable continuity and stability. Contingency theory offers an important corrective to the more popular focus on traits; but it is a limited theory of matching, fit, or alignment.

Carmen Rivera and Casa Myrna's board of directors selected Shiela Moore because they believed she would be a good fit with the next phase of Casa Myrna's development. She was professional. She had worked successfully in a larger, more complex organization and had helped implement a formal strategic plan. The fit with strategy and future was good. The long planning process had, in fact, moved the organization partway through the transition from grassroots to professional organization, as had the previous leaders, Kim Cofield and Michelle Drum. But the internal organization was not completely aligned. Contingency theory would note these disjunctions and wonder about Shiela Moore's success. Of course, character—the traits she brought to the table—and her flexibility in adapting to different situations overcame difficulties that contingency theory might have predicted. In effect, Moore's qualities amplified the strength of fit that contingency theory prescribes.

Path-Goal Theory

Path-goal theory (House, 1971; Schriesheim & Keider, 1996) challenges leaders to adopt styles that best motivate employees. There are three underlying premises: First, motivation depends on the expectation that one can successfully perform tasks; second, one's actions lead to specific outcomes; and third, successful work will be rewarded. Good leaders structure tasks so that employees believe they can do them; they highlight outcomes; and they create a variety of rewards for the realization of those outcomes. Leaders can go about their business in different ways. They can be supportive, directive, participatory, challenging, or some combination of the four, because the choice of leadership style really depends on the characteristics of subordinates. Some particularly need affiliation, some need structure, or control, or appreciation. Those who desire affiliation probably need a good deal of support. Those who work in uncertain situations may need directive leadership. For employees who need to feel internally in control, participatory leadership is effective because they work alongside their leaders instead of taking orders.

Path-goal theory presents the most psychologically oriented idea of leadership—style is matched to the cognitive-emotional profile of the workforce. This is a vital component of alignment. At Casa Myrna, the organization was built around the need to affiliate, which required Shiela Moore to be supportive. At the same time, in order to remedy fiscal uncertainty, she needed to break with Casa Myrna's egalitarian and informal norms. She elevated the financial officer and installed formal reporting processes. Note that at first she listened and listened until a critical mass of staff members felt allied with her, and only then did she introduce these changes. In other words, the alignment required for organizational change included both the emotional atmosphere and the psychological needs of the staff.

Leader-Member Exchange Theory

Leader-member exchange theory (Dansereau, Graen, & Haga, 1975) focuses on the dyadic interaction between individual leaders and followers, and it encourages leaders to develop customized partnerships with their direct reports. The theory's value is its focus on process; its limitation is that the process is both one-directional—what the leader does to create the partnerships—and outside larger group and organizational contexts. A leader's relation to one person is seen in isolation from relationships with others and norms built up around the executive team.

Alignment has at least as much to do with the relationships between parts as it does with the parts themselves. The coordination or alignment can have a more powerful impact on effectiveness than the quality of the leader or followers. A close-knit, well-coordinated team of relatively ordinary players can often beat a hastily gathered group of stars.

Shiela Moore's relationship with Jossie Fossas is instructive here. Moore realized that she needed sound financial practices to achieve orderliness, account-ability, and responsibility. Jossie Fossas's efforts had been largely thwarted in the past, and she was on the verge of leaving. During a series of long walks, Moore assured Fossas that she had full confidence in her abilities and made promises to support her work. Moore then continued in this style by establishing personal alliances with each key staff member whom she deemed talented.

There is much more to relationships between leaders and followers than exchange theory covers. In a later chapter, we describe the way such alliances are built and maintained and elaborate on the nature of the leader-follower relationship.

Transformational Leadership

Transformational leadership represents a contemporary version of the great man theory buttressed by a sense of the intense connection of such leaders and their followers. Gandhi, Martin Luther King Jr., the wartime Churchill, and Franklin Delano Roosevelt—these leaders were visionaries, whose leadership was based on ethical and national ideals and communicated in brilliant rhetoric and through acts of individual courage. They embodied their message in ways that immensely magnified their credibility and attractiveness. What is more, they had an intuitive grasp of what their followers would and could do, a strategic empathy, if you will.

James McGregor Burns (1978) introduced and popularized these ideas. Burns first distinguished transactional and transformational leadership. According to Burns, transactional leadership works within the current set of rules to get things done—it is "managerial." Transformational leaders get much more out of their followers by raising their level of consciousness about the importance of their work, by persuading them to subordinate or transcend their self-interest for the good of the organization and its mission, and by set-ting the bar of achievement higher and higher.

Transformational leadership is aligned leadership in two important ways. First, although the focus is not on relationship, transformational leadership is based on relationship. Leaders cannot persuade in such powerful ways without a powerful, explicit or implicit relationship with followers. Second, the notion of transformation is itself a form of alignment. It generally builds through virtuous cycles. The leader proposes actions in ways that catch the imagination of followers. As followers begin to join the leader, she is encouraged and makes further, bolder proposals, which further capture the imagination of followers, who come on board with greater number and enthusiasm, which spurs the leader to further . . . and so it goes. While this virtual circle is enacted, a seamless and unselfconscious bond builds between leaders and followers. Their every action seems aligned to each other and to their objectives.

When Shiela Moore began at Casa Myrna, many people were uncomfortable with her. She was from the health care world that domestic violence staff did not trust, a woman but not a proven feminist. Within a couple of years, she had helped transform Casa Myrna from a grassroots to a well-funded, better-respected, more professional organization, one with adequate infrastructure and innovative programs, one growing in size, influence, and financial stability. She accomplished this through a combination of making people better and replacing those who did not fit with those who did. In the process, there was a tipping point, when a growing majority believed in her, in the new Casa Myrna approach, and in themselves. The more they believed in her method, the more they succeeded. The more they succeeded, the more they believed in themselves. The more they believed in themselves, the more attached they were to the leader who had helped them feel this way. This was the virtuous circle that led to Casa Myrna's transformation—wonderful morale, smooth operations, and the expectation of continued success pervaded the organization.

Psychological Approach

Psychological approaches (Dansereau, Graen, & Haga, 1975) represent an application of psychodynamic psychology to the world of leadership. The writers in this group suggest that leaders are more effective when they understand themselves. Accordingly, effective leaders know what they do well and what they do poorly, what upsets them and distorts their ability to reason clearly, and when their confidence shades into narcissism, their enthusiasm into grandiosity—and how to catch their problematic tendencies before they create problems. Similarly, leaders would do well to understand their subordinates, especially what motivates them and what creates resistance in them. Implicit in psychodynamic thinking is the belief that character is deeply etched and very hard to change. Hence, leaders need to know, accept, and work within their own limits and those of their subordinates.

In contrast, family systems theorists note that character is not destined but malleable, particularly as contexts shift. In this view, different contexts bring out different aspects of individual character and let other aspects fall to the background. One context, for example, might bring out nurturing qualities. Another context might require directive tendencies and bring them out. Some situations bring out confidence, hard work, teamwork, and ethical conduct. Others bring out conflict, lethargy, and selfishness. According to family systems theory, however, people are not infinitely malleable. There is an interaction between their character and the context. Knowing the relationship between the two is the mark of a good leader.

Situational leadership is built on knowledge of this relationship, which varies with the developmental stage of the organization. Although situational leadership focuses on the management of increasing maturity in individuals and teams, that management is based on the manager's ability to recognize stage-by-stage development and to adapt to each new stage. In other words, not only leaders but also the relationship between leaders and followers changes from quadrant to quadrant and from context (situation) to context.

For purposes of alignment, it is important for leaders to know themselves and to know how they typically respond in different situations or contexts, and it is important for them to understand the systemic relationship between themselves and followers: the nature of a dyadic relationship, for example, and how that relationship is affected by the larger system.

Alignment, the Whole

As the story goes, when seven blind men encounter an elephant and describe what they "see," seven descriptions emerge that are accurate in the particulars but misguided in their sense of the whole. One man feels a leg and asserts, with great certainty, that it is a tree trunk. Another feels the body and argues that it is really a mountain. Yet another feels the trunk and argues that it is a great hose. The elephant itself gets lost in the process.

Leadership alignment is the elephant in the story. The leader must have the right character traits for the job, or so contingency theory tells us. This might mean courage and boldness in some organizations, for example, and steadiness in others. That is, character must match up well to organizational style, current organizational needs, strategies, and the like. Character plays out in particular styles. People of considerable ego strength, for example, can lead differently. Some are out front and charismatic; others, secure in themselves, work behind the scenes and satisfy both themselves and organizational needs by empowering others.

According to path-goal theory, leaders motivate followers by aligning expectations, outcomes, and rewards with workers' capacity to succeed. Aside from aligning character, style, and general situation, the successful leader structures specific situations to align them with the organization's goals and the workers' capabilities. Together, leadership theories begin to tell us how leader and organization fit effectively. Exchange theory tells us that effective leadership depends on more than structure; it requires relationship. It is through relationship that leaders bring followers into alignment with organizational goals and methods—and, as we will show later, it is through relationship that followers bring new leaders into alignment with organizational style and values.

Finally, with all the matching of leaders, followers, character, and capacity, psychological insight becomes the vital, intellectual fuel that permits leaders to align organizations.

If one were to align a leader who is determined and communicates well and whose personality and behavior (style) fit well with the organizational culture, who understands how to structure the organization's future and light up the pathway to success, who communicates frequently with direct reports and makes staff followers feel supported and understood, and who holds high standards in a way that is sensitive to both individual and group psychological needs—if one were to see such alignment, what would be witnessed is effective leadership.

Note

1. The great man theory is so prevalent and so ancient that it is hard to attribute it to any one person, but certainly people like Warren Bennis and Tom Peters have done their share in publicizing the theory in its contemporary form. See Peters and Waterman (1982).

References

Bennis, W. G., & Nanus, B. (1985). *Leaders: The strategies for taking charge.* New York: Harper & Row.

Blanchard, K., Zigarmi, P., & Zigarmi, D. (1985). *Leadership and the one minute manager.* New York: Morrow.

Burns, J. M. (1978). *Leadership.* New York: Harper & Row.

Dansereau, F., Graen, G. G., & Haga, W. (1975). A vertical dyad linkage approach to leadership in formal organizations. *Organizational Behavior and Human Performance, 13,* 46–78.

Fiedler, F. E. (1967). *A theory of leadership effectiveness.* New York: McGraw-Hill.

Greenleaf, R. K. (1977). *Servant leadership: A journey into the nature of legitimate power and greatness.* Ramsey, NJ: Paulist Press.

House, R. J. (1971). A path-goal theory of leader effectiveness. *Administrative Science Quarterly, 16,* 321–328.

Nadler, D. A., & Tushman, M. L. (1989). *What makes for magic leadership?* Boulder, CO: Westview.

Northouse, P. G. (2001). *Leadership: Theory and practice* (2nd ed.). Thousand Oaks, CA: Sage.

Peters, T. J., & Waterman, R. H. (1982). *In search of excellence.* New York: Harper & Row.

Rost, J. C. (1991). *Leadership for the twenty-first century.* Westport, CT: Praeger.

Schriesheim, C. A., & Keider, L. L. (1996). Path-goal leadership theory: The long and winding road. *Leadership Quarterly, 7*(3), 317–321.

Stevens, W. (1965). *The collected poems of Wallace Stevens* (7th ed.). New York: Alfred Knopf.

Zaleznik, A. (1977). Managers and leaders: Are they different? *Harvard Business Review, 15*(3), 67–84.

4

The Cultural
Narrative of Leadership

This is a time of great struggle and vitality in the nonprofit sector. As government funding for housing, health, community development, environmental, and workplace safety programs has decreased, nonprofit organizations, led by their largely self-taught leaders, have risen to fill the gap. Nonprofits are helping the people they serve claim responsibility for and control over their own lives, as best they can. A good part of the vitality comes from the freshness of these nonprofit efforts and the intimacy they have with the people and causes they serve. They arise to fill needs and to meet specific circumstances in specific communities that are every bit as demanding as economic markets.

What nonprofit leaders sometimes lack in formal education and management expertise, they make up in enthusiasm, energy, and, often enough, inventiveness. They learn quickly because they must; they build their ships as they sail; they innovate to solve the problems encountered along the way. In this sense, nonprofits and their leaders deserve key chapters in the story of American entrepreneurial enterprise.

Yet with the decline of public funding during the last decade and the increase in competition for financial resources within the nonprofit world, the gap between the skills and activities required of for-profit and nonprofit leaders has narrowed. Nonprofit leaders—both directors and board members—must spend more time raising money. As one commentator put it, "Resource shortages have stimulated a change in focus among leaders of social service agencies, moving them from a mission" and leadership in the larger community "toward a professional [managerial] orientation more concerned with self-preservation" (Eisenberg, 1997).

To succeed, leaders must fit their circumstances. Yet to a large extent, nonprofit leaders are being asked to fit narrowly defined standards set by outsiders:

government agencies and philanthropic foundations who fund the nonprofits, boards of directors and management consultants who advise them, and a cultural ethos that forms the larger backdrop to their efforts. To please funders, they must show results through formal program evaluations, now required by almost all funding sources, despite an absence of skill and an absence of funding set aside for the evaluation process itself. In other words, nonprofit leaders must demonstrate the kind of businesslike accountability taught at business schools.

The purpose of this chapter is to take a critical look at our culture's view of leadership, what we call the corporate canon, and loosen its grip on our collective understanding of what good leadership entails, enabling more ideas to be expressed and ultimately more kinds of leaders to succeed.

Cultural Narratives

Cultures have a good deal to say about how to be a proper leader. They do so through the media, through newspapers, magazines, books, and movies, and through educational institutions and training programs. In the case of nonprofits, funding institutions and boards of directors carry society's message quite directly. They exert pressure toward the style of leadership prescribed by a business-oriented world.

These messages are influential not only because they are brought by powerful people in powerful positions but because they are articulated within a legitimate cultural language, a cultural narrative. Both senders and receivers generally understand this language; both, even when they personally deviate from it, give that narrative considerable weight. It is the language they share.

A cultural narrative is the sum of a particular society's ideas about how people are supposed to behave, think, and feel—what constitutes a good person, a good marriage, and a good leader. It illustrates the thoughts or feelings deemed fundamentally characteristic of a place and time. It is most powerfully transmitted through stories—like teaching stories in traditional cultures or the Horatio Alger (1990) story of success through pluck and luck in late-nineteenth-century America. This is how the melting-pot theory, so visible in its imagery, explained what was supposed to happen to the masses of immigrants arriving from Europe. This is how Frederick Jackson Turner's (1985) theory of the frontier explained to generations of Americans why it was our manifest destiny to conquer the West and spread democracy across the American continent, no matter the obstacles—even as it taught us to ignore the genocide that accompanied the conquest.

Cultural narratives do not stand alone, each unique unto itself. In general, they are versions of universal themes. Thus they anchor archetypal images, such as the warrior leader or philosopher king, to specific times and places. They make sense of experience.

Hence in an age of empire, exploration stands as the story of courage, sacrifice, curiosity, and adventure. These stories serve a dual function, both mirror and meaning. At once they attempt to recreate past events in light of the current culture's needs, even as they create new perspectives and possibilities for interpretation. This interweaving of "the what" with "the why" gives a cultural narrative its power and permits a shareable world.

The story of the Mayflower is one of the core images in the American narrative, containing within it themes of estrangement from the Old World, destiny to discover the new, a compact that unites all on board (Pilgrims and nonreligious alike), settlement, proliferation, and enlightenment promulgated to the uncivilized. These plots persist in American culture, as they both remind and explain. Therefore, a cultural narrative is more than just a perspective. It is the means by which a culture puts forth, promotes, and imposes its standards on members. This is how a culture replicates itself, how it enfolds and survives.

The cultural narrative also brings leadership into specific cultural focus. One can read and understand the cultural narrative by reading the person who is called to lead it. In transitional historical periods, moreover, the cultural narrative generally presents both sides of important issues—ideas from the past, and ideas that are emerging. Erik Erikson (1969) describes Mahatma Gandhi as both the last representative of the trend in human history whereby "religious man" stood in the way of "political and technological man," and the first in a new trend "combining politics and religion." As the former, Gandhi was an ascetic who cultivated his inner reserves, a guru living in poverty, practicing abstinence, and preaching noninvolvement. As the latter, Gandhi organized workers and led campaigns of nonviolent civil disobedience that led to Indian independence. Gandhi's place in history is due in large part to how he transformed a cultural narrative in a time of revolutionary change.

The story of Moses is a good example of a cultural narrative. In the Torah, Moses is a reluctant and humble leader, insisting that he can't speak well enough to persuade Pharaoh to let his people go. But God reassures him and suggests that his brother, Aaron, will speak for him. Thus leadership can be shared. Not only must it be shared among the top group, but it must be agreed upon with each and all the people. This is the idea of the covenant, by which each person must freely join the community and its rules. The covenantal idea then becomes the basis of all ideas about how people should relate to God and to each other.

Later, still in the desert, the tribal elders advise Moses to deputize numbers of wise elders in order to help him rule because he cannot be accessible to all of the people. And when approaching the land of Israel, the aging Moses names his successor, Joshua. Moses is not permitted to enter the new land; a new type of leader, more human, less directly connected to God, is required for the future of the Jewish nation. These tales of decentralized, human-sized leadership, taking charge by virtue of agreement with free men, has been told year after year for millennia to Jewish congregations, informing children and adults alike about the type of leadership required for a particular type of community. Throughout the centuries in Jewish communities, leaders have aspired to this covenantal leadership (Elazar, 1995) and have been criticized when they diverge from it.

Many centuries later, during the Middle Ages, the ideal of leadership changed. At the time, there was thought to be a "great chain of being," in which all people had their place, to which they were born. They should not try to be other than who they were. Some were meant to be workers, others thinkers, still others leaders. Perhaps the noble King Arthur of Camelot best conjures up the image of such a leader.

The early idea that noble birth is critical to leadership has faded. George Washington, of an aristocratic Virginia family, is an example of privileged origins serving democratic ends. He fought against empire, and then, with the Revolutionary War won, he refused to be king. He was a nobleman turned democrat, a warrior in a time of war who turned statesman when that war was over, and a politician who went back to the agrarian way of life when his term was complete. Washington epitomized the dominant way of life—and what was held as virtuous—in the eighteenth century, embodying the narrative of leadership in his time.

American leadership narratives have focused on two types of men. One is the self-made man—the industrialist who, with "pluck and luck," has built an empire and created a fortune. Here one thinks of Rockefeller, Vanderbilt, Carnegie, Ford, and Morgan in the early part of the century, and Gates, Bezos, Turner, Soros, and Welch in more recent times. Our lionization of these men echoes Homer's celebration of Achilles and Odysseus. Not only do they build empires and accept our accolades, but they also articulate their philosophies for the admiring masses and institutionalize their philosophies in philanthropic foundations.

The second American narrative features the pioneer—the inventor, the rebel, the one who leaves conventional society to explore the unknown. Think of Daniel Boone, James Fennimore Cooper's Natty Bumpo, and Henry David Thoreau, and of Ben Franklin, Thomas Alva Edison, and the NASA space program during the early sixties. They represent the romantic strain in American culture, the belief that we began by escaping the cramped, rule-dominated world of Europe to find freedom in the vast New World wilderness. Throughout our history, this belief continually finds new ways to express itself: the westward migration; the agrarian rebellions against the stifling, dominating city; the environmentalists' struggle against uncaring corporations; the Silicon Valley rejection of bureaucratic practice in corporations.

These types occasionally cross, as in the case of Henry Ford, whose assembly-line methods revolutionized industrial production, but more often they stand in opposition to one another. At their best, these diverging archetypes are permissive. Together, they offer more than one mythical path to shape our imaginations and our sense of what is possible and heroic.

THE CURRENT CULTURAL NARRATIVE OF LEADERSHIP

In today's world, leaders are typically said to be confident, outgoing, and brilliant. They are articulate, driven, and creative, and like Harry Truman, they always accept responsibility for their decisions. While great leaders eagerly advocate change and are sometimes impatient with those who resist it, they are strong enough to tolerate both delays and ambiguous situations. Masterful strategists, good leaders are able to structure situations and to rally people to achieve their objectives. Unlike the image painted by Machiavelli, contemporary leaders are said to have integrity, which is what makes them credible with their followers.

Despite their current fall from grace during the corporate scandals of the early twenty-first century, America's business leaders still represent the standard against which others are measured. This is a period of free-market ascendancy and CEO cult status. The vast majority of Americans seem to believe that businessmen know best—no matter that this same majority is generally excluded from the halls of corporate power. Business leaders are said to be smart, tough, and daring, the victors in a Darwinian marketplace, and the benefactors of their own corporate canon.

By contrast, nonprofit leaders are seen to be well-meaning, not very talented or well-educated, social workers and community amateurs, cheered on by neighbors and supported by the largesse of our capitalist society. Most tellingly, they are not businesspeople. One commentator, Paul Light (1998, p. 2), makes this distinction:

> Consider for a moment the words one associates with the terms "businesslike" and "nonprofit-like." The former conjures up images of competitive, entrepreneurial, strategic, agile, innovative, and profitable, while the latter all-too-often sparks conversations about sluggish, under-funded, stressful, professionalized, duplicative, and inefficient. . . . Therefore, it is hardly surprising that boards and funders would rarely urge the nonprofit sector to be more nonprofit-like. Whereas, being businesslike has come to mean fast, lean, efficient, and strategic, being nonprofit-like is merely a condition of existence.

That, at least, is the cultural lore that often informs our evaluation of nonprofit leaders.

This creates problems. Although board members, foundations, program officers, and government funding agencies tend to come from the American mainstream, many nonprofits and nonprofit leaders—and their ideas about leadership—do not. Ours is a multicultural society. Urban communities are more likely to be dominated by African American, Latino, and Asian than by white Anglo-Saxon populations. And unlike the leadership of many corporations, foundations, and nonprofit boards of directors, our society includes women and children.

Different cultural and gendered imagery about leadership, however, tends not to make much of an impression on the mainstream cultural imagery. So even though almost everyone would agree that leadership requires the right person in the right circumstances, mainstream funders and board members generally revert to a uniform idea of leadership for nonprofits, no matter the cultural background, gender, or age of their leaders.

The imposition is both direct and indirect. The direct pressure is explicit about how you must act as a leader to receive support and funding. The indirect pressure says that you must act in a certain way to gain respect. Understandably, many, if not most, nonprofit leaders have internalized the mainstream view. So they war within themselves. On one hand, they believe in themselves and feel attached to the leadership style that brought about their early success. On the other hand, they harbor fearful beliefs that the imagery trumpeted in the media, in the leadership literature, and in their own boardrooms represents a deeper, truer idea of how they should behave and how they should think.

Of course nonprofit leaders are not solely caught up in this negative imagery. Among for-profit entrepreneurs, all but the most effective managers are diminished by way of comparison. Entrepreneurs, those heroes of American invention who are often considered the engine of our economic growth, are tolerated in the beginning but soon replaced by venture capitalists, investment bankers, and nervous boards of directors. Entrepreneurs are held to be disorganized, controlling, ignorant about business and organizational development, and hard to hold accountable. Like their grassroots and nonprofit counterparts, entrepreneurial leaders are disconcerting to bankers and managers—too enthusiastic and unpredictable. They just don't fit into the mainstream ethos, and in the end, they need to be developed as "leaders," converted, or marginalized.

The current picture of leadership is so pervasive among those who fund and guide nonprofits that it has become prescriptive and domineering. It is a canon by which leaders are evaluated. It is not entirely irrelevant or wrong. Who can deny the value in having a plan, a method, and a way to measure outcomes? Nor would any reasonable person say a leader cannot develop and grow with coaching and study. But when the canon is imposed in a one-size-fits-all manner, it wrongly deselects some leaders and has a distorting effect on others who abandon their own style and attempt to become something they are not.

When this happens to capable and innovative people, we squander one of our society's most precious resources: the energy, variety, and creativity of a large percentage of our leaders.

Hegemony

One of the most powerful theoretical strains of the modern age is historicism. First fully articulated by Hegel in the early nineteenth century, it has become the dominant view of the twentieth and twenty-first centuries. Historicism insists that all ideas, including the apparently objective ideas of science, are deeply influenced by the social, economic, and cultural forces of their time and place. Later in the nineteenth century, Marx emphasized economic forces as the underpinnings of ideological positions that shaped the political and moral theories of their societies. In the twentieth century, most prominently with Derrida (1982) and Foucault (1972), postmodernist thinkers argued that all ideas, small and large, reflected the interests of one social group or another, and that the most prominent, influential ideas reflected, both consciously and unconsciously, the interests of the dominant social classes. Together with the more obvious signs of power, such as wealth and military might, these dominant ideas contributed to what the postmodernists call the hegemony of ruling classes.

The notion of hegemony explains how a society's ruling class maintains itself through persuasion rather than through economic power or physical force alone. Hegemonic ideas embody, validate, and consolidate power in the hands of a few. Hegemony is complete when those who are dominated accept their plight as the natural order of things—as common sense.

On one level of analysis, the corporate canon represents the simplification of archetypal imagery to serve the ruling class. The problem with these shining stars, the archetypes, is that they can become stereotyped. Archetypes inspire; stereotypes squeeze the vitality from them. Once stereotypes are established, they limit both the range of motion leaders are allowed and the number or type of people who are seen as qualified as leaders. And there is a tremendous impulse in this country to institutionalize the stereotype. Then they are imposed on organizations and leaders, becoming the standard upon which leaders are measured, hired, fired, rewarded, and punished.

Apart from issues of fairness and justice, as a society we pay an enormous cost in terms of our life force, our diversity. First, because the cultural stereotype of leadership—the individual expression of the corporate canon—contains at root an overwhelming need for *control*, diverse expressions of leadership are constrained or disallowed. Exploration, risk-taking, leading with heart from vision and values—these are subjugated to the higher needs of loyalty, predictability, and closure. Second, and paradoxically, the corporate canon is ultimately self-limiting—because of its own success. Daniel Goleman et al. (2002) writes that the basis of self-deception is overreliance on our habitual consciousness. What has worked in the past becomes the only way to work. Thus, the corporate canon subordinates variety to its rule by success. Diverse and emerging models of leadership are held hostage by our consciousness of the one, the collective best practice of leadership.

Hegemonic views do more than oppress people directly. They become dominant to the degree that most people lose sight of the fact that they reflect one group's interests more than others'. They seem to represent the truth, and, in that way, they become the standards by which all of society's citizens judge themselves and others. For a brief time, we viewed leadership through the lens of Churchill's and Roosevelt's heroic stoicism, and later through the more romantic lens of Kennedy's Camelot. These views have been codified as "great man" theories of leadership. Those who approach these styles are deemed leaders or, when young, leadership material; those who look or sound different are outside the mainstream, or worse, subversive.

To fight the hegemonic views of their society, the postmodernists "deconstruct" the key ideas and images that shape the way people see and behave in their world, revealing how hegemonic views are partial and slanted in favor of some and against others. They show how such views tend to establish oppositions—good and bad, highborn and lowborn, smart and stupid, black and white, European and African or Asian, male and female.

Feminists, for example, have extensively and effectively dismantled theoretical and philosophical views that "privilege" men—that make men seem better, stronger, smarter, and therefore entitled or even obligated to hold most of the positions of power and influence. African American, Latino, Third World, and many other groups who have experienced a worldview that holds them to be less adequate than the "old white men" who rule and who enjoy the material fruits of contemporary societies have also deconstructed the views that press them down.

Some oppressed people have taken deconstruction as an opportunity to trumpet their own social ways over those of the ruling classes. The phrase "black is beautiful" sometimes captures this kind of attempt to overcome white dominance. Much of the research literature on female leadership similarly trumps male dominance by insisting that women's more egalitarian, nurturing, networking ways are better adapted to modern organizational realities. In its purest form, however, deconstruction does not trumpet one group or one ideological position over others. Instead, it takes apart a dominant view so that many views can flourish. This is multiculturalism at its best.

Perhaps the best illustration of what business wants from nonprofit organizations is found in *High Performance Nonprofit Organizations*, out of the Harvard

Kennedy School's Hauser Center for Nonprofit Organizations (Letts, Ryan, & Grossman, 1999). The book begins by noting the vital importance of nonprofits for the perpetuation of our civil society—nonprofits now make up "about 8 percent of the gross domestic product and 7 percent of total employment, with an annual payroll of $480 billion" (Letts et al., 1999, pp. 1–2). The authors are at pains to say that for nonprofits to fulfill their missions, they must learn to build capacity, which is current code for becoming more businesslike. Most of the book is dedicated to teaching business lessons for "high performance."

In an early chapter on "Cross Sector Lessons on Organizational Capacity," the authors state their fundamental proposition: "Businesses have developed a substantial body of information and experience on organizational capacity building, which could provide lessons and best practices" (Letts et al., 1999, p. 29). A list of chapter titles illustrates how capacity and high performances is achieved: "Quality Processes: Advancing Mission by Meeting Client Needs"; "Product Development: Better Ideas and Better Implementation"; "Benchmarking: An Organizational Process That Links Learning and Results"; "Human Resources: Developing Employees to Advance Organizational Goals"; and "The Nonprofit Board: Creating a Culture of Performance."

Pablo Eisenberg has sounded an alarm about the tendency to accept the truth of the corporate canon. He calls the trend the "corporatization" of the nonprofit sector. He writes, "Much of the nonprofit world has adopted some of the worst, not best, practices of corporate America. It has failed to distinguish between sound and ill-advised corporate policies, between for-profit and nonprofit activities" (Eisenberg, 1997, p. 332). One of the worst characteristics of the corporate sector that the nonprofit sector has adopted, he says, is what he calls "the cult of the CEO"—the tremendous emphasis on the chief executive. "While it corresponds to our national infatuation with stars and celebrities, it is dangerous to the long-term health of nonprofits because it diminishes collegiality and teamwork and detracts from the organizational mission. It builds egos, not institutions" (Eisenberg, 1997, p. 336).

A second problem with following the example of corporate leadership is that it has become increasingly shortsighted. It is narrowly geared to achieving "shareholder value" by meeting trumped-up profit projections and measuring them in quarterly statements. To achieve these short-term effects, boards provide immense bonuses to their CEOs. More than any other, this focus has led to the corruption of American corporate leaders and, perhaps as bad, inattention to building organizations that will be durable and creative over the long haul. When this short-term focus, this need to demonstrate results rapidly and through metrics, is applied to nonprofit organizations, it often robs them of their ability to grow at their own pace and to gradually win places in the communities they serve.

Current Nonprofit Leaders Who Fit the Cultural Narrative

To say that there is a corporate canon that excludes or burdens many nonprofit leaders does not mean that there aren't nonprofit leaders who fit naturally and well into that mold. In fairness, we want to sketch a few examples. Rick Little, for one, is a character of mythic proportions in the charitable world. He is a man of humble origins, plagued by early, life-threatening illness, who arose from his sickbed and resolved to help others rise as well. To do so, he persuaded the Kellogg Foundation to provide a grant of $63 million for an organization he had only so far conceived, the International Youth Foundation (IYF). It would be an intermediary organization, funneling money and technical assistance from foundations and corporations to programs that enabled young people to develop the skills, the confidence, and the will to rise from humble origins and thrive, and to give back to the communities from which they came. With time, IYF formed subfoundations in 60 nations, each serving what they believed were worthy, youth-oriented community organizations. Like his corporate counterparts, Rick Little formed this organization with "pluck and luck," with passion, tenacity, and skill. And corporate America, recognizing a kindred spirit, supported him unstintingly.

Alan Khazei and Michael Brown, who founded City Year in 1988, are two more exemplars of the American cultural narrative. At the time, they were roommates at Harvard Law School "who felt strongly that young people in service could be a powerful resource for addressing our nation's most pressing issues" (City Year, 2004). To realize their dream, they utilized the most contemporary methods taught to and espoused by the Harvard Business School. They began with a big idea developed through brainstorming and strategic planning sessions, including clear approaches to service delivery, project execution and program development, and fiscal responsibility and accountability. In other words, they caught a wave almost identical to the wave that fueled the dot-com boom of the nineties, with venture capital recruited to "scale up" good ideas that could make a difference. Within a relatively brief time, they had a modest number of programs up and running. Then City Year and its leaders caught fire and became the darlings of the philanthropic community. Their success was trumpeted throughout the media, popular and professional, corporate and nonprofit.

In a similar vein, at least three books—*Grassroots Leaders for a New Economy* (Henton, Melville, & Walesh, 1997), Paul Grogan's (2000) *Comeback Cities: A Blueprint for Urban Neighborhood Revival,* and Lisbeth Schorr's (1997) *Common Purpose: Strengthening Families and Neighborhoods to Rebuild America*— describe a movement that combines the technology of contemporary management science with venture-like investment and the needs and impetus of neighborhoods to "scale up" community development. *High Performance Nonprofit*

Organizations (Letts et al., 1999) provides a blueprint for such applications. Little, Khazei, Brown, and the others described in these books are talented leaders and deserve their success, but their success can also be attributed, at least in part, to the style by which they went about their business. They fit the American cultural narrative of leadership and, therefore, were deemed worthy of its resources.

Nonprofit Leaders Who Do Not Fit

On the other hand, there are too many nonprofit leaders who do not fit the mold and suffer the consequences. There is Harlen Smith (pseudonym), for example, a man of extensive administrative experience, who began a nonprofit to infuse a major American university with the ideals, understanding, and skills of civic participation. His organization was funded by a dot-com billionaire, who loved the initial idea but then insisted that his program officer almost immediately impose a hard-driving, entrepreneurial style of organization and leadership that was foreign to Smith. During the first two years, he spent 30 to 40 percent of his time dealing with the foundation, instead of with his organization. Unaccustomed to and uneasy with the extensive and formal, internet-based reporting arrangements the foundation wanted, Smith procrastinated and delegated and appeared far more disorganized than he had been in prior leadership positions. Criticized for his lack of management skills and attention to detail, he began to question himself; with time, his confidence was shaken, and the social skills that had been his hallmark began to deteriorate. He became less articulate, made fewer alliances for the organization, brought in fewer grants, and became almost reclusive.

The Innovation Center for Youth and Community Development was formed with the idea that young people had not generally been given a seat at the leadership table, that organizations for youth had been led primarily by adults who did not understand youth culture and, even though they meant well, often patronized youth. Those young people who did take positions of leadership were rarely taken as seriously as they should have been. Those who taught them leadership skills tended to teach them how middle-aged bureaucrats would lead. As a result, the young people were turned off and alienated. Fewer assumed or created leadership roles in a society that badly needs their engagement. Instead of imposing its idea of leadership, the Innovation Center searched for "best practices" among youth leaders themselves, then spread the word and helped to establish leadership training programs based on these naturally evolved best practices.

During the 1970s, many community drug rehabilitation centers grew up out of community hotlines that were built by street-corner leaders who themselves had been serious drug users. They developed unique approaches to therapy and organization, often egalitarian in a spirit similar to the early days of Casa Myrna. Government agencies, frustrated in their own rehabilitation efforts, eventually turned to these grassroots organizations, and poured millions of dollars into their programs. After a brief time, the agencies got worried about loose financial accounting, which they believed went hand-in-glove with the informal leadership style, and began to demand better management. Almost inevitably, the demand led to a leadership transition; the founding leader was replaced with a better manager; and many of the programs lost the spirit and exuberance that had made them successful in the first place.

HOW THE CULTURAL NARRATIVE IS IMPOSED

For decades, business and professional leaders have been instructing nonprofit leaders how to run their organizations. They have done so from positions of authority—sitting on boards of directors and presiding over foundations, whose support is often the lifeblood of nonprofit organizations and can be withdrawn as rapidly as it had been given. They have done so from the moral high ground that capitalism has gained since the cold war, with the astounding cachet that business leaders, MBAs, and untutored entrepreneurs alike had achieved during the great bull market. Together, they have formed a chorus to preach the gospel of accountability, planning, and measurement, among other core elements of the MBA curriculum. In a word, nonprofit organizations and their leaders should be more businesslike.

To survive, nonprofit leaders must focus on funding sources. To please funders, they must show results through formal program evaluations, which are now required by almost all funding sources despite an absence of skill and an absence of funding set aside for the evaluation process itself. Nonprofit leaders must demonstrate the kind of businesslike accountability taught at business schools. So it should not be surprising to learn that many younger, public-spirited people take business school, not social work or the "mean streets" as the best path to effective nonprofit leadership. Business schools represent the present-day equivalent of divinity schools for an American culture in which the managerial ethic is triumphant and transcendent.

So pervasive is the managerial ethic that even those organizations that pride themselves on standing outside the mainstream—for example, those who work with youthful leaders of social justice organizations—preach the gospel of strategic planning, outcomes research, management accountability, and marketing plans. Their justification is that it's essential to arm social protesters with the same kinds of tools that have made their establishment cousins successful.

Finally, entrepreneurs, those wonderful outlaws of American business lore, are also falling in line. They, too, frequently go to business schools and learn proper management techniques and behaviors. When they don't, they are often subject to "market discipline." These days, for example, venture capitalists generally insist on a majority voice on boards of directors. In those positions, they regularly replace founding entrepreneurs with professional managers. This has become such common practice that even the firing or demotion of well-known entrepreneurs rates only the scantest notice.

This brings us full circle in our argument about the homogenization of nonprofit leadership. Parallel to the disciplining of for-profit entrepreneurs, venture philanthropists have begun to discipline the entrepreneurial-minded nonprofit leaders whom they fund, teaching them about software systems for financial reporting and giving them crash courses in professional management in order to help them scale up small imaginative projects. Nonprofit leaders can be replaced with true professionals if they don't take well to the managerial discipline.

Nonprofit Boards

These attitudes are not confined to the recently wealthy. Executives from large, long-lasting, and stable firms, consultancies, and law partnerships join them in somewhat different forms. They are more inclined to join boards of directors, where some play relatively passive roles and others actively provide counsel to nonprofit leaders, who either seek their (for-profit) wisdom or say they do. The counsel is almost always in the vein of good management practice: Leaders should state clear objectives and hold their subordinates accountable for carrying them out; leaders should institute responsible financial practices and (where feasible) operational systems; and so forth. In other words, nonprofit leaders should learn to be good managers, in the image of the board members.

Foundations

Foundations provide considerable support for nonprofit organizations. They can be roughly divided into two camps: the more experienced and traditional foundations, like Ford, Rockefeller, Pew, Kellogg, Annie Casey, and Hewlett; and the newer, perhaps more aggressive organizations founded by what one author has termed the "new imperialists," Gates, Bezos, Walton, Omidyar, and others, who made their fortunes during the bull market of the eighties and nineties.

Much of the money targeted to nonprofits will come from those who have made their fortune during the last decade or two, entrepreneurs and investment professionals who followed the rags-to-riches pathways that are so central to American social mythology. As with their predecessors of a century ago, men like Rockefeller, Carnegie, and Mellon, the new millionaires and billionaires believe that they have discovered the formula for leadership and organizational effectiveness. Their belief is reinforced by the public media that glorify their triumphant methods and codify theirs as *the way to success.*

We met one newly rich venture capitalist, for example, who had only contempt for virtually anyone who was not a hard-driving, iconoclastic businessman and was busy hiring these types to replace sleepy and unimaginative "bureaucrats" in the nonprofits that he was now funding. Such men have been very successful. They are articulate and confident and, therefore, persuasive, which emboldens them to teach others, many of whom are eager to learn their lessons.

Many, if not most, of the newly wealthy businesspeople have already turned to philanthropy, wanting to give back to a society that has been so kind to them and, or so they believe, needs their help. All this is highly commendable. They do not wish to follow in the path of their predecessors, whose philanthropic activities seem passive and not oriented to radical change. They changed their own fields of endeavor—high tech, finance, even retail—in dramatic and rapid fashion. Why, they ask, shouldn't social problems yield to the same "out of the box" thinking and entrepreneurial methods? Instead of contributing money, alone, these "venture philanthropists" want to contribute their expertise and oversight. They want a (social) return on their investment. To guarantee their investments, they want orderly reporting, clear strategic plans, quantifiable measures of success, and, if possible, "breakthrough ideas" that work well in one location and can then be replicated in many other locations. In other words, the philanthropists insist that nonprofits work like the entrepreneurial businesses they built.

Often, "old money," with its professional staffs of foundation heads and program officers, is equally imposing. According to Peter Karoff (2004, p. 5), former CEO of the Philanthropic Initiative,

> Organized philanthropy is not a welcoming place. Large Foundations have almost no transparency, limited accessibility, are run by an old boy/girl network, work only in silos, and resist anything "not invented here." Further, they are lousy listeners, bureaucratic, unimaginative, slow, accountable only to themselves and risk adverse. They are mired in a 5% payout mode as though immortality is more important than the critical needs of today. They collaborate poorly with nonprofit leaders and among themselves, and refuse to invest seriously in the infrastructure of the field— such as experienced executive leadership—even though the infrastructure so significantly enhances nonprofit organization's ability to survive and to carry out its mission. What is more, philanthropic organizations have grown so enamored of "metrics" that they pay too little attention to the spirit of nonprofit operations.

In short, the business and foundation people too often present a one-size-fits-all solution to the nonprofit leaders, without asking who the leaders are and what makes each one effective—effective enough to have attracted funding in the first place. Certainly almost no one asks the leaders what lessons they might have for the foundations or for business enterprise. Yet nonprofit leaders have often created and run organizations on a shoestring, overcoming one obstacle after another in ways that businesspeople, if they knew, might admire greatly.

Government and Foundation Assessment

Like foundations, state and federal government agencies have increasingly demanded program and organizational evaluations from nonprofits that they fund. In most ways this is laudable. The evaluations are not just for the agencies. They require nonprofits to look at themselves, to determine if their goals are realistic, whether there is a market for their services, whether they are achieving their goals, and how well they are organized, operationally, to realize their goals. Yet implicit in most evaluation procedures are the forms of organization development and leadership style prescribed by the corporate canon.

Popular Literature and Consultants

As a culture, we are obsessed with leadership and enamored with its proselytizers. The bookshelves are filled with volumes that tell us how to be great leaders. In the 1980s, there were five articles a day being published about leadership—in English alone. By the 1990s there were ten. Enter "leadership" as the keyword for the Amazon.com database and 12,000 books leap to the screen. Add to this all the articles that weren't published, the memos in human resource departments, and, especially the leadership training programs that have sprouted up by the thousands. Almost all of these articles, books, and training programs are prescriptive. Few are descriptive. Almost none are written by nonprofit people.

They tell us the very best way to become a great leader. They do not even suggest that there are many legitimate and effective ways to lead. Taken together, these efforts constitute a veritable industry, through which so-called leaders are being processed like products on an assembly line. And the captains of this industry insist that nonprofit leaders pass through these processing plants.

They are, in fact, written by management consultants and business school professionals who earn their living providing advice and coaching to organizations and their leaders. While the majority of coaches and consultants are people of integrity who would be appalled by accusations of bias, they are generally unwitting agents of the cultural narrative. They talk, for example, of bringing "best practice" methods to their work. But best practice methods, far from being scientific, are almost always based on anecdotal evidence—what works for the writer/consultant, who spends most of his or her time working in the corporate sector. In other words, best practices are invariably taken from the corporate canon and then applied to nonprofit organizations.

IMPACT OF THE CULTURAL NARRATIVE OF LEADERSHIP

Years ago, Kai Erikson (1986) wrote an analysis of the Massachusetts Bay Puritans and the banishment of Roger Williams. Instead of focusing on the negative side of ostracism, he suggested that any society must have a way to say who belongs, who is in and who is out. The very act of defining someone as deviant permits a culture to say what is normative, that is, to describe its own character. In other words, deviance is functional. It permits one to know oneself.

Those deemed deviant are not as pleased about such distinguishing activities. They tend to lose out. They are ostracized (within a community, ostracizing takes the form of ghettos) or relegated to second-class status. As second-class citizens, they do not share equally in society's resources.

In order to improve their condition, they may aggressively assault the citadels of the culture's dominant group, which is a way to understand community-based protest movements, often led by nonprofit groups. Or outsiders can assimilate, which is a way to understand the efforts of nonprofit leaders to talk the language of insiders, what we have called the corporate canon, and even to convert to its verities. But the conversion is rarely complete. Even when one learns to behave like a full-fledged member of the dominant culture, there tends to be ambivalence, ambivalence that compromises one's effectiveness, and ambivalence that insiders can sense.

There is a price to pay for assimilation, conversion, or rebellion, no matter how earnestly undertaken. First, the one-size-fits-all approach squeezes out many effective leaders whose styles are several degrees off the central tendency. Again, the visionaries, entrepreneurs, and activists are taken to task for what they *aren't* rather than being supported and rewarded for their unique qualities.

Second, those who remain are forced to conform, and in the end, they are less effective. They become pale versions of themselves and of the prescribed leadership model, dedicating too much energy and attention to learning how to be the right kind of leader and to pleasing those who evaluate their work.

Third, the pool of financial resources available to nonprofits is reduced. Nonprofits really are different than corporations. They really are mission-driven. They emerge in response to social and community needs, which tend to make their customers and clients different as well. They are poorer and, lacking financial incentives, must motivate hired personnel and volunteers differently. They answer to different kinds of stakeholders, like community groups, which makes their approaches to accountability different. Being different, nonprofit organizations require different forms of leadership and different kinds of capacity building—or organization development—models.

Finally, there is waste of time and poor use of expertise in the relationships among leaders, donors, and evaluators. One can almost hear Rex Harrison incanting, "Why can't a woman be more like a man." Nonprofit leaders, like Eliza Doolittle, must swallow their discomfort and anger. At the same time, they are ready to leave the relationship as soon as they can, feeling neither empowered nor understood.

Granting money and holding people responsible, which is salutary when done in a respectful way, can, and often does, slip into a parent-child relationship in which the business or foundation people become alternately tolerant or patronizing and scolding or disappointed. When speaking with them in private one can virtually hear them cluck-cluck, as if to say, when will these kids grow up? In this relationship, nonprofit leaders, feeling judged, grow anxious and eager to please. Because they are the petitioners in this case, they keep their growing anger to themselves, and, with the anger, much information that funders and board members need in order to make good judgments. In private, nonprofit leaders grumble and fantasize about other ways to fund their programs, but they generally endure what they feel is paternalism and misunderstanding.

The ideal of an open, adult partnership, with essentially shared purpose and efforts and different but joined skills, can only be realized when the power differential is well managed.

Complexity

Although American culture prefers to think of leadership in a singular way—he is our leader—the truth is generally otherwise. Virtually every charismatic leader has lieutenants to get things done. Successful entrepreneurs depend on good managers to sustain their organizations and causes. And the most effective managerial leaders are often carried on the back of magnetic subordinates who help motivate others.

Leadership is a complex and polyglot affair. When leaders of different stripes complement and support one another, and when the great majority see little conflict in myriad styles, organizations thrive. Ask people who the leader is and, at first, they will name the person in the highest office. But press them just a little and they'll begin to name others. They will also tell you that such and such a leader only succeeds because of another, apparently lesser leader. Then they may go on to say that even the lesser leader succeeds only because of others, and that the others depend on the cooperation of everyone. And at times it is true that there is a swelling of energy from large numbers of people that seems to carry the action.

In any case, the corporate world is not what it seems (or seemed)—it doesn't live up to its own standards. The free market system, pushed to its limits, fails to self-regulate. Free market discipline has hardly stopped corporate leaders from hiding assets, lying about financial statements, spending company money on their own homes, and assigning themselves astronomical salaries and bonuses. What kind of model does this set? Is it possible that the mission- and morality-based motivation of nonprofit leaders is a surer guide to leadership behavior?

Alternative Narratives

Of course, the leadership idea or ideal has not been static. Over the last decade or two, there has been increasing emphasis on empowering others through delegation, removing barriers to involvement, convening stakeholders, affirming and appreciating the good in processes and people, creating networks, and so forth. These ideas, deriving a good deal of their animus from women and the literature on women's leadership, reached their apotheosis in the servant leader, invented by Robert Greenleaf. Yet, unless this idea—indeed any conception of leadership, including those emphasizing multiculturalism—is seen as one of many options, it can become rigid and ideological as well. The point is that there are many narratives but few receive much credence or play because of the hegemonic power of the cultural narrative.

In transitional historical periods, the cultural narrative generally presents both sides of important issues—ideas from the past and new ideas that are emerging. When the cultural narrative is broken, even for a moment, a creative free marketplace of ideas and possibilities is formed. There are currently many cracks, many forays or unprivileged narratives, such as the notion of distinctive forms of leadership among nonprofits. If we are on the verge of a paradigm shift, in our view, thinking about leadership will soon become greatly more nuanced and complex, embracing much greater variety in its forms and examples—and the core concepts of fit and alignment will become foundational for the latest best practices.

References

Alger, H. (1990). *Ragged Dick or, street life in New York with the boot-blacks.* New York: Signet Classics.

City Year Web site. (2004). Available from www.cityyear.org (retrieved July 30, 2004).

Derrida, J. (1982). *Margins of philosophy* (A. Bass, Trans.). Chicago: University of Chicago Press.

Eisenberg, P. (1997, Winter). A crisis in the nonprofit sector. *National Civic Review,* 86(4), 331–341.

Elazar, D. J. (1995). *Community and polity: The organizational dynamics of American Jewry.* Philadelphia: The Jewish Publication Society.

Erikson, E. H. (1969). *Gandhi's truth: The origins of militant nonviolence.* New York: Norton.

Erikson, K. (1986). *Wayward Puritans: A study in the sociology of deviance.* New York: Allyn & Bacon.

Foucault, M. (1972). *Power-knowledge: Selected interviews and other writings, 1972–1977.* New York: Pantheon Books.

Goleman, D. P., Boyatzis, R., & Mckee, A. (2002). *Primal leadership: Realizing the power of emotional intelligence.* Boston: Harvard Business School Press.

Grogan, P. (2000). *Comeback cities: A blueprint for urban neighborhood revival.* Boulder, CO: Westview Press.

Henton, D., Melville, J., & Walesh, K. (1997). *Grassroots leaders for a new economy.* San Francisco: Jossey-Bass.

Karoff, P. (2004). Saturday morning—A reflection on the golden age of philanthropy. *Just money—A critique of contemporary American philanthropy.* Boston: TPI Editions.

Letts, C. W., Ryan, W. P., & Grossman, A. (1999). *High performance nonprofit organizations: Managing upstream for greater impact.* New York: Wiley.

Light, P. (1998). *Sustaining innovation: Creating nonprofit and government organizations that innovate naturally.* San Francisco: Jossey-Bass.

Schorr, L. B. (1997). *Common purpose: Strengthening families and neighborhoods to rebuild America.* New York: Doubleday.

Turner, F. J. (1985). *The frontier in American history.* Melbourne, FL: Krieger.

5

Goodness of Fit

A merican corporate culture is of two minds about the importance of fit between leaders and organizations. The tendency is to identify the best leadership style and assume it will work anywhere—to believe that someone with "general management capabilities" can succeed in a leadership role in any organization, profession, or industry. At the same time, other concepts, often dismissed by advocates of the great leader theory, have entered the vocabulary of everyday life. Chief among these are fit and readiness. This alternate view holds that if you have the right person in the right place at the right time, your organization will hum like magic. This chapter will focus on the time and place aspects of that assertion.

We take the view that fit matters as much as skill, talent, and experience, and we go one step further to give full credence to degrees of fit. A fit that is too perfect leads to stagnation. Leaders must change in order to align with organizations, and organizations must change in order to align with the leader's strategic design or operational style. Close but imperfect fit combines the smooth functioning we associate with efficiency and effectiveness with the flexible adjustment to change we associate with creativity.

Howard Gardner (1983) has shown that people think in very different ways with multiple intelligences, including linguistic, logical/mathematical, personal, and musical. Each form is effective in different arenas, shining in solving certain problems and failing in others. Imposing or valuing one form over another is a surefire strategy for devaluing people and squandering intellectual resources. So it is with leadership. Each form has its place; organizations and societies that fail to value and utilize many forms of leadership are squandering social resources.

There are many forms of leadership, among them entrepreneurial and managerial, grassroots and corporate. Within each of these categories, there are wide variations. Some entrepreneurs, for example, are extremely detail-oriented and controlling; others move ahead with broad strokes and expect others to pick up the pieces of their bold, often wild initiatives. There are entrepreneurs who are good managers, and managers who are entrepreneurial.

Followers also have styles. People are able and inclined to follow certain kinds of leaders and not others. Some, for example, respond to inspiring orators. These same orators make others suspicious. Some people trust soft-spoken leaders who have recognizable goals that seem within reach. People are frequently responsive to leaders who hail from their own ethnic, racial, or professional group. These leaders are chosen because people identify with them and believe they understand their needs, sharing their imagery, humor, yearning, resentments, and hopes.

Furthermore, distinctive circumstances can shape distinctive forms of leadership. For example, women historically have not been permitted positions of authority in organizations. The challenge of getting things done and of being effective without authority has been a problem overcome to a degree with very creative forms of leadership. Women have learned to exert influence through the development and use of informal networks and to manage from one-down and peripheral positions by teaching and supporting those in formal positions of power. They have learned to lead by convening and facilitating others, and by removing obstacles from the paths of those charged with leading projects and making decisions. They have learned to mobilize and demobilize their networks according to the needs of projects. In recent years, management theorists have adopted such flexible organizational approaches and pioneered many of the leadership styles that have now become mainstream. Styles of leadership, then, are often formed in the interaction between potential leaders and potential followers.

The civil rights struggles of the 1960s and 1970s gave rise to a style of democratic political organizing among African American women—denied power and position by both white people and black men—that more closely resembles church gatherings and neighborhood associations than any corporate hierarchy. Many Jewish leaders take their character from their community's belief that, as a very small and different people, their organizations must go beyond specific functions to provide a kind of government-in-exile. Grassroots leaders of all kinds must often lift the morale and inspire hope and effort in communities that are in short supply of both.

Each of these leadership types can be effective, depending on the qualities, desires, and habits of both leaders and followers, and upon the organizations and cultures that mediate the relationships between leaders and followers—in short, depending on the fit between the leader's skills, style, and values and those of the organization and the community in which the organization resides.

A Theoretical Note

The idea that individuals and the context in which they live reciprocally influence one another has become a commonplace of social science research. The power of person-context interaction is so great that it literally shapes all levels of human behavior, from biological to political. To take an example from the literature on adolescent development, individual physical characteristics elicit varying responses from both peers and adults. Those who grow and mature rapidly, for example, are treated differently than those who develop slowly. At the same time, the social context influences biology. Better nutrition and health care, for example, hasten the onset of puberty. In other words, social context literally influences biological development. Early puberty then has social consequences, such as earlier childbearing capability, which, in turn, has an impact on social and community relationships.

Social scientists point to several ways that the context, or ecology, influences individual development. They call these influences "social demands" (Lerner et al., 2002), indicating how the social context encourages certain qualities in individuals and inhibits others. To name a few of these social demands: First, there are attitudes, values, and stereotypes regarding a person's physical and behavioral attributes. More specifically and importantly, there are the attitudes and attributes of those people with whom an individual must coordinate activities—must fit in with—in order to adapt to be effective in a particular setting. Furthermore, the social and physical assets or resources, provided by a community—these could be jobs, educational opportunities, after-school programs—help focus and bring out certain qualities in individuals, letting other qualities remain dormant.

The quality of match between individual and environment determines, to a significant extent, how well the individual will do. Here's how Richard Lerner (2002, p. 542) puts it: "Those children whose characteristics match most of the settings within which they exist should receive supportive or positive feedback from the contexts and should show evidence of the most adaptive behavioral development. In turn, of course, poorly fit or mismatched children should show alternative developmental outcomes."

All individuals and systems, leaders and followers shape one another. We know parental behavior and expectations influence the character of children and the course of their lives. But parents will tell you that their lives in general and the way they bring up their children are influenced by how their children respond to their parenting—and to qualities in the children, themselves, that seem to be hardwired. In other words, parenting is shaped by children. Together, parents and children exist in recursive relationships. A parent might encourage one kind of behavior; a child responds in a particular way, to which the parent adapts. Then the child adapts. This process continues until a pattern is reached, and for a while, one can observe repetition and sameness. Then something changes in the circumstances: The child develops new skills, enters school, or is influenced by other adults; or the parent takes a course and tries out a new way to express love or approval or a new way to practice discipline. Then there is some mutual jostling until a new pattern is reached. And so it goes through several changes due to development or circumstance. So it is with leaders and followers. This chapter extends this theory to leadership and argues that social context exerts a powerful influence on the nature and effectiveness of particular leaders.

Poor Fit

By the same token, poor fit between leaders and their social environment makes it almost impossible for them to succeed. Before describing what goodness of fit looks like, let's look at its opposite. Here, we are specifically not discussing poor leaders, but those considered excellent in one circumstance and, because the fit is poor, ineffectual in another.

The importance of fit is well known in sports. There are coaches, for example, whose teams perform brilliantly in one setting—let's say college basketball—who then fail in the professional ranks, or with another college team. Rick Pitino had spectacular success turning around basketball programs at Boston University, Providence College, the University of Kentucky, and, now, the University of Louisville, moderate success as coach of the New York Knickerbockers, a professional team, and little or no success with the Boston Celtics. Some coaches are good with young players—perhaps they are good teachers and need a degree of admiration and obedience. These coaches thrive when rapid success is not required and slow team development is sanctioned by owners and fans. They fail when they must produce quickly and when they have to work with experienced players who want more autonomy and on-court leadership themselves. And there are others who are good with the veteran players. These coaches may not like teaching or starting anew, yet thrive under pressure and rise to the need to produce quickly.

Casa Myrna Vazquez presents good illustrations of poor fit before Shiela Moore's tenure. When the organization was in transition between a collective and a more hierarchical and professionally managed organization, one leader after another departed in defeat and tellingly went on to become an effective leader in other organizations.

Joan Goldman (a pseudonym) effectively led a Jewish day school for twelve years. By her own account, she entered at just the right time for her skills and temperament. Joan followed the founding school head, a flamboyant, entrepreneurial leader, who brought the school from conception to operational reality. Joan says she doesn't like the early stages of organizational life. Concern for the school's survival makes her anxious and unable to bring her best to the job. She's not particularly good at giving speeches, raising money, and dealing with community politics. "I'm an educator," she says. She's good at selecting and managing teachers, teaching children, talking with parents, and developing curriculum. She even likes the nitty-gritty of day-to-day administration. So it's not surprising that Joan took over a badly organized school and made it succeed with efficiency, warmth, and good humor; and it's not surprising that her organization, warmth, and pedagogical skills helped the school grow, little by little, until enrollment surpassed the school's physical capacity.

At that point, the board and its new strategic plan outlined rapid growth to accommodate enrollment, a new building, and generally expanded educational programs. Joan knew that she did not have the proper skills for this phase of the school's organizational life, and she asked for continuing education courses, coaching, and the like in order to get up to speed. The board did not accommodate her because it was mired in a factional battle between those favoring rapid growth and those who wanted to slow growth to maintain the school's current character. The battle broke when the board elected a new chair who completely supported the rapid growth. Now there was a poor fit both between Joan's skills and the organization's needs—fund raising, leading a capital campaign, managing a larger, rapidly growing institution—and between Joan's temperament and that of the board chair, who, in the daytime, was a corporate president. She was aggressive, business-oriented, autocratic, and impatient, whereas Joan prided herself on her collaborative leadership style. In sum, the very skills, values, and temperament that made Joan an excellent leader for over a decade now fit poorly with the new phase of the school's life.

Jake Collins (a pseudonym) is a brilliant, charismatic, and creative leader. Three times now, he has started schools with great success and fanfare that have received national attention for their innovative programs and exuberant spirit. As a result, he has been elected to head national organizations. Informally, he is considered a leader and is treated with great respect, almost deference—and love. He elicits this kind of response from the lay leaders who employ him, the teachers he employs, and students and parents.

At his first two schools, his disinterest and ineptitude with administration eventually disillusioned people. He was asked to move on from both. He is terrific in the beginning, during the conception and early growth stages—creating curriculum, hiring wonderful people, providing and marketing a vision, calling forth funding—and he is a poor manager who is so sure of himself that he won't rely on others. One effective way to deal with this set of qualities would be to complement him with an operations chief. A better strategy would be to hire him under a contract for only a few years and prepare for a transition by grooming a next generation of leader. Equally instructive, Jake is a leader in national educational organizations that are loosely organized and run by others, where he is admired for his vision and creativity. Here, he is the right man for the job over a long period of time.

Finally, we would like to offer a complex illustration of mismatching from the corporate world. Sam Healey (a pseudonym) built a technology company with close to $700 million in annual revenue. In doing so, he combined entrepreneurial and managerial skills, technological savvy, grit, determination, and stamina. He is brilliant, personable, and often charismatic. The majority of people in his company loved working for him. Now, at another organization, Sam can't get many of the employees to take his lead, causing him frustration and, he confesses, "just plain confusion." He doesn't understand what's going on and confesses self-doubt.

When the venture capitalists, who dominated the company's board, hired Sam, they did so because of his ability to marry technological savvy to marketing and financial skills. The company had been profitable but small, and a little complacent. They were not growing. Sam's challenge was to transform the organization from a technology-driven to a market-driven company in order to take on aggressive growth objectives.

Originally, the company had been built around a brilliant software engineer, an MIT graduate who had invented several innovative products before graduating from college. He had collected a group of like-minded software people who happily took their lead from him. Although autocratic and irascible, he was the genuine article. His employees might grumble, but this combination of grumbling and reverence was integral to a culture that fit their image of a great technology organization. Finally, and this was important, they got to work on challenging problems and not the "ticky-tacky" problems that other firms imposed on engineers.

The transformation Sam wished to implement required engineers and managers able to meet market demands, which required them to submerge their intellectual interests in order to meet deadlines and customer specifications. The current group of managers and engineers balked at this prospect. What is more, the style of management best suited to a market orientation is collaborative and interactive—with engineers, marketing and sales, and financial people all working together to define products, determine project plans, establish objectives, and deliver results. Unlike the founding guru, master of his technical domain, the marketing leader needs to be collaborative. Even as final decisions and responsibility is his, he tries to create the best, the richest, and the most productive chemistry among constituents—customers, employees, and board members, who are clamoring for a big return on their dollar.

Where other employees had valued Sam's asking their opinions and genuinely listening, this group is disappointed in what they perceive as his uncertainty. Where he practices a model of respect, curiosity, and broad-based decision making, they see weakness. As a result, they shut him out of their deliberations, distancing him from the technological aspects of decisions. With time, his isolation and growing ignorance have actually made him uncertain about how to approach them. A vicious cycle has set in.

Sam is in his early fifties, with three children approaching college. He put away enough from his first company to pay for college and to retire in a modest way, but he wants to reap the benefits of all his hard work and success. He wants a big financial success in his current company—"My last," he intoned—in order to retire in style. In other words, his objectives and the urgency they imply fit badly with the organization's initial, slow-moving, problem-savoring culture.

Sam cannot change personnel fast enough to change the culture and still meet product deadlines. He says there are times when he believes he doesn't fit in his own company. He does not fit, and it is doubtful that he has the time and resources—the venture capital is burning at an alarming rate—to align the whole company to its future needs.

Goodness of Fit

The concept of fit has grown familiar to some, particularly human resource personnel and search firms who are asked to identify and place executives in organizations. But fit with what? To put it simply, the character and skills of leaders must fit with the needs and culture of the organizations they serve—and, frequently, with the larger culture in which the organization lives. There are some leaders and potential leaders who take a reciprocal view. They ask: What organization will optimize my chances of success? In the following section, we tell stories that illustrate how distinctive cultures and organizational needs shape the type of leadership that emerges.

THE INFLUENCE OF ORGANIZATIONAL CULTURE

To state the obvious, knowledge, skill, experience, and credentials within the organization's core competency create credibility for leaders. Physicians, for example, generally accept physicians in leadership roles, or at least give them the benefit of the doubt upon appointment, and often object strenuously to the imposition of a businessman as the head of a hospital or clinic. In psychotherapeutic settings, leaders must not only come with experience and credentials but probably a specific clinical orientation—psychodynamic, behavioral, whatever—in order to be welcomed. Twelve-step programs generally won't accept medically oriented leaders. Medical organizations, no matter how little success they have had with substance abuse, will not turn to those with considerable success as leaders of 12-step programs. Community-based organizations are suspicious of professionals; professionally oriented organizations are suspicious of those whose credentials have been won through experience on the street. Street smarts count much more in the former; degrees, internships, and the like count in the latter.

In the corporate world, brash and brilliant boy-men serve as the archetype of the technology leader, soft-spoken senior gentlemen serve as bank presidents, and aggressively flamboyant women or men serve as heads in the retail clothing industry. These stereotypes contain grains of truth. Imagine, for example, Bill Gates in a retail firm or Lee Iacocca in a bank. Entrepreneurial cultures will only accept and thrive with hard-driving, risk-taking, do-it-all leaders. Large, stable, older cultures more narrowly circumscribe their leaders' activities. Those who come up from the ranks are steeped in the organization's culture and fit well. Those brought in from the outside are brought in with the culture in mind.

Shiela Moore and Casa Myrna provide clear illustrations of the importance of fit between leader and organization. At first, the counterculture social workers at Casa Myrna were openly suspicious of Moore. Her skills were those of a manager, and she came from a medical background—what they saw, in fact, as a corporate medical background. According to alternative therapists, financial and management skills bear only a distant relationship to those that help heal battered women. Furthermore, medical centers were governed by what was then disparaged as the medical model, with its tendency to see and treat people in terms of pathology, to see the doctor as expert and the patient as a passive recipient of the doctor's wisdom, and often to blame or infantilize victims of domestic violence. This hierarchical, male-dominated practice was repugnant to Casa Myrna's staff. As a result, Shiela Moore had to prove that she understood—and valued—the staff's ways of healing before they would willingly follow her lead.

Casa Myrna provides a second illustration of organizational needs determining the selection of leadership. Carmen Rivera became board chair during the strategic planning process, a process that signaled the end of the old ad hoc organizational structure and processes. She believed the organization had reached a scale that demanded substantial infrastructure improvement and more systematic management. So she guided a search process to hire such a manager. Shiela Moore fit the future of the organization.

To counteract the resistance of the old culture, Moore developed a strategy of enlisting and supporting key executives. Jossie Fossas, the financial officer, was first. Then Moore included Fossas and key program officers—representatives of the founding or grassroots culture—on a team to implement the strategic plan that they had helped construct. Inside the tent, as it were, they promoted the new culture and the need for better accountability, clarity of roles, and an infrastructure to support rapid growth. Then, with an unexpected rapidity, the cultural assumptions shifted—"If we want to fulfill our mission, we need 'qualified' people in executive positions," they intoned in ways that surprised them even more than others. Within a year, the culture had been more or less transformed and, with it, the belief in who would fit its needs. The spate of new hires that followed—an IT director and a new clinical program director, among others—were, indeed, selected on that basis.

THE CULTURAL AND COMMUNITY CONTEXT

As we discussed in the previous chapter, there is a dynamic interaction between certain ideas about leadership that span the centuries and the particular ways that specific cultures shape those ideas. Although we described a national narrative, there are many subcultures, each with its ideas about what makes for effective leadership. Any person seeking leadership or being asked to serve within these cultures must more or less fit with those ideas. This process of fit is, in many cases, so automatic and so much an expression of character that the act of fitting oneself to cultural archetypes is effortless and unconscious. Many of the men of the Southern Leadership Conference who led the civil rights struggle, each a church leader in his own right, may fit that description. For others, like Shiela Moore, achieving the fit is, in various degrees, intentional and hard-won.

The research literature on African American women who rose up to positions of leadership during the civil rights movement of the 1960s illustrates the particularity of leadership within a distinctive culture. The title of one article says it all: "Invisible Southern Black Women Leaders in the Civil Rights Movement: The Triple Constraints of Gender, Race, and Class." The author, Bernice McNair Barnett, goes on to set the scene:

> Even while suffering the daily indignities heaped on them by their location in the structure of society, many southern Black women were much more than *followers;* many were also leaders who performed a variety of roles comparable to those of Black male leaders. Although seldom recognized as leaders, these women were often the ones who initiated protest, formulated strategies and tactics and mobilized other resources (especially money, personnel, and communication networks) necessary for successful social action. . . . (Barnett, 1993, p. 163)

These women performed their roles in the only way possible in that time and place. Several authors describe the roles taken by female organizers as emerging from both the strengths and limitations of their social conditions (Elliot, 1996; Gyant, 1996). They argue that for black and other minority women, caretaking is heightened by both the general culture's emasculation of men and their own wish to protect and promote their children and their communities. Many black women have become social activists after fighting local, specific battles on behalf of their own children, then for children within their neighborhood. As Nancy Naples (1998, p. 114) puts it, "Latinas, Native American women, and Asian-American women have well-established traditions of community-based work designed to defend and enhance the quality of life within their communities." In effect, black women foreshadowed the late-1960s emphasis on making the social political.

Black women organized protests through networks, relationships, and cooperation, much as they organized church functions, not through hierarchical positioning. That is the positive pull of culture. On the negative side, both white and, perhaps even more so, black male culture forbade black women from assuming formal positions of authority. As a result, Patricia Parker suggests (2001) that black women continued to behave in a collaborative and informal style and to avoid competition and conflict, particularly with white and male leaders.According to Nancy Naples, multiple layers of oppression, ironically, have given black women an advantage over white women because they have a more developed sense of the need for equality. Naples says that minority women's activism has several qualities distinct from other women's activism. Many became involved because they wanted to improve their child's environment, either regarding school quality or neighborhood safety, or by improving welfare and health systems. Black and Hispanic women became activists out of their concern for improving the lives of their low-income communities where solving pressing problems in health, education, poverty, and the environment, among other issues, was a matter of survival. The added struggles against racism and poverty caused these women to get involved—and they played crucial roles in the survival of their communities.

Several authors focus on the way the oppression, itself, shaped black female leadership. Because of the discrimination they have faced, Cheryl Townsend Gilkes argues, black women are better suited than black men to fight for social causes: "The position of Black women at the bottom of both the status and income hierarchies produces an interesting paradox in their politics of liberation. They have a better and more comprehensive view of the dynamics of oppression. . . . Historically, the Black community has recognized the power of Black women's powerlessness" (Gilkes, 1988, p. 74). Black men, as ministers and politicians, were viewed with skepticism and as a source of instability, but black women were responsible for everyday life and for maintaining stability at home and in the community.

The Role of Church Leadership in the Development of Women's Leadership

The church, religion and spirituality have historically played a role in black women's leadership in a variety of ways. Women developed many leadership and activist skills in church. Its patriarchal hierarchy has prevented women from assuming leadership positions as pastors and in other black organizations—and spurred them on to seek equality. Spirituality and faith, central to many black women's leadership styles, have given them strength to persevere.

Coordinating Activities. Historically, black women had roles as social networkers in churches and served as coordinators of church activities. Leadership skills were frequently developed in church activism. "African American women who exercised strong membership in church communities were also historically prominent in secular organizations, in which their activism was a powerful force in sustaining the movement for social change" (Barnett, 1993, p. 132).

Faith. Many of the women leaders in the civil rights era had moral and religious upbringings. "Women were motivated to participate for various reasons. One important reason was their belief and faith in God. . . . Because the church was the center for mass meetings, it provided women the opportunity to become leaders." Faith played a large role in activist Fannie Lou Hamer's leadership. She had a spiritual fervor that drew people to her. "Without her faith in God and the essential rightness of her cause, Fanny Lou Hamer could easily have been dissuaded by the adversities and defeats she suffered," Williams states in *Servants of the People: The 1960s Legacy of African-American Leadership* (Williams, 1996, p. 197).

When leading a cause, such as civil rights, the ultimate goal can seem elusive, its attainment often in doubt. Yet, the servant leader is sustained by, and draws strength from, an abiding faith—faith in God, faith in self and in others, faith in the vision and in the integrity of the cause. Fannie Lou Hamer often alluded to her trust in God and how that belief was a sustaining power in her life. She, as did Martin Luther King Jr. and many of the southern activists, came out of a religious background with a deep spirituality. Faith plays a defining role because it assures the servant leader that even in the midst of fear and confusion, amid turmoil and uncertainty, appropriate actions and responses will somehow be revealed. . . . Fannie Lou Hamer's inspiration was firmly grounded in a spiritual context and sustained by her Christian faith. Her religious beliefs were the source of her strength. Personal faith, which has historically and traditionally sustained African Americans under brutal conditions in their sojourn through slavery and even now, was a strong palliative against the pervasive poverty and racism that surrounded Hamer and could, in a less determined person, have weakened resolve (Williams, 1993, p. 144).

Servant Leaders. Williams defines Hamer as a servant leader, and weaves Robert Greenleaf's ideas of servant leadership into her description. Hamer was committed "to serving others through a cause, a crusade, a movement, a campaign with humanitarian, not materialistic, goals," writes Williams (1996, p. 145). Hamer eschewed personal gain to achieve a greater good; she was guided by a prophetic, transforming vision, was willing to lead in the face of adversity, relied on her intuition, and was persuasive.

Participatory Democracy. Most black women leaders have embodied this leadership style; Ella Baker has been hailed as its champion. This decentralized leadership style is cited as the underlying strength of the civil rights movement. Ella Baker knew that she had a different leadership style than the black male leaders: She was a strong supporter of participatory democracy and admitted to having no ambition to be in formal leadership roles:

> As an astute and seasoned organizer, Baker believed that the most effective strategy for sustaining activism among local people would be to develop a decentralized, group-centered approach to leadership which would minimize hierarchy and involve grassroots people in the decisions affecting their lives. In describing her own approach to activism, Ella Baker once commented that "the kind of role that I tried to play was to pick up pieces or put together pieces out of which I hoped organization might come. My theory is strong people don't need strong leaders." (Crawford, 2001, p. 109)

Black women in their homes, churches, social clubs, organizations, and communities throughout the South performed valuable leadership roles during the modern civil rights movement in the United States. Although race, gender, and class constraints generally prohibited their being the recognized articulators, spokespersons, and media favorites, these women did perform a multiplicity of significant leadership roles, such as the initiation and organization of action, the formulation of tactics, and the provision of crucial resources (e.g., money, communication channels, and personnel) necessary to sustain the movement. Sisters in struggle, they were empowered through their activism (Barnett, 1993, p. 17).

Other Cultural Variables

Culture in organizations varies along many dimensions beyond ethnicity and race. One is whether processes are bureaucratic or entrepreneurial, and another is whether procedures are loose or tight. These are also aspects of fit. Just as an Anglo man would have a hard time leading a Latino domestic violence organization, an entrepreneur would struggle trying to budge a bureaucratic organization into rapid, risk-taking action, and a leader who by experience and temperament likes order, upon entering a loosely structured organization, might institute clear-cut rules and procedures only to provoke wide-scale resistance if not rebellion.

Two cases of leadership in nonprofit agencies supporting children, one in Massachusetts and one in North Carolina, shed light on fit within a cultural and community context. In Massachusetts, Suzin Bartley's leadership is almost perfectly attuned to her state's blend of progressive social programs and Irish-dominated politics. She is passionate about protecting children. She is a political pragmatist. She is "connected." Bartley is the granddaughter, niece, cousin, and friend of generations of Irish politicians. One might say that the Massachusetts State House is the community in which she was raised, and the community she can call on in times of need.

Suzin Bartley has helped build the Children's Trust Fund (CTF) of Massachusetts from a start-up to an extensive, statewide effort to prevent child abuse by supporting parents and strengthening families. Each of the 50 states has a CTF, but the Massachusetts version is generally considered the national standard-bearer. As an umbrella organization, it funds, evaluates, and promotes the work of over 100 agencies that serve thousands of families. CTF sponsors innovative programs such as Healthy Families that brings young paraprofessionals into the homes of teenage mothers in an effort both to decrease pregnancies among young teenagers and to teach mothering skills that protect the children of these mothers. Through its Fatherhood Initiative, CTF has intensified efforts to raise public awareness about the important role fathers play in their children's lives. CTF also funds parenting education and support programs and the Massachusetts Family Centers.

The home visitors that Bartley hires for the Healthy Families program are based in agencies throughout the state. During their orientation, they are taught how to interview, form relationships, and support teenage mothers. But unlike most other social workers, they are also instructed to make connections with their state representatives and taught how to do so. They invite elected officials to parties, provide photo opportunities, and form relationships. In this way, they serve as political liaisons. When CTF funding has been threatened, Suzin has called not only on her powerful, high-profile board members to go to bat for her but also on her legion of home visitor "ward healers" to talk to their representatives and, in some cases, to call in their small but sometimes meaningful chips. This fit well with Massachusetts's political culture; the existing structure could be used effectively in the service of young children with a high risk profile for physical abuse.

In North Carolina, Lindalyn Kakadelis is the executive director of the Children's Scholarship Fund (CSF), which provides scholarships to private schools for poor children in Charlotte. Her leadership style is as suited to the working and middle class population of Charlotte, North Carolina, as Suzin Bartley's is to Massachusetts.

Lindalyn Kakadelis is a humble woman whose husband is minister of a conservative church. Kakadelis believes in what she is doing—helping poor children "escape" the public schools and enter faith-based institutions. At meetings, not confident in her own abilities, her style is to let others take charge. But lack of confidence in any "leadership abilities" does not stop her from working tirelessly for her beliefs. As a result, she pulls many other—also humble—people with her. They like her, feel comfortable with her, and trust her.

Dennis Williams, a former public school principal, formerly interim superintendent of schools for Charlotte-Mecklenburg County, the 18th largest school district in the country, and now executive director of a youth organization that "brings Christian faith to the schools," is "completely confident in Lindalyn." When asked in a focus group that Lindalyn had gathered if he would be interested in continued involvement with CSF, Williams said, in a slow, quiet, but unhesitating way, "I'd stay involved with anything led by Lindalyn. She knows that." This is all the more remarkable since Kakadelis is a white southern woman and Williams is an African American man. Falinda Farley, an African American mother of seven who sang for Tammy Bakker's TV ministry, "seconded the emotion."

Lindalyn Kakadelis is a leader by definition, in that people follow her lead, but that's not it exactly—they join her in a common cause. If she is the one in front, they follow. When they are in front, she follows. She serves on Dennis Williams's board, for example. Her followers don't look up to her; surely she doesn't look down on them. She has little positional power, but she's confident that if she calls, if she asks something of them, they will come through—not for her, but for the cause. This was how she had been elected to the Charlotte-Mecklenburg school board and to other leadership positions. The idea and the practice of leadership are fluid and situational, not fixed and not located in a person.

Her failures, however, may be equally instructive. When she tried to attract the rich and well educated—to contribute to CSF, for example—she failed. People would not even return her telephone calls. None of this simply rolled off her back. Instead, it hurt her feelings and reinforced her low opinion of herself.

For CSF to survive and grow, it would have to develop a sustainable funding base, which meant finding ways to reach the moneyed community. Lindalyn Kakadelis would readily let go leadership of CSF if it could thrive under someone else—she had plenty of other work, plenty of other causes, to keep her busy, she said. Dee Schwab, a member of Charlotte's moneyed community and friend of a philanthropist interested in supporting CSF, was the right person for the job, that is, to head the CSF board and eventually to hire an executive director who better fit the professional image that donors preferred. Dee had gone to the same country day schools and colleges—the University of North Carolina or Duke—and served on the same boards as those CSF was now trying to reach. Her manners were their manners. The books, movies, and vacation spots she mentioned were familiar to others of her group. She spoke with the same accent and in the same speech rhythms as they, which were clearly distinguishable from Kakadelis and Williams. Upon agreeing to the job, Schwab rapidly began to shift the CSF image, to explore new, more professional-looking office space that would make potential donors comfortable, and to develop classy marketing materials. These are "the little things that make a difference," she said. In this next phase of CSF's organizational life, she was no doubt the right person for the job. She fit CSF as well at this stage as Kakadelis had during its grassroots beginnings.

Zeitgeist

The zeitgeist—literally, spirit of the times—is a variation on the cultural demands already discussed, but it adds the element of time. In Chapter 4, we described the current cultural narrative of leadership, ending with the observation that we may be on the verge of a paradigm shift in our cultural leadership narrative. Comparable shifting ideas characterize communities and other social sectors, prescribing and proscribing certain qualities.

In the early 1990s research on the demographics of American Jews reported that the birthrate had dropped below two per couple, which meant that the Jewish population, already small, was declining. This was compounded by what many saw as a disastrous rate of intermarriage with Christian Americans: 52 percent nationally and up to 75 percent in areas of the South, Southwest, and West, which was where Jews were migrating. Synagogue membership was also declining; even among those who remained on the membership rolls, attendance was sporadic at best; and knowledge of ritual, observance, and history was extremely low. The long-sought road to acceptance in American society—the first society to accept Jews on equal terms and with a minimum of anti-Semitism—was exacting a potentially terrible toll: assimilation so great that it seemed to threaten the survival of the Jews as a distinct people. A near panic set in. That was the zeitgeist.

In response, 12 very wealthy men gathered to see what they could do to help. They decided that they would create an organization that would fund and support new Jewish day schools. This was 1997. Their purpose was to nurture a cadre of knowledgeable, dedicated people who would at least preserve the core of the historical Jewish experience. To head their organization, they tapped Josh Elkin, a midforties rabbi, who had himself led a Jewish day school. Elkin and the organization he formed, the Partnership for Excellence in Jewish Education (PEJE), have been wildly successful, helping to start up countless new schools, to support ongoing schools, to convene and train Jewish educators throughout the country, and to gain at least some support from other Jewish organizations ordinarily wary of new, competitive initiatives in the field.

Josh Elkin is hardly a leader of Mosaic proportions, capable of leading the Jews out of Egypt. In fact, he is small of stature, gentle by nature, and happy to have others take center stage. But he is the right man at the right time. He is smart, articulate, and passionate in his Jewish identification. He also has an odd combination of traits. On one hand, Elkin is passionate in his approach to the cause of Jewish day schools. On the other hand, he is a compromiser and a reconciler who is able to bring people together and affirm many sides of contentious situations. He can see many sides of an argument—some even accuse him of indecisiveness. But he is great in a boardroom. With his sponsors, he submerges his specific passions to their demands. Thus he continues to raise funds for PEJE. Yet he is impatient by temperament. When confronted with detailed planning efforts that threaten to go on and on, he balks. "Let's get it out the door," he'll exclaim. There's no time to waste with obsessive research and planning. By turning his back on perfectionism, he has proven an excellent entrepreneur, moving forward and forward against whatever odds exist.

In effect, Elkin is an almost perfect fit for the current crisis zeitgeist. He is rooted in Jewish traditional values, which makes him acceptable to virtually all strains of Judaism. And he is contemporary enough to try all kinds of organizational methods in order to take on the challenge of saving the Jews from continued loss of identity.

During the bull market of the 1990s, many newly wealthy individuals emerged from both the high technology and financial sectors and wondered how they might contribute to less fortunate members of their society. They were not sure how to do so but believed that the nonprofit organizations they would support should mirror their own entrepreneurial spirit. They wanted to identify and help nonprofit organizations that were lean, efficient, and innovative and that had capable leaders with big ideas that could grow rapidly and exert a major influence on American society. City Year is a well-known example of the type of nonprofit supported by these social venture leaders.

A variation on this theme is the intermediary organization, which brokers between foundations and wealthy individuals on the one hand and nonprofits on the other. These intermediaries sprung up and thrived with awesome rapidity during the 1990s. Rick Little, for example, founded the International Youth Foundation (IYF). With a stunning initial grant in the vicinity of $60 million from the W. K. Kellogg Foundation, he built an organization that funneled money from both foundations and corporations into foundations in 60 nations, each a subsidiary of IYF, each dedicated to identifying and supporting nonprofit organizations and public agencies providing services to underprivileged youth. Rick Little is an idealist with considerable business savvy, a charismatic speaker and a relentless organizer, who is as much at home on the dusty streets of a Mexico City slum as in the boardrooms of the Ford, Rockefeller, and Clark Foundations and of Procter and Gamble, Coca-Cola, Lucent, and the Bank of England, all sponsors of IYF.

Peter Karoff is yet another kind of intermediary leader. He is not a young idealist. He earned his spurs as a businessman, building a successful insurance business, and as a citizen, working for countless causes and sitting on dozens of nonprofit boards over decades. In his early fifties, Peter Karoff cast off his business to start The Philanthropic Initiative, which helps wealthy individuals "invest" in causes that suit their values and means. Even more than Rick Little, Peter Karoff had built up credibility in both worlds, neither of which exactly fit his temperament. He is, by nature, a matchmaker, and that is what the times called for.

These social venture and intermediary leaders have responded to a powerful cultural trend, providing it guidance and manpower. They have proven to be the right people in the right place at the right time; in other words, they fit the zeitgeist.

THE PULL OF THE MARKET

Like corporations, nonprofit organizations have markets. Funding and popular demand for certain services, for example, can become "hot." Some people happen to be in the right place when demand for their services escalates. And some leaders with a flexible and opportunistic bent take advantage of such market openings. We have seen both versions of such good timing in innumerable fields. For example, there were grassroots drug treatment, domestic violence and child abuse centers, and hospices that benefited tremendously when state and federal funding turned their way. There are other organizations that happened to be well positioned when state governments insisted on consolidation—they wanted to deal with fewer nonprofit organizations. Advocates, a mental health agency providing care for both formerly hospitalized mental patients and developmentally delayed adults, was well positioned when state government insisted on such consolidation—they had funds, plans, and a leader eager to take advantage of the market to spread what he believed were the tremendous skills of his agency. Many small organizations have benefited by such market turns, but, of course, they benefited over the long run only with effective leadership. For every Casa Myrna, for instance, there were many other domestic violence agencies that closed their doors within a year or two of opening.

Stages of Organizational Development: The Right Fit for Each Stage

As we have suggested throughout the book, the type of leadership organizations need changes as the organizations move through developmental stages.

For example, many startup or grassroots organizations are almost completely led by single leaders. As they grow, however, power may be shared in two ways. First, it may be shared with functional executives who complement the leader's entrepreneurial enthusiasms with a more systematic approach. A COO or a CFO may be hired for this purpose. With increasing scale, some organizations form leadership teams. Second, boards often move from a rubber-stamp to a strong governing personality and function. This shift happens frequently in response to financial and human resource problems created by entrepreneurial leaders or leadership transitions—boards will step in to govern the process and will remain powerful, monitoring and holding functional leaders accountable. Then, if powerful leaders emerge, they may win over their boards, stock them with their own choices, and essentially make their boards a rubber stamp again—until the next crisis or succession issue.

To examine the stages of organization development a little more closely and see the potential fit between leader and organization at each stage, we will focus on concrete examples taken from a study of how Jewish day schools evolve (Dym, 2003).

STAGE 1: THE BIRTH OF A VISION

Developmental Challenge 1: Clarifying the Vision

To begin, the challenge is to move from a limited idea to a clear vision, a vision that is compelling enough to move people to the next stage of planning.

As with most organizations, new schools generally begin as an idea, a vision, a yearning in the mind of an individual or small group. In one instance, a father has a fierce desire to pass on the tradition in which he was raised. In another, parents want to give their children what they lacked. In a third, parents want to extend a satisfying preschool program into the elementary school grades. In a fourth, a parent-educator wanted a more progressive, up-to-date curriculum than is available in the existing day school. In a fifth, people have read about the declining Jewish population and high intermarriage rate and, with mixtures of anxiety and excitement, set out to do their part in preserving the identity and continuity of the Jewish people.

As these "visionaries" continue to dream and to talk with others, their dream takes on increasing reality and urgency. For some, it becomes an obsession. They think about it day and night. It must be realized. They bring others into the conversation and the initial planning.

Leadership fit: At this conceptual stage, the leader must be a dreamer of sorts, able to imagine and articulate an idea and to begin drawing others to that vision. She need not be all that practical or experienced.

STAGE 2: FROM VISION TO PLAN

Developmental Challenge 2: Developing an Attractive Plan and Effective Leadership

There are two crucial challenges to meet in order to move from idea to concrete plan. First, the vision must be turned into a blueprint for future action—from personal discussions to practical plans—and constructed attractively enough to draw families, teachers, administrators, and donors, as well as to keep up the spirits of the founding group. Second, effective leadership must emerge and consolidate its role.

To launch schools, founders—or leaders—have to translate their visions into concrete plans and then act on those plans. During this stage, the founders make initial decisions about who they are and what they want to accomplish, and they build their plan. Some do so in isolation, speaking mostly to themselves. Others continue to expand their knowledge and the circle of participants. The latter group is likely to conduct some kind of feasibility and demographic study to determine, first, whether there is a demand and potential funding for the school and, second, where it should be located. Some perform these activities in informal ways; others hire professional firms to conduct the studies. In some cases, one or two people do everything, following no orderly process discernible from the outside and often taking years before they are ready to launch a school.

In one city, a founder, wanting to start a Jewish community high school, talked with all pulpit rabbis, principals of current elementary schools, and leaders of Jewish communal institutions—virtually anyone who would listen—trying to build support and to develop common ground. Since her main mission was to begin the school, not to infuse it with a particular denominational flavor, her emphasis was on gaining support. Since she had financial support, the support of community leaders was uppermost on her agenda. And, with time, hiring a school head capable of bridging denominational divides was critical. His hiring also made the vision real. The first fund-raising success and the hiring of the head of the new school mark vital substages in the concretization of the school development.

Others, steeped in nonprofit and corporate cultures, follow formal planning procedures. One founding group, for instance, formed several committees—on incorporation, finance, philosophy, site selection, and curriculum—and developed sophisticated bylaws, reflecting their knowledge about how to run effective schools. They created a formal rule that only half the board could consist of parents, thus guaranteeing the perspective of those with less immediate needs from the school, and bringing influential, older community members into their orbit. In an effort to avoid the controlling ways of founders—themselves—they decided to change board presidents every two years.

Although the latter group met the challenge in the more efficient way, it is important to acknowledge that many less professional founders form serviceable plans and carry their evolving organizations to the next stage. Generally, the style is entrepreneurial and informal. Roles are not differentiated. People fill in for each other. Action is often helter-skelter. Leadership either emerges and broadens in this heady mix of activities or, in the most isolated groups, simply remains in the hands of the initial visionary. Management capability and style begin to evolve through the planning process. Resources are sought without systematic plans and processes. Excitement builds, as do some anxieties based on beginning the real work. Now the idea seems more daunting to some—the launch is at hand—and more feasible to those who are reassured by a plan.

Leadership fit: At this initial stage, both a pure entrepreneurial and a combined entrepreneurial-managerial style work very well. Once organizations are built around either style, however, the next leader will have to fit into that style or realign the organization to fit with a new choice.

STAGE 3: LAUNCHING A NEW SCHOOL

Developmental Challenge 3: Making the School a Reality

The challenge here is to turn the plan into a reality, an operating school, in which classes are conducted, students learn, tuition is paid, other sources of funding are sought, and the preliminary rules of the road are established.

Initial money has been raised. A head of school has been hired. Incorporation is achieved. Planning and execution take on a new, more urgent reality. The school must be financed. Faculty must be hired, supervised, and trained. Curriculum must be found, adapted, and developed. Space must be located—generally rental at this point. And families must be recruited. All of this continues in a somewhat frantic manner, with the visionary leader or founding group still doing a great deal of the work.

For some, the move from planning to launch awaits a professional. With fewer controlling founders, even those with many ideas of their own, the internal construction of the schools is largely left to the professionals. This is because they firmly believe that the success of the school depends on the pros. This was true in Toronto, St. Louis, and Phoenix. In a Boston day school, a founder and school head were one and the same.

But the internal ecology of the organization is partly shaped by several dynamic processes: how much founders and heads of school differentiate roles, how much the roles and personalities complement one another, how much the founder can let go, and so forth.

If the professional, the head, has been hired, he or she takes on an increasing amount of responsibility, and orderly processes may emerge rapidly. If the school begins without a principal or with an interim principal, the founders take on operating responsibility. Even with principals in place, however, many parent volunteers are reluctant to relinquish control at this exciting moment. Control struggles may emerge and mark the next years of the school's life.

In general, though, volunteers and professionals become teams, filling in for each other, talking constantly. In the absence of established rules and systems, improvisation and creativity are the order of the day. This is both the most anxious stage—a commitment has been made—and the most exciting. When people look back to the romance of beginnings, often this is what they look back to.

Leadership fit: This stage calls for strong but flexible professional leadership. The leader must begin to put in processes, hold people accountable, and establish rules but, at the same time, must allow for considerable variation and change among teachers, students, and parents. The leader must have an ability to tolerate uncertainty—in most cases, not knowing whether student recruitment and fund raising will guarantee the school's survival. And the leader must play many roles: teaching, managing, fund raising, and recruiting. At this point the versatility and flexibility of the leader trumps management skills.

STAGE 4: CREATING A GOOD SUSTAINABLE SCHOOL

Developmental Challenge 4: Professionalizing Management and Developing Ongoing Funding Sources

The challenge is to move from a grassroots or entrepreneurial organization to a professionally managed organization that is sufficiently funded.

The majority of startups, nonprofits and corporations alike, fail within the first few years. It is easier to start than to sustain new ideas and new institutions. Now founders and professionals, together, must manage a transition from the idealistic, entrepreneurial beginnings, when everyone seems to do everything, to a stable organizational structure. In more professional organizations, roles are more defined and differentiated; people are held accountable for their performance; structures and processes (e.g., committees and information systems) are established to support teaching, recruiting, and fund-raising practices; and a supportive culture is built. Perhaps most important, management experience is building.

During this period, there is often a struggle between a visionary founder or group of parents, loath to let go control of the school they so passionately built, and the professional staff. When the board and the founders are the same group, there is no one to mediate the conflict. When the board is independent of the visionary founder(s), the board can and often does mediate. The struggle is often resolved through either leadership transition or the development of a more formal strategic plan, with indicators of effectiveness built in. Sometimes the visionary founder is left in place and complemented by professional support. The transition may take place smoothly or with great pain, leaving wounds that resurface later.

Leadership fit: This is the time when the balance between professional and entrepreneurial leadership shifts; management skills trump versatility. For the school to grow and thrive, the leader must, first, identify personnel needs; second, either elevate and mentor or hire them; and, third, delegate responsibility to them.

STAGE 5: EARLY MATURITY

Developmental Challenge 5: Managing Growth and Establishing Sustainability

After schools are established, they often continue to grow at a rapid rate. At the beginning of this period, management and infrastructure capabilities, as well as financial resources, are limited and need to be developed at speed and with care.

At this stage, the character of the school has been established, and its staff is largely in place and expanding. Information and other infrastructure systems have been introduced and consolidated. Essentially, people know where to be and what is expected of them. This is true for both the professional staff and the board, which has, by now, established a committee structure, a tradition of governance and a clearer relationship with the school head. Generally, this is not an altogether stable period. It is a period of considerable growth, though not so much aimed toward creating something new as toward expanding what has been established. For example, more classes and grades are added, requiring more teachers and, subsequently, administrators; in some cases, middle schools have been added.

Leadership fit: At this stage, either a thoroughly professional management style has already been established or the school is floundering. The leadership style may have many variations, according to the personality of the leader, the denomination of the school, and the geographic location, among other characteristics. But, as one examines successful schools, management, not entrepreneurial or charismatic, styles prevail.

STAGE 6: MATURITY

Developmental Challenge 6: Harvesting the Field

The challenge is to get the most out of what people have built: to utilize, enjoy, and celebrate.

In this stage, the initial goals have been achieved, and people can feel proud. The school has developed a rhythm and functions in an almost automatic way. Routines reign. Relationships built over the years remain fairly steady, some supportive, some not, managed by the routine. There is the potential to become bureaucratic, even rigid. This is a time when people may look back, longingly, to the beginning, with its spirit of adventure, its close relationships, its adrenaline-filled late-night meetings. But it may also be a stable, safe place that permits individual teachers, students, and families to thrive, to experiment and learn in safe, sustaining ways.

Leadership fit: The ideal fit at this stage is a leader who feels comfortable in and supported enough by the stable organization to begin to implement long-term growth projects, such as capital campaigns to build new physical plants, and innovative plans, such as new, creative curricula. This is a reforming and community-oriented leader, not an entrepreneur or a revolutionary.

STAGE 7: STABILITY

Developmental Challenge 7: Continuously Changing and Renewing

A new and successful organization can move along quite successfully for a number of years, relatively unchallenged either internally or in its market niche. In doing so, it can grow a little complacent, without sufficiently evaluating and renewing itself. In general, this renewal only happens when there is a challenge, from within or from without, such as the loss of students or the threat of a new school being formed.

There is a tendency for all human systems to grow conservative with time. Bureaucratic tendencies that emerge can harden. Innovation wanes, is even discouraged. Traditions become limitations: "This is how we do it here," people intone when faced with requests for change. This applies to curricula, teacher training, board procedures, marketing, and fund-raising activities alike.

But some people grow discontent with the old way and challenge it, sometimes by leaving and beginning a new school, sometimes by advocating their differences within. These challenges threaten the school. In response to the threat, the school examines itself on some or all of the dimensions that have ossified. When enough people become self-reflective in this way, a period of experiment and new growth often blossoms forth. There is a renewal. This process of renewal is iterative. If the school lives a long enough life, it will be required to review and renew itself with some regularity, either due to external challenges or due to regular, intentional self-reflection and planning.

Leadership fit: As with the previous stage, the ideal leader is one who is comfortable within the current organization and determined to build for the future. There's a twist, though. This leader must be able to overcome inertia and resistance from traditionalists. This form of leadership must be strong and, to an extent, inner-directed, that is able to take a direction in spite of what other important people say and in spite of organized forms of opposition within boards, parent groups, and faculty. It should be no surprise that this leader is often brought in from the outside rather than one who is thoroughly part of the school culture and systems.

MOVING IN AND OUT OF FIT

Fit comes and goes. In a later chapter, we will describe the cycles of fit and misfit, or alignment and misalignment. For now, we want to illustrate the point with a brief case summary.

The day school case illustrates a sequential fit process, according to several qualities. For example, the school founders (generally a small group of parents), with their abundant time, ability, and willingness to take on operational responsibility, are often the perfect fit for the beginning an organization. Their micro-management, however, makes it hard for new heads of schools to make their mark and establish their style. Often, initial heads are not strong enough to establish themselves. Without strength, versatility, and flexibility, they are the wrong people for the job at that stage. Then, frequently, board leadership gains understanding and grows weary of operational responsibility. "We have jobs and families," they can be heard to say. So they seek a strong and experienced professional, who, with the waning of entrepreneurial energies and fire on the part of the founding board, becomes the right person for the job. With time, this leader may grow too attached to what she has built, and needs for growth and vibrancy require a new type of leader. At every stage, the leader may be very competent, but when the goodness of fit is lost, the leader must change and grow, or a new leader must be found. In many of the best organizations, leadership development and assignment—the question of fit—is a continual concern. Fit is as critical to organizational success as the individual qualities of the leaders.

The Value of Not Quite Fitting

To conclude, we would add one caveat by way of preview. Although goodness of fit is clearly of benefit to organizations and their leaders, there is value in not quite fitting. Without complete fit, there must be change. Leaders and organizations must adapt to one another. This can and should be a creative process, in which the leader stretches to meet strategic, operational, and cultural norms that challenge his or her assumptions and abilities, and in which the organization stretches to meet the challenges posed by the leader. Still, the underlying dynamism of fit is central to the notion of alignment.

References

Barnett, B. M. (1993). Invisible Southern black women leaders in the civil rights movement: The triple constraints of gender, race, and class. *Gender & Society, 7*(2), 162–182.

Crawford, V. (2001). African American women in the twenty-first century. In *The American Woman, 1999–2000* (pp. 107–132). New York: Norton.

Dym, B. (2003) *School development and community integration.* Unpublished research paper produced for the Partnership for Excellence in Jewish Education.

Elliot, A. (1996). Ella Baker: Free agent in the civil rights movement. *Journal of Black Studies, 26*(5), 593–603.

Gardner, H. (1983). *Frames of mind: The theory of multiple intelligences.* New York: Basic Books.

Gilkes, C. T. (1988). Building in many places: Multiple commitments and ideologies in black women's community work. In A. Bookman & S. Morgan (Eds.), *Women and the politics of empowerment.* Philadelphia: Temple University Press.

Gyant, L. (1996). Passing the torch: African American women in the civil rights movement. *Journal of Black Studies, 26*(5), 629–647.

Lerner, R., et al. (2002). Applied developmental science of positive human development. In *Handbook of psychology: Vol 6. Developmental psychology* (pp. 535–553). New York: Wiley.

Naples, N. (1998). *Grassroots warriors: Activists mothering, community work, and the war on poverty.* New York: Routledge.

Parker, P. (2001, August). African American women executives' leadership communication within dominant-culture organizations. *Management Communication Quarterly, 15*(1), 42–82.

Williams, L. E. (1996). *Servants of the people: The 1960s legacy of African-American leadership.* New York: St. Martin's Press.

6

The Alignment Map

For leaders, their organizations are front and center. Leaders must align themselves to organizational purposes, operating methods and culture, and the market within which their organizations exist. And leaders must help align their organizations to their own purposes and to the needs and resources of the markets and communities that represent their environment. Success comes when leaders, organizations, and communities or markets are all aligned with one another.

In order to strike a balance between the power of simplicity and the truth of complexity, we have created a grid with twelve cells. For the leader, the leader's organization, and the organizational context—its community or marketplace—we describe four arenas of focus: basic nature, underlying principles, means available to make progress, and overriding purpose and direction. We conclude that the fundamental challenge of leadership is the alignment of these components.

	Leader	*Organization*	*Community/Market*
Basic nature	Character and style	Organizational type	Patterns and norms
Underlying principles	Personal values	Organizational culture	Larger culture
Means available	Individual skills	Organizational resources	Economy and industry
Purpose and direction	Personal objectives	Mission and strategy	Community needs and market demands

The Leader

A person considering a leadership position and an organization evaluating a potential leader must ask both whether her skills, style, and objectives are a good match for the organization and, to the extent that they are not, whether each is flexible enough to accommodate the other. We identify four major qualities of leaders.

CHARACTER AND STYLE

Character has long been the focus of those who write about leadership. It has been said that everyone has three characters: one she really has, one she thinks she has, and one she exhibits. By character, we mean all three, forming a complex of salient personal traits that individualizes a person. While there may be some universal qualities of leadership, such as analytic and emotional intelligence, dedication, resilience, and a capacity to look forward and welcome change and innovation, there are myriad distinctive personalities and leadership styles, each of which may be attuned to distinctive organizations and organizational climates. A person may be particularly active or passive, passionate or dispassionate, analytical or intuitive. She may be passionate with an Italian, Jewish, or Hispanic flavor, or laid-back with the same ethnic flavors. Any of these may work, if they fit. If a leader's character and style can be aligned with the organization, the person leads.

In the lexicon of leadership, there are many useful typologies of character and style, such as the Myers-Briggs Type Instrument, the categorization of Type A and B personalities, and the identification of mythological or spiritual forms from ancient traditions. Angeles Arrien's (1993) naming of warriors, healers, visionaries, and teachers, based on her anthropological work among indigenous peoples, has entered the mainstream of leadership training. David Riesman (2001) long ago popularized the notion of other-directed personalities, who take their cues primarily from others, and inner-directed types, who tend to trust their own perceptions and attend first and foremost to their own values and ideas. Familiar Freudian categories also represent different leadership types: obsessive types, for example, are those who micromanage and pursue control. Our point is that character and style are key components of leadership alignment.

In an organization that grew up around a passionate and charismatic leader, a cool, analytic person might find it difficult to fit in, or might have to realign the organization—new personnel, new procedures—to make best use of her character. Entrepreneurial temperaments, which are generally aggressive, risk-taking, hands-on, and energetic, are essential to grassroots and other startup organizations that wish to grow rapidly. A preference for caretaking, with the humility, empathy, and concern for others that come with it, fits best with service organizations. Those who prefer to work behind the scenes, to facilitate other people's efforts and give them credit, can only lead organizations that appreciate their value and employ others who can and like to be out front.

PERSONAL VALUES

All leaders are guided by their values, and these values must be aligned with those of their organizations. Imagine a leader who has a stoical philosophy and a matching personal style—spare, lean, and unembellished—being hired into an organization accustomed to lavish spending. If alignment meant converting employees or bending the organization to the leader's will, then the leader would probably exert so much energy, use so many chits, and exhaust so much goodwill that there would be insufficient energy left to conduct business. On the other hand, a value connection frees leaders and organization to focus on the organization's specific objectives.

There are a variety of ways to think about leaders' values that also help us see how they align or fail to align with their organizations. For one, there are values specific to organizations. Some organizations are built around raising the consciousness of women or ethnic groups, about the importance of music in life, about the need for social justice, or about caring for the indigent.

For another, there are values that are more like cultural commonalities than ethical standards, such as the shared assumptions about good and bad, valuable and worthless, in various religious and ethic groups. In some Jewish organizations, for instance, the value placed on Jewish continuity is assumed and the leader must be passionate for this purpose. Feminist values such as a shared sense of oppression, coupled with the need for greater equality and safety, are prominent in many domestic violence shelters.

A third set of values concerns means and ends. There are leaders who value ends almost exclusively, and believe all should be sacrificed to get there—certain revolutionaries, and those who are single-minded about achieving short-term results, for example. There are also those who believe that the way you conduct yourself is an end in itself, and that means are even more important than ends in a truly ethical world—pacifists and members of the ACLU are inclined this way. Then there are those, like the leaders of the Children's Therapeutic Day School, which we will introduce in the next chapter, who have a passion for integrating means and ends, believing that anything less is both ineffectual and unethical.

In nonprofit organizations, values are primary. The leader generally represents that mission, may even embody it, and surely must advocate for it in public. Values are not an aside that an executive makes to build morale, please a regulatory agency, or place a particular mark on a business operation. Lack of authenticity is readily detected by staff, volunteers, and donors alike. And while the leader's values are of great importance in all organizations, they are of particular—focal—importance in nonprofits.

Nonprofit leaders and their organizations do, in fact, have missions that mean something to them. Leaders exhort staff to greater effort on behalf of their mission. They attract and motivate volunteers because of their mission. They salve their wounds during hard times by reference to their mission—"At least," they will say, "we are working for a good cause." Effective nonprofit leaders embody passionate missions.

Nonprofit leaders bring their missions out into the community. They are generally the main advocates for their organizations' purposes and services. For many organizations, the executive director's advocacy is its major marketing activity, and advocacy is a core ingredient in the executive director's job description. It is made much easier because she believes in what she is advocating. Advocacy and mission-based leadership may also come easier to nonprofit leaders because they are often folded into a personal story about the leader's youth and professional beginnings. One leader whose organization helps learning disabled children talks of his painful encounters with schools as a youth. Another notes how her example is one of making it against the odds. The volunteer president of a trail association speaks with visible emotion about how hiking has been essential to his physical, mental, and spiritual health. The most effective leaders tell stories that connect their own personal experience with the people they serve and the staff they lead. These leaders embody their stories and bind people together in common hope, sorrow, frustration, and resolve.

The corporate equivalents of these stories are the rags-to-riches tales of Horatio Alger fame exemplifying the power of myth-making with oneself as the protagonist. While the entrepreneurial tale is compelling to some, the nonprofit tale tends to reach out to a larger proportion of employees because of its universal appeal.

The broader reach of nonprofit leaders has much to do with the way they pay attention to their audience. They identify with their audience and, even if they have been more successful than the majority, they expect their audience to identify with them. Often the identification derives from a common culture, history, neighborhood, or cause. Corporate leaders may listen to their boards, but few listen to any but a small circle of their employees. The best for-profit leaders in this regard embody what Frances Hesselbein, former CEO of the Girl Scouts of America, calls authentic "voice" (Helgesen, 1995, p. 80).

Nonprofit leaders, because of the very nature of their roles, tend to listen to their constituents—some of whom are employees and volunteer staff. To be effective leaders, they must listen when their constituents talk as attentively as a CEO must listen to Wall Street's response to her quarterly reports. In other words, the principal frames of reference for corporate and nonprofit leaders are different; this makes a big difference when they try to invoke mission statements and common purpose in the service of increased productivity or organizational change.

Few for-profit organizations are mission-based, requiring what James MacGregor Burns (1978), Robert Coles (1993), and other theorists call moral leadership. Moral leadership has as much to do with the qualities of the relationship between leaders and their constituents as with the qualities of the leaders themselves. Here's how Burns describes it:

> Leaders and led have a relationship not only of power but of mutual needs, aspirations, and values; second, that in responding to leaders, followers have adequate knowledge of alternative leaders and programs and the capacity to choose among those alternatives; and, third, that leaders take responsibility for their commitments—if they promise certain kinds of economic, social, and political change, they assume leadership in the bringing about of that change. (1978, p. 4)

Corporate executives could learn a good deal from nonprofit leaders about how to address their employees and constituents, how to connect with them through common stories and cultural symbols, and how to advocate for commonly held purposes, thereby gaining a certain legitimacy for their leadership that they currently hold primarily by virtue of their position.

INDIVIDUAL SKILLS

There are some obvious skills required of leaders. For example, if growth requires fund raising, then networking and public speaking skills are important. Early in an organization's life, however, the ability to gather people around an unproven organization may be more important than public speaking. Later, the ability to manage large numbers of people, to delegate, or to work with vendors may be critical to building organizations to scale.

In other words, the particular skills required of leaders vary according to the organization. During periods of rapid growth, the ability to articulate a vision and rally people around it, to manage change and take risks, and to attract funding may be primary. Very early in the life of nonprofits, single-minded dedication to mission may be a more important ability than managerial skills and the ability to implement procedures or document processes.

As we discussed in Chapter 5, the appropriate skills vary according to cultural and professional context, developmental stage, organizational values, market demand, and zeitgeist. Also, as we discussed in Chapter 4, there is a commonly held idea, increasingly fed by leadership training programs at business schools and elsewhere, that leadership is a specific set of skills that can be taught. Clearly, certain leadership skills are, in fact, appropriate for many if not all organizations. Many large organizations tailor leadership training programs to their particular needs and cultures. They identify high potential candidates and teach them the General Electric or Hewlett Packard "way" or, less familiarly, the Girl Scouts of American or Youthbuild "way." These ways generally include indoctrination into the values and cultures of the organizations, rotation or tours of duty through various units, and specific skill training in planning, motivating, delegating, and the like. These efforts intentionally align leadership skills to what are perceived as the leadership needs of their organization's future.

PERSONAL OBJECTIVES

Personal objectives must be aligned with organizational purposes. The job has to be a vehicle for satisfying individual objectives. The leader may wish to do good, to grow prominent and powerful, or to learn, as a stepping-stone to future professional goals. Maybe a stable living is the objective. Whatever the personal objectives, they must be possible within the organization's objectives, style, and strategy, or the leader is in the wrong place.

By way of example, if a leader who is 63 wants to leave a legacy to future leaders whom she has mentored and a stable, well-functioning agency, but the organization is being positioned for rapid growth toward somewhat uncertain ends, then there is a mismatch. If a leader enters with an aggressive agenda that is not shared by the board or by employees, there is a mismatch. Conversely, if a leader's objectives are primarily idealistic and her mission-driven organization cannot afford a big salary, then there is a match.

The leader's personal objectives must be aligned with her organization's objectives. Above all, the personal objectives of leaders must be aligned to organizational mission and strategy. They must match up with organizational culture. A leader with very modest objectives will not fit with a hard-driving, ambitious organization; a brash leader whose objectives have to do with success at all costs will not play well with an organization that prides itself on being measured or sophisticated. A leader who needs a big salary—children in college, unexpected expenses—and a resource-strapped organization won't fit well together. Some nonprofits are organized to feature their leaders in a very public way; some are not. Flatter organizations that give many people access to leaders work for those who are comfortable with wide spans of control.

Some organizations insulate the leader who prefers to spend time on the outside. Marian Heard, CEO of the United Way of Massachusetts Bay, entrusted Pat Brandes with operational and strategic responsibilities so she could focus on working the community, raising money, and speaking out for the United

Way's causes. She has had little involvement or interest in the day-to-day side of organizational life. Shiela Moore's wish to make a broader impact and to develop a reputation in the broader Boston community fit very well with Casa Myrna's need for greater publicity. Similarly, Suzin Bartley's desire and ability to live in the Massachusetts political milieu fit with CTF's need for political positioning and funding; furthermore, the new awareness and rage at child abuse called upon her wish to speak out. Meanwhile, Peter Karoff's pleasure in making things happen from behind the scenes fit his organization's purpose and allowed philanthropists to take center stage.

SOME ALIGNED LEADERS

Peter Karoff, whom we met in the last chapter, is well suited to leadership of an intermediary organization. Like other such leaders, he is an accomplished matchmaker. Like marriage brokers in traditional communities, he likes to bring people together. Even when not working, he does so at social occasions. He takes pleasure in other people's success and lacks the need to be the protagonist in the plays he authors. This is his character and his leadership style. Peter is more concerned with facilitating social action than starring in it. This is a value he holds. When he listens to you, you feel very important, very capable. This is a skill he has. He has a huge personal network and an almost encyclopedic knowledge of nonprofit activities from which to draw. This, too, stems from his social skills and a lifetime of commitment to social action causes. And he is immensely adept at framing a conceptual link that joins people and organizations to one another. This is another skill. He had built and led an insurance company earlier in his career, but by middle age, public service had become his passion. The Philanthropic Initiative, which helps wealthy people align their charitable impulses and capacity with a clear philanthropic vision and good social investments, has been a perfect vehicle for Peter Karoff's own objectives.

Alignment entails mutual adaptation. Shiela Moore brought Casa Myrna into a more professional organizational style employing clear lines of accountability, calm deliberation and decision-making processes in the executive team, and roles defined by areas of expertise. Yet she also adapted, that is, aligned herself to Casa Myrna. She did so as she became knowledgeable about issues of domestic violence. She learned to appreciate and provide room for the programs to operate more or less as they had, which was not as closely ordered a process as she would have preferred. She became a passionate advocate of Casa Myrna's mission, which was a different role than she had played in previous jobs. In other words, the job at Casa Myrna brought out aspects of Shiela Moore's personality that had been dormant or undeveloped.

Pat Brandes of the United Way combines qualities that don't always go together. She is passionate in her advocacy of clearly articulated values about social justice, yet she dislikes conflict and feels compelled to make things go smoothly, and she is very practical.

For years Brandes lived with her husband and three children in a low-key lifestyle built around an alternative school. Gradually, she volunteered for one activity after another until she was practically running the school's operations. When that challenge diminished, Pat went to business school, where, much to her surprise, she graduated first in her class. She was offered excellent corporate positions that did not fit her values and did not even seem exciting to her. So she chose the United Way. The United Way's focus on supporting community-based nonprofits fit her values, and there was a chance to make a big difference after playing on a small, almost private stage. At first, however, the United Way's emphasis on charity was not a fit with values she practiced in her alternative school, empowering people versus outright giving.

Pat Brandes did not enter the United Way as a major leader, but her capacity to make things happen, first in small arenas and then in larger, quickly catapulted her to the top. Within a few years, she was in charge of day-to-day operations and strategy for charitable giving. Pat Brandes was an almost perfect fit with the United Way at that particular time—in the larger Massachusetts community, which was shifting its emphasis in nonprofits from charitable giving to leveraged change. Her combination of passionate advocacy with practical, businesslike strategy and her ability to bring people together were just the right leadership qualities to move the United Way through an essential organizational strategic transition. She befriended everyone from Marian Heard, to board members, to young staff members, to clients.

In sum, Brandes aligned herself to the United Way and the United Way to her design. She helped realign the United Way's strategic emphasis to fit her own idea of how to empower community-based organizations that served those living in poverty. She aligned herself to the organization, first, by making herself an indispensable manager, equally at home with spreadsheets, best-practice research, and neighborhood health centers. She went to school, as it were, to learn the practical methods of leveraging charitable giving. And because she genuinely liked the corporate scions of Boston society, she taught herself to work the boardrooms with the same kind of comfort she had once brought to the alternative school.

Thus, there are many types of organizations and leaders. The fit between them must be good for leaders to be effective. The fit is never perfect. Leaders must therefore align themselves to organizations by adapting themselves to the organization's structure, process, culture, and strategy—and by aligning the organizations to fit their style. Both processes are necessary for effective leadership.

The Organization

In our discussions about how leaders align themselves with their organizations, we have covered the qualities of organizational life that are most in need of alignment, but we would like to briefly separate and describe each.

ORGANIZATIONAL TYPE

In psychology, character refers to those deep, enduring, almost hardwired qualities that make us who we are, as opposed to personality or style, which can change over time and according to circumstance. Organizations may also be said to have such a character. Here we are thinking of the structure and culture that shape the activities of organizations. So the structure of a grassroots or entrepreneurial organization can be minimal and fit perfectly its need for everyone to fill in here and there, but an organization dealing with lots of employees, funds, and outside funders must have more orderly and more transparent ways of holding employees and itself accountable. A fast-growing organization in a fast-changing environment must have an agile decision-making process.

Sam Healey fit poorly into the high-tech company originally built around a software genius. For the first five years of its existence, the entire structure was built around the genius's ability to provide answers for virtually all questions and to inspire others to technical innovation. To that end, there were weekly meetings, in which he would ramble on about both scientific and philosophical subjects. He would visit each technology team each week to discuss the problems they were working on. Incentive systems emphasized technological innovation, not getting to market on time or collaboration. There was no real executive team. The structure consisted of seven technology teams, each with a leader who reported directly to the genius.

Healey was accustomed to working with a senior team, with each member managing a department and collaborating with the others. Because he was attuned to market demands, the marketing vice president was second in command and had considerable influence over technology development—Healey's motto was, "Develop what the customer wants." When Healey tried to implement a comparable situation at this new company, the team leaders of the technology groups refused to report to anyone but him. Although his marketing vice president was current on the technology, Healey was not. He could order a change, but the long-standing structural tradition made alignment tremendously difficult. It is hard to change the character of a company. But Healey, too, was set in his ways and in his character and limited by his skills. He needed to give over the marketing-technology interface to others, but the very act violated the company's values and its structural preferences. Leadership was virtually doomed to failure.

David Kantor devised a typology of family systems that may help us further elucidate the notion of organizational character (Kantor & Lehr, 1975). He wrote about closed and open systems. By closed, Kantor meant traditional families organized around clearly stated, relatively fixed rules, rituals, and processes derived from moral and religious traditions and certitudes. They have tight external boundaries that help to protect the rules from unorthodox ideas. They are almost invariably headed by fathers, whose authority is more or less absolute, though it can range from benevolent to autocratic. Next in command comes the mother, then the oldest child, and so forth. Open systems tend toward greater flexibility in hierarchy and rules, and place emphasis on adaptability, open boundaries, cooperation, and sharing. Kantor is careful to say that each type works, and neither is better than the other. They simply represent very different characters. Each makes decisions, processes information, plays out emotional attachments, raises children, and does everything differently than the other.

Each is also more or less effective in different social milieus. The traditional system works best in a stable community, the open system in a changing community. When families—or organizations—change milieu, their character type may be more or less adaptive. This is true, for example, of immigrant families with their traditional characters that are often rent apart as the parents cleave to the old ways while the children push to be like Americans. There are comparably good and bad adaptations as organizations relocate themselves or establish branch offices in new communities or foreign cultures. Organizations may also be characterized as open or closed.

There are other organizational characters as well. There are what Peter Senge (1990) has termed "learning organizations" that call upon certain kinds of flexible, collaborative leadership. There are collective organizations. There are family businesses that frequently and in each generation tend to have a definable character. And each calls for a different kind of alignment with both leaders and the communities in which they exist.

In general, the structure and culture of organizations may be found in the distinctive ways that they make decisions, manage projects, recruit and train new employees, and create incentives for desirable performance. Some organizations are centralized, which works well with leaders who need to translate ideas rapidly into action, whereas other leaders, who prefer to delegate and let the implementation of their strategy unfold over time, may find comfort in decentralized organizations. Organizational structure may be hierarchical or flat. Its culture may be deliberate or immediate. In some, every move is carefully considered. In others, everything seems like a crisis.

To all these things, the leader must be more or less aligned, changing herself to fit the organization or changing the organization to fit herself, in order to be effective.

ORGANIZATIONAL CULTURE

Culture in organizations refers to the values and norms—made manifest in patterns of behavior—that distinguish it from other social groupings and permit its members to say, "This is us." Culture shows itself in the way people talk with one another, the way they dress, and the way they make decisions, both formally and informally. It reflects what the members of the organization value and rejects or marginalizes those who don't share those values.

We describe some organizational cultures as laid-back, others as hard-driving; some as careful and prudent, others as daring and innovative; some as stable, others as chaotic or continually changing; some as democratic, others as autocratic; some as political or petty, others as rewarding real merit and achievement. Much of a culture is obvious when you first enter a system, particularly as a new employee or a consultant. People say things like, "This is how we do things here." They may be affirming or damning the cultural norm, but they are surely cuing the newcomer as to what is acceptable and what is not, what leads to alliances, to the inner circle, to (culturally defined) competence and success.

Leaders must more or less align themselves to the organizational culture. An insistently democratic leader like Sam Healey will founder on the rock of a (benevolently) autocratic culture. A hard-driving leader looking for rapid organizational change will encounter trouble in a stable culture that has emphasized lifestyle work habits. A male leader who values competition and individual achievement will have trouble in an organization built by and around women who value group achievement and the minimization of individual glory.

On the other hand, alignment need not and generally should not be perfect. Perfect alignment between the values and style of the leader and an organization's culture works beautifully in brief spurts, as for example, when everyone is focused on the achievement of a major goal and works in unison toward that goal in a culturally prescribed style. But the complete alignment of leaders and organizations can also lead to stagnation and make it difficult for leaders to respond to changing conditions or changing objectives. At such times, leadership change may be experienced as a kind of abandonment and betrayal of an implicit agreement. Large segments of the organization may resist changes the leadership believes are necessary. Control struggles may ensue, blocking and deteriorating organization effectiveness.

So, in fact, it helps to have an implicit agreement that leaders and their organizations are meant to be sometimes in alignment, sometimes out of alignment. And organizational cultures can be built around this kind of agreement. Stories are told that chronicle, justify, and even glorify such alternations. They can go like this: "We move along pretty smoothly until the boss gets a new idea. Then all hell breaks loose, and no one knows exactly what to do. But she's usually way ahead of us and right on the mark. It was important to shift gears.

So we don't like it when she starts on one of her jags, but we pretty well accept it and don't get so upset anymore."

ORGANIZATIONAL RESOURCES

Obviously leadership style and objectives and organizational objectives must line up with available resources. The executive director of a particularly innovative and growth-oriented nonprofit organization, when asked how she was doing, said: "All right, considering what's going on. I'm just trying to help us survive the depression." Few of the programs she normally ran had gotten funded. So she had downsized both the organizational objectives and her staff. Her staff is very versatile, however. Where they had been serving as an incubator for innovation—conducting research into best practices that could then be brought to many small, community-based organizations—they could also facilitate change through direct consulting practices. In the organization's conception, such hands-on activity was considered a slow and plodding practice. They preferred to leverage their resources. But, for lack of internal resources due to a lack of external resources, they adapted their mode of operations. Thus leadership provided impetus to align strategy to the reality of internal resources—and to the resources provided by the larger community.

There are many kinds of organizational resources: human, financial, technological, and intellectual, to name a few. The better the leader assesses these resources and aligns the organization to what they make possible, the better the organization functions.

ORGANIZATIONAL MISSION AND STRATEGY

The heart of any organization is its mission—what it is set on earth to do, as it were. The mission may be divided into objectives. Then, strategies are chosen for their ability to help the organization achieve its objectives, leading to the fulfillment of the mission. The mission might be to create a community where now impersonal housing units are inhabited by people who are indifferent to one other. An objective might be to get people to know and care about one another. A strategy might be to form neighborhood organizations that bring people together in work and play and common cause. Then, tactically, the organization must decide how it is going to form the neighborhood organizations—meetings, shared projects, and the like.

The leader's raison d'etre is to guide her organization toward the fulfillment of its mission by clarifying objectives and developing strategies, requiring others to design and implement tactics, and to hold them accountable for their efforts.

Leaders and their organizations are not always in sync. Sam Healey's major objective was to make lots of money for shareholders, which he—and his board of directors—thought meant market-oriented strategies. But the majority of software engineers and middle managers disagreed. Their objective was to make the most elegant machine, which suggested a strategy focused on product development. Each strategy means a very different allocation of time and resources and a very different orientation to customers. Leader and organization were not aligned.

One very typical problem in organizations is the contradiction that exists between their own mission and strategies, on one hand, and their internal processes, on the other. Many nonprofits, for example, aim to empower their clients in social, political, economic, and other ways. These very same organizations often depend on substantial volunteer activities from these same clients and other interested people. Often, however, the organization of work disempowers them. Leaders may be autocratic. Volunteers may be given menial tasks and few opportunities for advancement. Their voices, along with those of most employees, may not be listened to. As a result, these organizations regularly founder on the rock of disillusionment among staff and volunteers.

In organizations built on developing innovative approaches to social change, some leaders may encourage employees to be creative and take risks, and then reprimand, marginalize, or fire people when success is not achieved. Many organizations, from schools to high-technology companies based on the centrality of continual learning, introduce strategies that create more barriers than incentives to learning. For instance, they create career paths that move almost exclusively through management. As a result, some of the most innovative clinicians, software engineers, or lawyers become managers. Too often, this produces poor to mediocre managers and a concurrent loss of brilliant, creative sole practitioners, whose skills and temperaments are not best married to management.

Community/Market

Organizations live within communities and markets. In Chapter 5, we emphasized the importance of fit with the larger culture. Here, we want to very briefly describe several key elements of the organizational context.

PATTERNS AND NORMS

It is easy to understand that community-based organizations must align themselves with their communities. The effort to help children, abused women, teenage school dropouts, or unemployed men and women within a Latino, African American, or Asian community must be aligned with the norms and values of that community or it will not build a base of volunteer labor or be funded in an ongoing manner. Its services will be refused and ultimately unsuccessful. In contrast, leadership that aligns with community and other group cultures increases the organization's chances of success. We described such leaders in Chapter 5: the African American women who coordinated so much of the civil rights voter registration drives; Lindalyn Kakadelis and the Children's Scholarship Fund of Charlotte; Josh Elkin and the Partnership for Excellence in Jewish Education. Each understood and worked with the patterns and norms of the community served.

LARGER CULTURE

Communities and societies can be likened to markets. They will buy certain kinds of advocacy and certain kinds of service at different times and won't buy it at others. In the case of service agencies, such as legal aid, abortion counseling, or domestic violence shelters, the relation between organizational objectives and community needs, desires, and tastes is obvious enough.

But the same market will also respond to nonprofit services that are less directly connected to individual clients. City Year, for example, trains community-based and middle-class youth to work together to improve neighborhoods. It has clearly caught the public imagination, as reflected in its rapid spread and funding. Youthbuild, with its emphasis on poor teenagers taking charge of their own lives, has appealed to a society that fears it has encouraged a dependent subculture. Within a couple of decades, under Dorothy Stoneman's leadership, it has grown from its origins in East Harlem into an international organization, with branches in 40 states and several nations.

Both governmental and philanthropic funding depends on ideas that are current. Organizations that fit current ideas about social change, artistic development, or educational achievement tend to get funded. Naturally this gives them a much better chance to succeed. Leaders who align their organizations to national and regional funding trends tend to succeed. Of course, this kind of alignment can be so opportunistic that it violates the organization's own goals, culture, or strategy. In such cases, alignment of leaders and funding sources throws the organizations out of alignment and jeopardizes effective use of the funding.

ECONOMY AND INDUSTRY

Community and larger social resources play a large role in the success and failure of organizations. In the simplest sense, good economies tend to be good for nonprofits, and vice versa. Yet some nonprofits—say those dealing with unemployment—may thrive in difficult economies. There are many less obvious resources. For example, although the Jewish day school movement is poised for rapid growth, there is a dearth of qualified heads of school and qualified teachers and of curriculum to integrate secular and traditional Jewish subject matter. Without teachers and curriculum materials, it is hard for these schools to compete with the excellent public schools in their areas. Organizations that depend on certain kinds of expertise, labor, volunteer effort, and technical materials all rise and fall, in part, on the resources available outside of their immediate organization.

COMMUNITY NEEDS AND MARKET DEMANDS

Neighborhood and other locally based organizations succeed or fail based on their fit with their communities' values. Chapter 5 discussed this theme at length.

Beneath the Surface

Alignment is a dynamic process, with the components affecting each other in sometimes predictable, sometimes unpredictable ways. The process is always in motion, always changing. A map of component parts cannot fully capture the spirit of alignment, but it can help isolate elements and relationships, enabling diagnosis and perhaps remedial action when things aren't flowing smoothly.

In the previous chapter we introduced Suzin Bartley as being well aligned with her organization, a public/private agency dedicated to the prevention of child abuse, the Children's Trust Fund. She joined when the organization was in its infancy, when her freewheeling, entrepreneurial style matched the organization's need for rapid growth. She openly reveals her deep moral conviction about the need to protect children from the ravages of abusive adults and from poverty's many insults, yet her passion is leavened by the practicality and political acumen she acquired as the daughter and granddaughter of Massachusetts politicians—qualities that play well for an organization funded chiefly by the state legislature.

Despite her ambitions for herself and her organization, Bartley is skeptical about her abilities and worried about her job's ability to suck energy and time to the marrow, taking her away from a family she loves. So she resists the call to bigger assignments. When offered the leadership of huge state agencies with great prestige, she has refused. They would not only take too much of her, she says, but their size would not play to her strengths. Among other things, they would require too many people, too many layers, and too much delegation. She likes to be hands-on. She is an intimate person who thrives in a setting like CTF.

Bartley's character and leadership style, her skills and personal objectives, and her values match up brilliantly with the character, resources, organizational process, and organizational culture of the Children's Trust Fund, and both match up with the Massachusetts social and political climate. The result is that CTF is a great success, the most successful CTF in the nation, and Suzin Bartley is a prominent and much sought after leader. This chapter provides a framework to understand her success and that of other well-aligned nonprofits.

References

Arrien, A. (1993). *The four-fold way: Walking the paths of the warrior, teacher, healer, and visionary.* San Francisco: HarperSanFrancisco.

Burns, J. M. (1978). *Leadership.* New York: Harper & Row.

Coles, R. (1993). *The call of service.* Boston: Houghton Mifflin.

Helgesen, S. (1995). *The female advantage: Women's ways of leadership.* New York: Doubleday/Currency.

Kantor, D., & Lehr, W. (1975). *Inside the family.* San Francisco: Jossey-Bass.

Riesman, D. (2001). *The lonely crowd: A study of the changing American character.* New Haven, CT: Yale University Press.

Senge, P. (1990). *The fifth discipline: The art and practice of the learning organization.* New York: Doubleday/Currency.

7

The Dynamics and
Cycles of Alignment

Having provided a map of the alignment territory, indicating its major components, parameters, and pathways, we now want to go further—beyond our own map—and describe the territory itself. The territory is dynamic. There are continual, complex interactions between leaders, organizations, and the larger communities in which they live. These dynamic interactions may be described as cycles of alignment, misalignment, and realignment.

Organizations as Dynamic, Living Systems

Healthy organizations behave like living organisms, with semipermeable boundaries in constant interaction with the world in which they live. Information comes through the boundaries—news about resources and opportunities, ideas about how to manage people and processes, thinking about technology that can speed things up and change the way we see the world—and organizations change accordingly. Change occurs internally, as an adaptation to information from the outside, and externally, as organizations modify their stance in the world.

Because change is inevitable and constant, organizations move in and out of alignment, just as people do. Consider, for example, the growth of a boy in a two-year span, from a five-foot-one-inch child to a six foot-three-inch adolescent. No longer a boy but not yet a man, he doesn't feel entirely at home in his body. His sense of himself, his identity, his movement, and his coordination have not caught up with his height. Of course he has trouble on the basketball court, but he also doesn't know how to stand when he is near his now much shorter mother, or among tall people who used to tower over him. His self-image and physical being are out of joint. So it is with organizations that grow rapidly—they too can become awkward, nervous, and uncoordinated.

In general, living systems do not change for the sake of change. Even genuine innovation is rare. More often, they change because they see the need to adapt or they conceive a goal that requires change. Even then they are reluctant to change and tend to pursue their goals in their current form and style. When they do change, they do so minimally, striving to maintain their character. It can be said, in fact, that organisms change in order to remain the same. That is, they adapt just enough to maintain their balance, their livelihood, and their character. This is equally true for microorganisms, individual people, and organizations.

However much organizations resist change, they must change and do so in a way that sustains the integrity of their purpose. By their nature, then, organizations are learning systems. Organizations accommodate new markets, new funding realities, and new socioeconomic conditions, and as they adapt to these new conditions, the process changes them. Seeking survival and growth, they become different.

As they change, organizations lose the alignment they had achieved. Misalignment is a natural phase in the organizational life cycle, not a failure. Rather than criticizing others, leaders can look for the heart of the adaptive change and guide it forward, with praise and support for those who are moving the organization *out of alignment.* Just as a growth spurt in an adolescent is ungainly but ultimately advantageous, an applecart upset in an organization can be a sign of health. When an executive director adds highly qualified new board members who have no previous connections to the agency, who in turn instigate needed reforms, the old guard on the board may put up a fight. They may feel bypassed and no longer valued, or far worse, implicated in what are now seen as the sins of the past. They may think, "If these reforms are really needed, we must not have been doing our jobs when we were in charge."

For a while, governance may devolve into contention. For the executive director to enable the agency to reach a new level of alignment requires her to stay the course during the disruption, to manage her own anxiety, and to shift her awareness from polarization—old versus new, continuation versus change, adversaries versus allies, and so forth—to "holding both." Leadership of a dynamic, living system requires cohabitation with complexity.

ALL PARTS ARE CONNECTED

All of the parts on our alignment map are dynamically connected with one another. If you change one—or if one changes—others change as well. As these change, still others are set in motion. We will illustrate with two cases:

The principal of a private school for disabled children suffers a minor heart attack that results in a major change in his outlook on life and his values.

He had been the undisputed center of authority for the school, outgoing, decisive, demanding—and neglectful of his health and family. Suddenly, as he recovers from his heart attack, he becomes more balanced, more willing to delegate, more thoughtful, and a better listener—though some would say he is no longer as intense and present. A vacuum has been created, and the other members of the executive group, the chief operating officer, the chief financial officer, and the two program directors, don't believe themselves individually capable of significant leadership responsibility. Each prefers to work with the other three as a team.

It happens that the team effort is successful and replicated throughout the organization—teams are formed to handle enrollment, bus scheduling, and parent relations. This, in turn, creates the need for greater collaboration among employees at all levels. This not only changes the organization's culture but also raises questions about the organization's values. The emergent leadership team begins to appreciate process and cooperation for their own sake as well as for their utilitarian value. They begin behaving in a more democratic way. More people feel affirmed. With this internal democratization of the work-place, the organization shows a different face to the external world—more people represent the organization outside. This, in turn, raises issues of account-ability and consistency, forcing the organization to implement a much stronger infrastructure to replace the hierarchical, supervisory structure that had existed before.

Here's a second illustration. A government agency begins funding a neigh-borhood drug treatment program, imposing requirements for greater account-ability than the program had provided in the past. This is an organization founded by a charismatic leader, who, it was said, "couldn't manage his way out of a paper bag." He hadn't the temperament or interest in orderly processes or in holding employees accountable. Now the agency is demanding detailed tracking of both services and finances. It happens that one of the staff, one who had risen from volunteer to administrative assistant to second in command, is very good at managing both the infrastructure processes and the people. The demands of the government agency emphasize her importance. As her star rises, so does her ability to organize people and systems. And, as government funding increasingly dominates, the money the founding leader brings in from donors pales by comparison.

During the year prior to the manager's increasing prominence, the board of directors, which had once been a rubber-stamp board, felt compelled to rein in the looseness of the founder's management. They began to support the manager's ascendancy. For a while, the manager and the founding director work in very com-plementary ways, but eventually he grows jealous of her increasing authority and begins to find fault with her, claiming that her businesslike ways were leading the organization away from its original community-based spirit. The board listens with a cold ear. Emboldened by the government agency's clear stand, the board eventually asks the founding director to step down.

Within months of assuming the executive director's job, the manager consolidates a new, very different alignment in the organization. Her skills, character, values, and objectives—more modest than those of the founder—set the tone. From an entrepreneurial, loosely organized, helter-skelter style of organization, it becomes well ordered and smoothly functioning, with a culture of cooperation (to replace the culture of hero worship) and a broader-based decision-making structure. And because she had been a volunteer, the organization is able to enhance its volunteer labor pool and cut back on fixed expenses.

What is happening in these two cases? In the first, the leader's personal crisis initiates a cascading series of changes in the organization's character, culture, values, and resource allocation, which in turn leads to different interactions with the community, whose "feedback" sparks further alterations in the organization. In the second, external changes initiated by a board and a funding agency exacerbate internal changes already in process, which pick up pace.

Changing one aspect of alignment does not *always* lead to multiplying effects. Frequently, changes in one arena may change only a few others and not much more. In the case of the more withdrawn leader, for instance, his role is simply picked up by one or two others who like the organization as it is—they had risen through its ranks and feel successful in its culture. Consequently, they change little. Sometimes outside efforts by foundations and government agencies to change organizations meet resistance and harden the organization's commitment to its present state.

Systems theorists tell us that all systems, from cells to individuals to groups, organizations, communities, and societies, have closely linked tendencies to maintain themselves, as is, and to resist change. The effort to maintain character is variously called homeostasis (in biology), negative feedback loops (in cybernetics), replication (in evolutionary theory), and constancy loops (in family systems therapy). Because of this inherent tendency to maintain character and resist change, the cascading effects described above rarely happen in such clear and rapid order, except when precipitated by crises. Because of the inherent tendency to adapt to both internal changes—like a maturing child or organization—and external changes—like new regulatory systems, technologies, or funding sources—it is possible to build on adaptive changes to multiply effects.

It is much easier to influence organizations in the midst of change than to build on small changes. During adaptive moments, systems are temporarily out of balance, out of alignment. Such moments are the focus of much change theory. The physicist, Ilya Prigogine, for example, notes that systems out of equilibrium are particularly vulnerable to change—often major, unpredictable change (Prigogine & Stengers, 1984). We might say that the organization whose leader had a heart attack was such an organization. The action-research theory of Kurt Lewin (1948) speaks of "unfreezing" a prevailing state in order to "break open the shell of complacency and self-righteousness" before "moving to new levels." Educational theorists, like Eleanor Duckworth (1987), talk of these misaligned or transitional moments as "windows of opportunity."

An implication for leadership is that when major changes are required, it is often best to wait for the organization to move out of alignment of its own accord, or to begin changes in arenas that are most vulnerable and most likely to lead to the type of cascading impact we described in the two examples of realignment. This is an application of martial arts principles—accelerating organizational momentum from behind and directing it toward a desired goal. Hence the importance of acute observation in leadership: the ability to identify when and how an organization is in motion and ready for realignment.

Development and Cycles

Like humans, organizations pass through stages in the course of their development. Each transition, from stage to stage, naturally throws the organization out of alignment. The challenge at such times is to find ways to integrate the old and the new in a way that permits the organization to move forward feeling strong, bringing with it its old character and resources, but reconfigured to meet the new realities.

The Casa Myrna case study provides a good illustration of how organizations move in and out of alignment. To digress for a moment, let's return to the comparison with individual development, applying Piaget's developmental model, beginning with a child adapting—or accommodating—to something new in her environment. As she does so, and does so repetitively, the child begins to internalize what she has learned. She assimilates new reality. It becomes part of her. That is, new behaviors and perceptions—new relations to self and world—become part of her way of being, what seems like her character. As these new ways are assimilated, they come into contact, often conflict, with old ways. This is the moment one calls a developmental crisis. The two views of reality must be reconciled. In this dialectical process, a new synthesis, forged from the old and new, is eventually achieved. This new synthesis then forms the cognitive basis—the map of reality—that guides the child's behavior. But it does not last. Eventually, the child accommodates to something new, again, and the process starts all over again.

So too with organizations. Casa Myrna began its life with one view of reality—how life works, what makes it worthwhile, what brings on difficulty—and built its initial organization as an antidote to what it saw as life's troubles. With time, it had to accommodate to all kinds of new realities. Some had to do with the demands of funding organizations. Others concerned the nature of abused women and their families, often containing teenage boys. As Casa Myrna adapted to new elements in its environment, it began to change, not, at first, with a plan, but awkwardly and uncertainly. When Casa Myrna began a strategic planning process that reconceived its vision and how it would fit in its community, it created a new reality that had to be reconciled with the spirit and programmatic methods of the original organization. Under Shiela Moore, a synthesis was formed.

THE RELATIONSHIP MODEL

A second developmental model, also dialectic in form, based on the developmental course of couple relationships, can also be applied to illuminate the dynamics of alignment. The relationship between leaders and their key employees and founding boards can be intense, urgent, and important, taking on many of the characteristics of a marriage. In both relationships, each partner is dependent on the other for support, success, happiness, and productivity; each is often jealous of the company the other keeps; each must adapt to the other—perhaps more than either likes. And, like couples, leaders and their organizations go through cycles of romance, struggle, and reconciliation.

The relationship model was developed in a book by Barry Dym and Michael Glenn (1993) entitled *Couples: Exploring and Understanding the Cycles of Intimate Relationships*. The book describes the developmental phases that couples pass through and how those phases repeat themselves in continuous cycles. During the first phase, the stage of expansion and promise, the partners are enthralled with each other, bringing out the best in each and creating a virtuous cycle. The more she appreciates him (or he appreciates her), for example, the more he acts in ways that please her. The more he pleases her, the more she appreciates him. As a result, he not only loves and appreciates her but also likes himself more than usual. He is at his best, and it isn't just to please her; it just seems to emerge. So each of the partners seems to receive not only the other's love and appreciation but the gift of each's own best self. The experience of this virtuous cycle is so special, so compelling, that new partners take it as a promise, even a contract. The contract says, in effect, that I'll keep playing my part if you'll keep playing yours. And for a wonderful while they do, feeling as good in what they give as in what they receive.

The second phase is the stage of contraction and betrayal. The partners pull back into their skins and renew their normal life, seeing friends, returning to engagements with work or family. After the intense, more exclusive beginnings, the renewal of other relationships can be threatening. Partners cope with this threat in a variety of ways. The more one partner pulls away, for example, the more the other tries to close the gap through kindness, cajoling, or threats.

When these strategies meet only partial success, the partner who remains exclusively engaged for a longer time can feel abandoned. The one who tries to pull the other back can look jealous, controlling, or at least insensitive to the other. Moreover, the person pulling away can look cool or rejecting.

They fight and make up, and a pattern sets in. The next time one of them pulls away, or is too insistent on retaining intimacy, or commits some other violation of the original contract, there is another fight. In place of the original virtuous cycle, a vicious cycle begins, bringing out the worst in the partners. Efforts to dig themselves out only make things worse. One might say, for example, "I'll be better if you will," only to be met with an angry retort: "You didn't used to make everything so contingent," or "You're so controlling—this is the real you." This stage can be so difficult that many couples never pull themselves out. Many new couples break off before commitment deepens.

For those couples who continue their commitment, there is a third stage, the stage of resolution, in which the partners gain perspective and are able to hold both of the previous stages in the same hand. In effect, they say, "You and I are more complex than we first thought. We are our best and our worst sides." As they learn this lesson, they develop a strategy: The more they are able to affirm the best in each other and to limit the worst, the better they can be together. At first, the achievement of this perspective is such a relief that it helps them climb out of their miseries. But they remain for only a brief period in the state of resolution.

The elation that comes from escaping the stage of contraction and betrayal propels the couple into a renewed stage of expansion and promise. A new moment of romance is at hand. As mere mortals, however, they invariably grow disillusioned again and plunge once more into the stage of contraction and betrayal. Successful couples then pull themselves into another period of resolution, which, if they are determined and skillful, lasts longer this time, longer still the next time, and so on, until resolution is the main stopping place in the cycle, with periodic forays up and down into the other two states of being. This relationship model also applies to leaders and their organizations, as will be described in the following sections.

Stage of Expansion and Promise

Early on in their existence, within organizations that eventually survive, there is usually a moment of conjunction among their missions, visions for a better future, strategies, and operational styles. Outsiders may not see such coherence. They may witness frantic activity, emotions that shoot through the roof and into the basement, and an absence of clear roles—everyone pitching in, and no one standing on ceremony. Of course the conjunction is imperfect at best. People are trying this and that, almost anything that works, almost anything that allows the organization to survive. But the effort feels good, it feels exciting if not sometimes scary, and it feels coherent, like a family trying to make it together. And generally, this early stage of intensity does bring out the best in individuals. Situations and colleagues demand a lot and get it because there is no safety net and no one else available.

These are the days that are generally written into the organizational lore. People and events take on mythic dimensions in the stories that are told year after year at picnics, reunions, and award ceremonies. The lore itself comes to exert a powerful influence, forming the foundation of the organization's culture, much as the "contract" does for couples during the stage of expansion and promise.

During this semimythical period, the leader's character, skills, values, and objectives more than align with the organization—they are embodied in it. The leader personifies the organization, and vice versa. They are inseparably connected. Part of the reason for this is very simple: The organization is still small; in the startup mode, the leader's influence is everywhere. Even as the organization grows, it is the leader who brings each new staff member in personally, who articulates the organizational vision, who pays salaries and who sacrifices herself as much as or more than others. Early staff people, paid and unpaid, join the cause, as represented by the leader. It gives meaning to their lives. They have a sense of belonging, a sense that what they do matters—and it does. So, like the partners in couple relationships, they feel themselves expanded, bigger than they normally are, more capable, more important, more related, part of something larger than themselves.

And the more they feel this way, the more the leader feels this way. As she turns others on, she is turned on and joins in their enthusiasm and their willingness to sacrifice for the cause. Their skills supplement and complement hers. She is grateful for their efforts, and she buries discontents for the time being. Her values receive validation, even celebration from staff members who, after all, have thrown their lot in with her. Almost everything about her character and skills is working better at this moment. Just as to others she seems embodied in the organization, so it is that she finds it hard to find the line between herself and the organization, her personal and work life, her personal and social desires—all of these seem seamless. It is a seamlessness that is alternately painful and exciting but, in sum, exhilarating.

Stage of Contraction and Betrayal

As with couples, organizations cannot stay forever in this "newlywed" condition. Community conditions change. Service offerings and style go in and out of fashion. Economies, reflected in fewer purchased services or less foundation and donor support, may dry up for years. New personnel may create unanticipated effects, as when organizations put in information systems or when a new program director has a very different way of working. And as we have seen, something in the personal life of the leader may shift and reverberate in the organization.

The most predictable change, however, is related to normal development. At some point in the course of their lives, organizations pull back from the wildness of their grassroots origins. They start to see the efforts of their pioneers as amateurish. In place of the helter-skelter early days, a growing contingent begins to call for more orderly processes. They want staff to be more accountable for their actions and outcomes. They want financial controls. They want professionalism. Slowly in some organizations, more rapidly in others, there is turnover. The pioneers begin to leave or are eased out, to be replaced by more professional staff people. Where hard-won experience, street smarts, and a willingness to experiment had characterized the founders, now formal training, degrees, and regular hours are the norm.

As the cry for professionalism and order increases, and staff who believe in it and gain their stature from it multiply, the original leader is increasingly seen as a loose cannon, a naïf, and an amateur. From the professional perspective, often reinforced by foundations, donors, and newly appointed board members, the leader can seem almost adolescent in her need to control what happens and her tendency to lapse into pouting or tantrums when things do not go her way.

The board may be a particular thorn in the leader's side. At first, it was more or less a rubber-stamp body or a circle of friends, each enlisted and appointed by the founding leader. Now, facing fiscal difficulties or the need to expand services, the board becomes more aware of its fiduciary responsibility and feels more urgently engaged. The board, like a lover awakening to the importance of neglected work, workouts, or family and friends, pulls back. The leader feels abandoned, then betrayed. With time the struggle grows, marked by accusations and demands. The balance of power has shifted as the board acts like the employer, holds the leader accountable, and reins her in.

Now serving the board, the leader, usually a very independent person—the kind who is attracted to entrepreneurial leadership in the first place—begins to act as independent people do when others are in charge. Counterdependent behavior ensues: refusals to do even ordinary things that the board requires. Struggles break out that look more like parents and their adolescent children than leaders and their boards of directors. The more controlling one becomes, the more the other acts out, by doing things "my way." The more the leader insists on one way, the more the board both controls and considers replacing the leader. If this is made explicit or made known through rumors, the battle becomes even more pitched. This battle can go back and forth at length until there is a resolution. As with couples, a vicious cycle, bringing out the worst in all parties, now replaces the virtuous cycle that had brought out the best. Often the struggle is only resolved by replacing the leader, installing a professional manager in place of the entrepreneur.

Partly as a cause of the struggle and partly as its result, there is a declining certainty about the organization's original purpose. People wonder whether it was naïve to think they could accomplish so much in the first place. They question whether they can survive without being more realistic about their goals, their methods, and the people they trust. As doubt creeps in, people grow more conservative, more cautious. They see problems where before they mainly saw solutions. They begin to invest less of themselves—their hopes and dreams, their willingness to risk, and their time. Or they begin a somewhat frenzied and exhausting alternation of investing more and less.

Some organizations steady the course by finding a more conservative way to conduct their affairs, but as they do, they stop growing. They may even begin to stagnate and decline. If they try to right the course, they are too cautious and controlled to jump-start their faltering enterprise. In this climate, people work at less than their optimum effectiveness. Many of the original staff, volunteers, and board members feel dispirited. They may blame the newcomers, those representing a more professional mode of operating. Meanwhile the newcomers can feel both like saviors, finding new funding, and interlopers, taking both the organization's reins and its soul in the name of efficiency. Or maybe their founding leader really is to blame. Maybe she has outlived her time and usefulness. She seems so ineffectual with these new people and in this cautious world. In either case, the core of the remaining staff frequently feels abandoned and betrayed by the leaders, those who had once seemed heroic.

Many organizations do not recover from this period of contraction and betrayal. As with couples, 50 percent of both nonprofit and for-profit organizations go out of business within the first few years. They have lost the spirit and the alignment of the earlier days, when all rallied behind their leader and her vision, and they have not yet built a new alignment.

Perhaps the grassroots leader has not yet made the full adjustment, but with time, learning, and mentoring, she can. Perhaps the new leader has not been able to realign the organization in the professional image. It is not uncommon for organizations—remember Casa Myrna—to go through a series of leaders until the organization and the leader can align themselves in this next developmental stage.

Stage of Synthesis

Some organizations do move on. They gain perspective, realize that there was much of value in the old ways of doing things, and see that there is also much of value in the professionalism that they have been seeking. They often say that there was wisdom in the founding leader, and that her drive and vision were necessary. They begin to see her and the original coterie—some of whom remain—as early heroes. This is where the organizational lore is codified— more than in the early days, when people were so immersed in their work that they had little ability or inclination to see it clearly.

As the organization begins to synthesize the virtues of both early stages, a new alignment is reached. We saw this kind of alignment at Casa Myrna, where Shiela Moore lent herself to the organization's original purposes but replaced many of its original staff, reorganized the processes, and modified the culture in order to build on those original purposes.

In other organizations, the founding leader remains, now complemented by more professional managers. The Big Sisters Association of Massachusetts is a good example of this process. The founding leader, Gerry Martinson, had once done everything, from fund raising to picnics. She had deeply and personally touched the lives of every staff person. In large part through her leadership, Big Sisters grew bigger and stronger. At the same time, more and more began to fall between the cracks. There was insufficient supervision and accountability. The organization took on a ragged look. Funders were not certain that Big Sisters was the best way to spend their charitable dollars. In response, for the first time, her board of directors, under a new, accomplished, and professional president, Renee Landers, stepped in. They insisted that Martinson take less of a role in the organization's daily operations, and they provided her with an excellent manager, Mia Roberts. Landers and the board of directors made Martinson's choices clear. If, with Roberts's help, Martinson can let go of daily operations and spend her time with strategy and fund-raising, Roberts will continue in her chief operating officer role. If not, it is possible that she will step in as chief executive officer.

Suzin Bartley, of the Children's Trust Fund, represents a different organizational and leadership resolution. As CTF began to struggle with comparable issues of growth, Bartley wondered if she should or could remain at the helm. She and her organization then went through a series of alternating experiences, in which she would delegate and step away, get frightened at what she saw, and step in to control even more. Then, realizing that this was not the solution, she would delegate again, back away, return to again exert control, and so on.

Bartley, however, is a woman with a strong introspective streak and an ability to seek counsel in others. Eventually, she saw very clearly the dance that she and her organization were engaged in. She decided she needed a top-notch manager to complement her skills and, after a couple of false starts, she found one in Jerry Doherty. He is not a generic manager, though. He has spent a lifetime working with and for troubled children and is almost as committed to the CTF cause as Bartley is. Because of his long commitment to and experience in the field, his sturdy and modest personality, and his clear willingness to be number two, Doherty has not been a threat to Bartley, and he has not threatened the very close relationships she has with her other executives. He frees Bartley to tend to the legislature, to creative programming, and the like. He has fit in every bit as much as he has taken over a large swath of the CTF leadership. His management skills have steadied the CTF ship. Through his efforts, Bartley's willingness to learn, and the staff's desire to balance Bartley's charismatic persona with Doherty's calm management style, CTF has found a synthesis without a leadership change. CTF is every bit as well aligned now as it was in its early days, but differently.

In general, the stage of synthesis marries the passion and promise of the early days—though in a somewhat more muted form—to the orderliness, but not the caution, of the following period. The culture has changed. Most of the structure and processes have changed. For example, staff does not have as much access to the leader. Decisions are often made by executive teams rather than by the entrepreneurial leader, on the fly, perhaps in consultation with trusted followers. People may not work long hours all the time, but they have learned to work more efficiently—even the remaining pioneers are old pros now, mentoring others and passing on the lore, the values, and the vision of the founding period, but in a different voice, more savvy, a little older, with more perspective and less urgency. They now know that they won't win the war in a day or a year. They are less outside the system and more regular participants in the system.

New Cycles

After reaching a synthesis, the new alignment and the leader tend to look very good: The character, resources, values, and objectives of leader, organization, and community are in sync. It seems like a sturdy alignment. Unlike the one based on the frantic energy of the entrepreneur, this one seems institutionalized: structurally, through formal processes; culturally, through brochures with mission statements joined to programs and projects; and strategically, with both structure and process anchored in strategic plans and a steadier stream of financing. People believe this will last; even if a new leader were to leave, she could be replaced. After all, the mystery is gone. The organization understands itself, knows its needs, and knows who fits and who doesn't fit.

But alignment never lasts. There are two likely paths, which may take place separately or in sequence. First, the organization and its leadership may be so pleased with the return to alignment and effectiveness, so excited by the possibilities it offers, that they enter into a second period of expansion and promise. Once again, people and processes are working well, bringing out the best in almost everyone—all in the service of a mission that once again seems very clear and reachable. This period may last for a while, but never for a great length of time—no more than a few years. For one thing, people extend themselves too far during this stage—nothing seems beyond their grasp or beyond their ability. They move out of their sweet spot and eventually flounder. The first time, they may recover and flourish. Perhaps the second time, too, and the third. But, sooner or later, they blunder in a big way, lose confidence or have insufficient resources, and begin to fall in such a way that they enter a second version of the stage of contraction and betrayal.

A second path skips the repeat of the stage of expansion and promise. Even with the organization in its sturdiest form, many things can happen to throw an organization out of alignment. Change emerges once again, rendering leadership incapable of indefinitely sustaining alignment or of leading the organization back to alignment after brief departures and disintegrations. Once again, economies can fall. The services or products provided by an organization can fall out of favor with customers or with funders. Efforts to adjust demand internal changes, which require new personnel, which in turn can cause a cascade of more changes. Before the changes can be choreographed or coordinated, they seem to go in random directions, and the organization looks more like a gangly adolescent, all arms and legs going in different directions, than a well-oiled machine. As alignment eludes leadership's early efforts, subsequent efforts can be herky-jerky, reactive, and piecemeal. There may be a mad scramble, in which each reaction brings an equal and opposite reaction. Confidence is lost. Old solutions fail to work. New solutions aren't evident. A second phase of contraction and betrayal is at hand.

As before, though, many organizations gain perspective, stop their free fall, and begin the process of integrating old and new, once again, eventually reaching a new synthesis. To bring about the new synthesis, they assess what is new: conditions to which their organizations must adjust and new goals to which they aspire. Second, they identify people in the organization equipped to go forward, and in effect follow these designated trailblazers, easing their way. Third, leaders invoke the entrepreneurial spirit of the original organization or of other contemporary organizations. As the newly central people and projects are married to the lore and the resources of a more entrepreneurial style, synergies begin to form. Success builds on success; people and processes bring out the best in each other. All of this once again may require new leadership or the next incarnation of the older leader, who, in some ways, trusts the new breed even more than herself.

Solution Space

What is surprising is that developmental crises created during the state of contraction and betrayal provide leaders with their greatest opportunities for rapid change. The organization's stable patterns have broken down. There is confusion, disorganization, and desire for a safe harbor—desire, in effect, for new synthesis. When leaders keep a creative perspective and remain calm enough to identify and support those forces that are moving in the direction of the organization's mission, they are most able to guide the organization toward a new alignment.

References

Duckworth, E. (1987). *The having of wonderful ideas and other essays on teaching and learning.* New York: Teachers College Press.

Dym, B., & Glenn, M. (1993). *Couples: Exploring and understanding the cycles of intimate relationships.* New York: HarperCollins.

Lewin, K. (1948). *Resolving social conflicts.* New York: Harper.

Prigogine, I., & Stengers, I. (1984). *Order out of chaos: Man's new dialogue with nature.* New York: Bantam Books.

8

Community
Therapeutic Day School
A Beautifully Aligned Organization

The Community Therapeutic Day School (CTDS) of Lexington, Massachusetts, is a beautifully and intentionally aligned organization. It illustrates how leaders, organizations, and their community context or market can be coordinated as a seamless, effective whole. In order to explicate its success, we have culled the elements that we describe in this chapter from its origins, its operations, and its underlying values.

Leading by Attention to Mission

The Community Therapeutic Day School was built from scratch. CDTS was initially the brainchild of Bruce Hauptman, a psychiatrist, who soon shared the conception and the task of building the school with Nancy Fuller (later Hauptman's wife); Alan Shapiro, a former Head Start teacher; and Trudy Goodman and Tom McCormack, two relatively untrained but game and highly talented mental health workers. CTDS began in a little room in a broken-down area of the Massachusetts Mental Health Center. Now CTDS enjoys a solid reputation in New England and abroad, and there are 36 full-time staff members. "The three of us [Hauptman, Fuller, and Shapiro] share a passion and a common focus," says Fuller, one of CTDS's three codirectors. That passion is to build and sustain a healing community for both the troubled children it serves and the staff who work in it. Everything they do follows from that idea.

GRASSROOTS/ENTREPRENEURIAL ORIGINS

The founders share many of the qualities of entrepreneurs. They built their own furniture when they couldn't afford to buy it. They discovered and built their own administrative procedures and clinical practices—on the fly. Their originating ideas, derived from the British psychoanalysts Winnicott and Bion—holding children in a close, loving, firm environment that would permit them to venture forth from their isolation, pain, and awkwardness—were changed over time, as they were translated into programmatic reality.

From the start, Hauptman and the others have been insistently nondoctrinaire. As dedicated as he has been to this idea of "holding," Hauptman has never been controlling. He has consistently given over the operations of CTDS to others, and particularly to Fuller. This simple act, consistently applied over almost 30 years, has set the tone at CTDS. Within certain, clear parameters, every leader, staff member, child, and parent has ideas that must be respectfully heard and considered.

COMMON GROUND

The three founders and codirectors of CTDS are all gifted clinicians and teachers, steeped in classroom experience with troubled children. No matter what else they do, they continue to build their clinical knowledge, renew their experience, and discuss it among themselves and with others. Fuller moved largely out of the classroom when her son was young, and Shapiro began to direct educational and clinical activities. The shift felt simple, organic.

Their swath of common ground has permitted them to appreciate their differences and to depend on each other. None of them seems inclined to do it all or to protect turf.

The Spirit of Respect, Democracy, and Innovation

The founding leaders originally shared an antihierarchical bias, and they tried to establish a collective leadership. Fuller, by far the most inclined to everyday management and administrative detail, believed that one person had to be responsible, and that it should be her. Since the very early days of CTDS, she has, in fact, retained managerial leadership. She is the closest CTDS has to a chief operations officer. Despite her role, a form of collective, not undifferentiated, leadership has emerged. Fuller, Hauptman, and Shapiro each worked their way into very distinctive roles.

Shapiro may have been the fiercest in his democratic longings. Beginning in the late 1960s, he had worked in public schools through the Head Start program. There, he claims, the boss's word was all that counted, and he hated that. CTDS became his answer to what he experienced as an oppressive, disempowering workplace. To illustrate how an alternative view entered and then became embedded in the CTDS culture and decision-making structures, he tells a story about the early days of CTDS when an important decision had to be made.

At one point, Shapiro, McCormack, and Goodman had one idea about how to structure a classroom, but Hauptman had another. Out of habit, Shapiro was essentially ready to go with Hauptman's idea, but Hauptman demurred. He told his younger colleagues to "go try it." That set the tone at the school. It became a symbolic moment. And such moments are critical in the history and development of leadership styles, cultures, and organizations. The story is often retold to teachers. The point is, don't be afraid to have ideas, to articulate them, and to try them out. To support this idea, teaching and clinical supervisors continually ask younger colleagues, "What's your idea? Try it. Tell me how it works." These phrases have been repeated so many times that they are now almost a mantra. Where once Hauptman, then Shapiro and Fuller said it to others, now each generation of staff says it to the next, and everyone says it to the children. This is how everyone becomes a leader.

"One of the reasons I stay here," said Linda Butler, now a senior staff person of 18 years tenure, "is because there are no intimidating hierarchies. Anyone's voice is listened to and respected equally. . . . I don't mean we are all equal in our decision-making power, but we are all equal as people and deserve respect. I am the same with the younger people. I listen—and learn."

People are given room to develop their own distinctive styles; they are encouraged to be creative. Paraphrasing Suzuki Roshi, a traditional Zen master, Fuller says: "The way to control your cows is to have a large pasture." Both the leaders and staff agree that the organization builds on their strengths. Everyone gets to build out from what they do well, and to do so as far as they seem able and willing.

Leadership by Teaching and Mentoring

In the beginning, Hauptman was the clinical leader. He trained the others, teaching them every single day in both formal and informal settings for a couple of years. Since then, it has been up to Shapiro and Fuller, and others, to do the same. Shapiro now works with all the teachers and communicates the organization's objectives, values, and culture. He often teaches through stories. It is part of the Yiddish culture in which he was raised and of the Buddhist tradition to which he has gravitated during his adulthood. The "go try it" story, in which Hauptman encouraged Shapiro and others to take initiative, to experiment, and to dare, is a core aspect of his leadership and the culture they have built.

Clinical Supervision Is the Crucible of Learning and Culture. Everyone receives close clinical (and organizational) supervision, which is where both professional effectiveness and cultural mores are taught. These experiences are generally both clinical and deeply personal. This reflects the CTDS belief that there are no clear lines between personal and professional behavior. To be a good professional, they believe, you must be a good person. You must be generous and collaborative. You must be aware of yourself and your impact on others, whether conscious and intentional or inadvertent.

In some ways, there is nothing new about this idea. Ever since Freud insisted that psychotherapists had to participate in a training analysis, clinicians have struggled to minimize the ways their personal history, thoughts, and feelings impinge in distorted ways on their patients. What does feel defining at CTDS is the way that its leaders have tried to expand this clinical idea to the running of the whole school, including therapist-patient and teacher-student interactions, plus all activities among staff, between staff and parents, and between staff at other, referring institutions. There is, in effect, an unwavering effort to maintain a consistency of behavior and values throughout every aspect of CTDS's functioning.

In addition to individual supervision, each person participates in group supervision, in which individuals present cases to the others and to a senior clinical supervisor, often Shapiro. It is in these group meetings that CTDS values, culture, and preferred communication processes are modeled and passed on. The senior clinician teaches the CTDS approach with its emphasis on holding and providing safe haven for children that allows them to come out of their shells and experiment with new behaviors. At the same time, the senior clinician models that same behavior, holding the younger clinicians, providing enough safety for them to discuss not only the technical but the personal difficulties they encounter in improving their clinical competence. This does not mean that the groups are tepid and nice. In fact, many difficult, incendiary issues are raised. But they are raised in a respectful atmosphere. They are discussed until some solution is found. They are followed up during the next meeting, in individual supervision sessions, and in hallway encounters. Praise and appreciation are heaped on those who really get the CTDS method. Activities that violate that method— unkind, unexamined, or patronizing behavior, for example—are confronted.

Leadership as Support

According to Linda Butler, there is "a hierarchy of responsibility not of command, so everyone feels backed up." Over and over she returns to this theme—what a relief it is, how it allows her and others to take chances, and how it has created a holding environment for its people. In some ways, this is the primary reason she and others have stayed for so long.

When difficulties or confusions arise in larger groups and concern larger matters of policy or strategy, Shapiro, Fuller, and Hauptman will say, singly or together: "This is ours to decide—we'll deal with it." This appears to be a relief to others, particularly since the leaders, as a matter of principle and habit, come back quickly to the larger group with their decision or consideration.

Support and Lessons Through Culture and Structure. The leadership's commitment to supporting staff that, in turn, support children, is heavily reinforced by the CTDS culture. In small and large group meetings, the availability of support and the need for everyone to lend a hand is continually connected to the ultimate therapeutic and pedagogical aims of the school.

The culture, in turn, is supported by the school's structure. The structure is oriented to holding and advising people and producing rapid, clear decision making, which is another way of providing support. People are not left hanging when they bring clinical or policy questions to the leadership. As a result there is minimal chaos and confusion, which is a major accomplishment in a school that serves such troubled children and their often troubled parents. If there's a clinical problem, staff will raise it immediately to their supervisors or directly to the leaders. They are urged to do so and criticized if they fail to do so. Immediacy and rapid problem solving are explicit and important CTDS processes. "You know that there will be a supervision session or class meeting within a day or two," said one staff member when asked what she does with thorny issues, such as a parent wanting something different for her child than the school seems to provide. Or, as that same staff member puts it, "The structure is in place as much for the adults as for the children. . . . I don't think I could work with children like this without it."

Leadership by Demonstration; Embodiment

Each of the three leaders models the type of behavior they want to see in their staff. Hauptman is continually encouraging with staff members. He supports their independence and insists that they demonstrate the courage of their convictions in their work. When they are at a loss and ask for his help, he is willing to offer clear, decisive advice. Fuller brings a combination of managerial talent and a kind personality. She manages relations with state agencies, for example, in a meticulous and immediate manner so that no one else has to bother. They simply expect her to get the work done, to grease the institutional skids, so that others can teach and do therapy. Her door is open, her mood calm and inviting. Everyone feels safe with Fuller; she often serves as a mother figure to young staff people, listening intently to their fears and uncertainties, offering gentle but firm advice.

Alan Shapiro is by far the most intense, restless, and immediate of the leaders. If there is something to be done, he does it now, and people see him doing so. This is precisely how Shapiro is at home, the way he does the dishes, pays bills, and responds to telephone calls and letters. It is deeply ingrained in his character, and deeply reinforced by three decades of discipline built through the practice of Tai Chi and Buddhist meditation, and he has institutionalized this passion at CTDS.

He is in motion throughout the day, and he's especially fond of teaching by doing. He roams the halls like the mayor of a small town, saying hello to everyone, asking after a husband, a relative, a family celebration. As he does so, he is talking with the children and the teachers. He makes little interventions as he goes, literally holding a child and asking him, eye-to-eye, how a particular project went, then stopping, for a moment, to review a curriculum plan with a teacher or to arrange a staff meeting with one of the senior staff people. In every encounter, there is a sense of connection and immediacy. Many problems are solved during these walks through the halls. Except when issues are complex, there is no sense in waiting. Issues are dealt with then and there. One might expect such immediacy to seem a little too intense, a little overwhelming, yet these hallway meetings are each relatively calm. Each detail is considered significant; each relationship, and each person, is valued. More than anything else, this may be Shapiro's gift: the ability to make each person and each moment feel important.

The whole organization is dedicated to modeling the behavior they are trying to teach the children. This means candid, respectful conversation, warmth and acceptance, and curiosity and openness to new ideas. In describing the three leaders—but also herself and other staff members—Linda Butler said, "At CTDS, kindness and respect are demonstrated, over and over again, by the leaders." Fuller insists, "We lead by modeling for people. We model integrity, honesty, professionalism, playfulness, and sharing of our personal lives." She says this with an intensity that belies her ordinary calm, relaxed manner. This seems to be at the center of her beliefs. Hauptman concurs. Shapiro seems to have devoted his life at work and home to this idea of living one's beliefs.

Embodying Pluralism and Complementarities in Leadership. CTDS is so consistent in its efforts to live its values, one might imagine a rather constrained atmosphere in which there is a prescribed way to be. This is true. One must lead, hold, decide, and affirm. But it is also vital to do so as oneself, to be oneself. CTDS is a pluralistic society that celebrates differences, even idiosyncrasies, among people. Everyone loves to tell stories about the others; many are funny, most emphasize quirkiness and eccentricity, always with the underlying respect that is central to CTDS.

Hauptman, Fuller, and Shapiro make no attempt to be similar. They affirm and depend on their differences and the way they complement one another—the way that each one's skills make up for the others' lack of skills—and this has given others permission to do the same. No one is encouraged to be all things to all people, or to be the "all-around" teacher-therapist. Each has a role, and each performs that role knowing—this is also taught through stories—that other people, playing their own roles, will fill in the holes.

These three insistently equal leaders exhibit a range of models for the staff of 36 teachers and psychotherapists. Hauptman is a little shy, very intellectual, and entrepreneurial. He likes the world of finance and organization development. He is a psychiatrist with all the legitimacy that his medical degree confers in the larger psychotherapeutic, educational, and government communities, and he has used this status to help build CTDS. His clinical opinions are also highly valued. As Butler puts it, "When there is a knotty and worrisome clinical problem, I often go to Bruce; he offers clear, decisive guidance, sort of takes the final decision on his back. We feel, 'Bruce has spoken.' We don't have to worry about it anymore."

Fuller is warm, highly organized, and more easily engaged than Hauptman. People relax in her presence. She also understands boundaries, limits, and rules. She is, according to Shapiro, the best problem solver in the group. She can bring ideas to life by working with state and local systems. The combination of warmth, clarity, and organization has made Fuller the organizational director. She manages personnel decisions. She's the operations chief and the public face of decisions, announcing them and ultimately enforcing them. She also thinks of herself as in charge of operations, the person who "ties things together . . . sees the big picture . . . thinks long term," and others would agree.

Shapiro's presence is charismatic, funny, smart, warm, and in-your-face. Moment by moment, he is the leader. He sets the cultural tone and carries on Hauptman's tradition of mentor-leader and exemplar. People watch him and learn both how to and how not to do things. He can be stern one moment and warm and funny the next. Yet you know the rules when you are around him. He is jokingly referred to as the principal because of his clarity and his willingness to act quickly, and because he can be "scary."

Hauptman summed up the differences this way: "I'm more comfortable with loose ends. This discourages premature decisions and encourages creativity." In fact, Hauptman tends to be the creative center of CTDS. Fuller "likes to make sure all the loose ends are tied up. This is very reassuring to staff. They know where they stand." Shapiro "likes closure." This lends an extremely immediate atmosphere to the day-to-day operations of CTDS. The three put great value on people knowing where they stand. It lends security and permits them to take stands and to try new approaches.

Together they cover the traditional organizational bases. Hauptman is like the CEO, leading in matters that touch the larger community and general strategic direction. It is almost always Hauptman who conceives new programs and policy. It was his idea, for example, to take CTDS into the local public schools, thus spreading its capability and forming stronger partnerships with the schools. Fuller and Shapiro, together, are chief operating officers, managing the everyday details of the CTDS operation. Fuller is primarily in charge of administrative matters; Shapiro is in charge of the school. In addition, Shapiro joins Hauptman as chief salesperson: Hauptman sells to financial and political institutions; Shapiro sells to schools, parents, parent groups, and the like. Together, the three plan strategy, marketing, sales, and operations. Fuller is the court of final appeal, the one who feels responsible for everything that happens. Hauptman is a little like the grandfather, Shapiro and Fuller the parents.

While they make many large decisions together, each is empowered to make many decisions individually. They don't hamstring themselves through cumbersome processes; they trust one another.

UNITY OF PHILOSOPHY, PSYCHOLOGY, AND PRACTICE

However much they value diversity and difference, CTDS is dedicated to a seamless unity of philosophy, psychology, and practice.

Philosophy. This is an organization that believes deeply in kindness, generosity, curiosity, and concern for each individual; these values must be seamlessly woven into everyday behaviors.

Psychology. They believe that, when acted upon, their philosophy creates a climate in which troubled children—all children—can relax, trust, and therefore, learn. They believe that access to information helps children learn. This norm of accessibility is practiced everywhere, not just for the children.

Practice. Everything they do reflects their values and theory of what promotes learning. Consequently, the culture of classrooms, professional development seminars, and executive committee meetings is the same. The way teachers are treated fits the bill. The leaders inquire frequently about home life, act as good listeners when difficulties emerge or when joyful experiences take place, and provide flexible working conditions to fit family situations. People greet each other warmly, often kissing and hugging and kidding around. This is from a teacher: "There is such an interweaving of work and personal life. They [the leaders] care about everything. They know what's going on in your life because they take the time.... They sit with you, and you know their interest is sincere."

Active Openness to Outside Influence and Change

Generally, the kind of consistency practiced by CTDS and its leaders comes with insularity and a cultlike adherence to its mores. Even as the leaders have taken on a legendary status for staff and for many parents, they have been remarkably free of cultlike behavior and the insularity that is normally required to maintain that kind of status. Throughout the history of CTDS, its leaders have never isolated themselves but have sought the wisdom of outsiders. They have insisted that staff take continuing education courses—outside of CTDS—and bring what they learn back to CTDS, either teaching seminars themselves or bringing other teachers to the school. They have brought in influential clinicians who challenge dogma, and during an organizational crisis they brought in a management consultant.

CTDS's leaders are equal parts adaptive and dedicated to their way of doing things. When, for example, key early teachers left and staff growth in general was required, they hired new teachers, who did not know the CTDS way. As a result, Shapiro and Fuller found themselves operating in a more hierarchical way, which they disliked. Cliques, factions, and fighting erupted. So they brought in a consultant, who helped them build a more formal organizational structure from the communal, egalitarian structure and processes of the initial organization. Within the formal structures, the old, more egalitarian processes were gradually reinstituted. For example, they have an executive team, but all have a say and others are often invited in. The same holds for task groups, clinical supervision groups, total staff meetings, and the like. The changes, which were attempts to deal well with both increasing size and responsibilities of organizational growth, were equally attempts to sustain the culture of caring and unity that made the growth possible.

CONSENSUS-BASED DECISION MAKING

Decisions require consensus. The CTDS leaders never vote. This doesn't mean they always come to agreement, but there seems an implicit agreement to go with the general sentiment or to go with the person who has the energy and commitment to carry out a particular project. When they can't come to a comfortable consensus, they may put decisions off, but not too long. They don't procrastinate; it does not fit their dispositions. They return to the conversation, sometimes time and again until a compromise is reached or until they entrust one or two of them to carry the ball, while the opposing people watch with as little skepticism as possible. According to Linda Butler, "They always reach a consensus."

Furthermore, experience is valued. "Experience speaks with a lot of weight," according to Butler, whose voice, over time, has gathered weight as well. This is an old-fashioned idea. The leaders have earned respect by virtue of tenure and talent. There isn't a need to topple people at the top. John Glenshaw says, "I feel about Nancy, Bruce, and Alan that they've been at this a long time."

Candor and Transparency

There is great emphasis placed on candor and transparency. The leaders exemplify and insist on this. They will disagree publicly about professional matters and work things out without rancor in public view, and expect others to do so, as well. According to Fuller, "We share almost everything with staff, so there should be few surprises."

Clarity of Expectations

Rather than a workplace expectation of correction, scolding, and firing, staff members say, "I am confident that I know how to fulfill their expectations. They have been clear. The head teachers, whom I mainly hear things from, have been clear. They teach me; I certainly know what they expect." From another: "If I made mistakes, they would help me out."

A Familial Culture

"This is a familial experience," says a teacher who has been employed at CTDS for about two years. "The quality of leadership comes from that idea. There is a hierarchy but it isn't corporate. There's lots more give-and-take. We're all here to help each other. The leaders aren't looking over our shoulders. They trust us, give us room to try things. . . . We're expected to do our jobs, and we do. . . . As in families, a lot goes unsaid, but you know what you're supposed to do."

Retention of key personnel is a key issue in the corporate world. Although corporations have given up on the idea of loyalty, in the nonprofit world, loyalty and attachment are alive and well. People stay, not for financial incentives, but because they believe in the organization's mission and because they have found a home in the nonprofit organization. They are aware that they could command more money elsewhere, but they choose to stay because there are so many other, intangible benefits. Staff salaries, set by the state, are very low. Knowing this, the leaders have begun a foundation to supplement salaries and to develop a pension plan.

Staff members work very hard. Some are clear that they are, in some ways, exploited by being asked to work too many hours. But so do their leaders, which makes it hard to refuse them. People say, "It's hard to say no to . . . ," not because that person was taking advantage but because the leader also works so hard and cares so much for the mission and for them.

There's something of the good parent here. The three leaders are very different kinds of parents. Hauptman is supportive, endorsing, and a little distant. Fuller is warm, motherly, supportive, firm, and close. Shapiro is clear, strong, supportive, in-your-face, and at your side.

Keep It Small

It would be easy to expand CTDS significantly, and Hauptman would like to do so. Shapiro and Fuller resist. They want to maintain the intimacy, which they think is essential to the work and to the community that makes the work possible. With little fuss, Bruce concedes the point. They will be true to their mission: building and sustaining a healing community for both the troubled children and families it serves and the staff who work in it.

9

The DNA of Leadership

Moment-to-moment activities of leadership involve interactions of people. These interactions become patterned. Leaders and followers don't invent new ways to work together each day. They build a comfortable—or uncomfortable—style of work and repeat it over and over again. It is in these regular, powerful patterns of contact between leaders and followers that we see leadership at its most basic level. In effect, these patterned interactions represent leadership's molecular code, its DNA.

Leadership involves interactions in which leaders make requests and followers comply (or not), and in which leaders respond to stated or perceived entreaties from their organizations. The sum total of these simple interactions, or transactions, does not tell the whole story, however. Leadership transactions are held in place by much more elaborate interactive sequences and by complicated groups of forces. Leaders hire followers with the premise, explicit or implicit, that their orders will be carried out. Followers accept this premise and have needs of their own: They expect leaders to exercise their roles in ways that advance their individual and collective interests, or at the minimum, to "do no harm." So there is a contract—either formal or informal—and a legitimacy, accepted by leaders and followers, behind the regularity of transactions.

Forming Contracts

The relationship between leaders and organizations begins with selection: Each must find and choose the other. Both sides must look for fit. From the leader's perspective, questions concern the degree to which an organization fits the leader's objectives in life—both professional and personal: Will this organization make good use of the type of person I am, the type of leader I am, and the skills I bring? Do its values fit closely enough with my own? Explicit values may not jibe with enacted values, moreover, so candidates must look beneath the surface. At the same time, the organization must look for fit. It must see if the character, skills, values, and objectives of potential leaders—those they espouse and those they act out—really are aligned with the organization's.

As with successful couples, finding the right partner is the key to success. As important as it is to work on difficulties, to respect differences, to endure low periods, and to stay with commitments even when doubts surface, none of this is of much value without an initial sense of fitting together. So it is with leaders and their organizations.

What is more, couples will often enough say that the process of reciprocal selection wasn't as simple as it might have seemed. As with any courtship, there is a dance involving many elements, including the experience of the immediate past.

Also as with courtships, there might have been other potential partners for each. Each has a history of relationships and measures possibilities against that history, wanting to optimize what was good in past relationships and minimize what didn't work. Organizations with great leaders often find it difficult to find another who measures up and, when they do select a new leader, find it hard to stay with that leader. More often than not, the person following a beloved leader is, by intention or inadvertence, an interim leader, a "sorbet leader," whose purpose is to cleanse the palate rather than provide caloric substance. Conversely, organizations whose last experience of leadership was troubled may also have impossibly high expectations and search for an ideal leader, a savior to bring them out of their current difficulties.

If the initial act of leadership is a reciprocal selection process, the next is an early stage of alignment. As leader and organization come together they form contracts. The formal employment contract specifies what the organization expects from the leader, and during the negotiation process the leader also specifies what kind of support is needed from the organization. In addition, there are many informal contracts between the leader and the organization as a whole, and between the leader and individuals within the organization. Some of these concern grand matters, such as the expectation that a leader will usher in an era of change, but during the course of interviews, many small, often unstated, promises are made as well. "I will be attentive to your innovative work," a potential leader might imply to a program director. "I will support your vision even when my more conservative colleagues don't," the program director might hint. These informal contracts determine, as much as the formal contracts, whether the leader-follower relationship will be aligned.

The leader must walk a fine line between alignment and lack of alignment. She must emphasize her alignment with the organization's purposes and norms in order to gain credibility. Yet most effective leaders will not enter feeling or acting fully aligned. Leaders are almost always selected to make the organization better, and so leadership means both fitting in and changing the organization.

This particular dance usually involves at least a two-step process: first aligning, then changing. Those who seek change before establishing alignment build resistance. Those who spend a great deal of time forming alliances within the old norms may find that they have been too much inducted into the culture's norms to be effective agents of change. Some leaders establish a complex relationship between alignment and difference from the start, working day by day with people from a complex position between changer and adapter.

The early formation of relationships between leaders and their staff determine a great deal about the future success of leadership. If, for example, leaders form relationships too much on the side of alignment, followers may feel abandoned and betrayed when leaders reveal their "true" agendas later on. If, on the other hand, leaders are too forward-looking in ways that do not connect with followers, then they may alienate people from the start.

LEADERS AND FOLLOWERS SHAPING EACH OTHER

During the processes of selection and contracting, leaders and followers do not relate to one another as constants. Rather, they change in relation to one another, as they negotiate, as they try to bend each other to their many and complex ends, and as they try to grow more competent in dealing with one another.

In all systems, leaders and followers shape one another. As discussed in Chapter 5, for example, parents and children adapt to each other. Just as parental behavior and expectations influence the character of children, the responses and personalities of children influence the parents. Stated boldly, parenting a child with a chronic illness, such as asthma or diabetes, can be an entirely different experience than parenting a child without such limitation. Parenting is shaped by children—as are parents themselves.

Together, parents and children enter into what systems theorists call recursive relationships, or larger, regularly repeating patterns of interaction. A parent might encourage one kind of behavior, for example, hard work in school. A child then responds in a particular way, let's say by just getting by. Then the parent responds, perhaps by feeling anxious and irritated and by putting pressure on the child to work harder. In the face of the pressure, the child, without saying much, continues to work in a bare minimum way. This process continues until a pattern is reached and, for a while, one can observe repetition and sameness. The more the parent pressures, the more the child learns to ignore her and do as she wishes. Or, to turn the situation around, the more the child refuses hard work, the more anxious the parent grows and the more she pressures. Cause and effect are muddled, but the pattern is clear.

Then something changes in the circumstances. The child is engaged by another adult and begins to work hard, or the child makes friends with others who work even less. Then the old pattern is thrown off balance; for a while, parent and child spin out of control—until a new pattern is formed. Or, suppose the frustrated parent takes a course or goes to therapy and, in place of applying pressure, begins to engage the child around activities they both like, without judgment. Again, the old pattern spins out of control. During this time, the child might "act out" even more than before. But if the parent persists, a new, and probably effective, pattern will emerge and consolidate with her child.

So it is with leaders and followers, who inevitably fall into patterns that, once formed, are difficult to change. By way of illustration, an executive director depends heavily on the advice of her chief financial officer, who worries about costs. After discussions with the CFO, the executive director repeatedly orders several of her direct reports to cut costs in their departments. Having been through this process many times before, the direct reports no longer argue but go back to their direct reports and ask for small reductions in their budgets, which they then use as bargaining points. Eventually, they will concede to cut some costs but not as much as the CFO might have wanted. After bargaining with her direct reports, the executive director reports back to the CFO, who backs off because he has won at least a small victory. This process repeats itself regularly, particularly in the period when the CFO and the executive director are preparing for meetings with their board of directors.

To apply the concept of recursive patterns to alignment, we can illustrate with a familiar situation. A quiet member of the team does not believe that the leader wants her to express her opinion, and after the weekly staff meeting she shares her thoughts with a talkative colleague and other people in her own department, often in a critical way. When the leader learns of her discontent, she does not confront her, even though her department has grown increasingly separate and unresponsive to the leader's direction. This sequence of behaviors has repeated itself and become ritualized; even when the department head agrees with the leader, he does not speak up, suspecting that the leader does not really mean what she says.

Let's imagine a further sequence. Periodically, the leader believes she must have the close cooperation of the dissident department head and has a talk with him. She admits that she hasn't provided him with as many resources or as much support as she has others and vows to improve in that regard. He is pleased at her admission and begins to participate in discussions at senior management meetings—for a while. Then support from the leader or willingness to cooperate from the department head, or both, begins to wane, and one act begets another; together, the two tendencies lead to a downward cycle, which reestablishes isolation. The departmental isolation becomes the norm and lasts for a while. An important project makes cooperation crucial, and again the leader apologizes and promises to do better. The department head cooperates; for a while, there is progress, and the cycle repeats.

These patterns of interaction, some simple, some complex, some representing effectiveness, others representing ineffectuality, are recursive cycles held in place by the larger immediate context and by events that have taken place over time.

THE FOUR ROLES IN A LEADERSHIP SYSTEM

In their work on family dynamics, David Kantor and William Lehr (1975) developed a scheme to simplify the understanding of complex interactions, the four-player system, which is applicable to the interactions of leaders and organizations and is a particularly useful way to describe the DNA of leadership relationships. It is also a corrective to the overly simple way that we tend to conceive these leadership interactions. For example, we generally see leaders taking initiative, framing the vision and formulating strategy, then delegating, persuading, and inspiring others to carry out that vision and strategy. In fact, leaders often take advice or ideas from employees, then exert their influence to realize those ideas. Here, they are second in the interactive chain. Some leaders are prone to initiate; others follow the lead of the talented people with whom they surround themselves; still others tend to convene people and encourage them to build plans and solve problems. This, then, is another way to describe the variety of effective leadership styles—here in a microcosmic way.

According to the four-player system, there are four basic roles people play in groups: the mover, who initiates action; the follower, who supports the mover's initiative; the opposer, who opposes initiatives; and the bystander, who steps back, gains perspective, and comments on the process in the system as an observer of sorts. A single person can and does play all of these roles over time and even in a single conversation.

Here's a typical interaction. A program director makes a suggestion (mover), which another program director says won't work (opposer). A development officer makes another suggestion (also a mover), which is opposed by both program officers. The executive director comments that people are too concerned with their own territory and don't build on each other's suggestions (bystander). He continues: Figure out together which project works best with our strategic priorities and come back to me with a shared suggestion (mover). Leadership involves perspective (bystanding) and insisting that others collaborate on a shared solution (following one another). Eventually, they will come back to him with a plan that he will probably accept (follow).

Consider a second interaction. The executive director says he has met with some important donors who would like to see a particular project initiated (the mover suggests the idea but needs not be the originator of it). The CFO comments on how important it is to please these donors (follows). The program directors wonder whether the project fits their current capabilities (mild opposition). The executive director says we'll make sure they do (reinforces his initiative). The program directors agree to the work (follow).

In effective systems, roles are flexible. Each person can and does play several. As relationships fall into routines, however, individuals tend to play only one or, at most, two roles. Some regularly find themselves in opposition. Some comment and comment from the periphery, never entering the fray. Others keep initiating ideas and proposals. This can work reasonably well, like a well-oiled machine. Effective leaders and organizations even make very good use of what others find annoying, regular opposers. Leaders will say about them, for example, that they keep us honest. Chief financial officers, for instance, take such oppositional roles almost by institutional imperative. The effectiveness of such a routine can break down however, when new situations require flexibility, such as when the need for speed requires regular opposers to follow or bystanders to join in.

A more damaging side effect of these patterned interactions is that people tend to become negatively identified with their roles. Initiators are said to be control freaks, unable to let anyone else take the lead. Followers are said to be weak, passive, and insecure. Opposers are thought to have trouble with authority. And bystanders are considered disengaged, unable to dirty their hands or be intimate. When people become identified with these roles or interactive positions, the system has grown rigid and leadership will fail.

Leader A may initiate action: "I'd like you to write that idea up as a project plan." The follower may comply, first in words—"Sure."—and then in action. This sequence of initiative and compliance is our picture of everyday leadership, and it may play itself out over and again, with one follower after another. It is equally likely that the follower is, in effect, the leader. "I'd like to try out this idea," says a staff member. "Is that okay?" "Yes," says leader B, putting the stamp of approval on an employee's suggestion. This sequence may be more typical of leader B. To complicate matters, leader C typically solicits ideas from employees, listens carefully, and then alters them a bit. "Go do it, but I want you to change this and add that." It is important to note that both leader B and leader C actually follow or support the ideas of their "followers." Leader D may typically listen to and reject lots of suggestions—until the right one comes up. Leader E may often comment on the process in her executive team, until they become more productive. When these patterns are flexible, there is information, creativity, and flow in organizations. When the four-player interactions become too rigid, leadership becomes stagnant and ineffectual.

Although the illustrations above have focused on the interaction of small groups, they are equally applicable to whole organizations. Imagine that each of the interactions above were taking place among senior managers or within a senior management team. In that case, we can think of whole departments interacting. For example, the executive director's staff might typically advance new initiatives. In other words, as a team they are a mover. Program directors charged with implementing these initiatives, with support, even insistence, from their middle managers, worry about the feasibility of the initiatives and oppose at first—that is, until the executive director promises that they will receive the resources necessary for implementation. Once their fears are assuaged, however, their groups become followers. Often staff groups such as human resources, legal affairs, or auditing function as bystanders, looking in on and providing commentary on the process for the good of all.

These interactions almost always become routinized. They are the way things get done in organizations. Through constant repetition, in matters large and small, each organization develops a relatively standard, if unconscious, four-player pattern. Each person plays a part in this choreography, and leaders are as much a part of these patterns as anyone else. If they try to get things done outside of these patterns, they are likely to meet resistance and fail. On the other hand, leaders that permit the routine to grow rigid will also fail because the organization will be unable to adapt to new personnel, new customer demands, and changes in the environment.

The important personal and interpersonal point to be made about the four roles is this: Stagnant situations are characterized by the limitations of roles one can play; vibrant situations permit and even encourage people to play many roles.

The most effective leaders play all four roles at different times. Popular imagery may cast the leader as the mover, but she must often listen to others, like one idea or another, and accede. Often, leadership comes from the follower's position. Similarly, the leader may listen to lots of ideas and keep rejecting them, finally saying that none work. Here opposition is an essential ingredient of leadership: Choosing what not to do is as important as choosing what to do. Finally, a leader might step back and observe or take the long view—bystanding is a necessary and often unacknowledged role.

Even more important than the idea that leaders play many roles in everyday leadership is the idea that leadership may be characterized as a set of repetitive interactions or as a set of relationships—not as a person. For example, one leader may typically solicit ideas and listen for a long time before supporting one or another, at which point others—usually different from the originator of the idea—pick up on the leader's choice and move it from thought to action. This sequence of conversation, suggestion of ideas, rejection of ideas, support of one choice, and implementation of that choice may take place over and again. Beyond the dimension of positional power, it is not possible to identify the leader as an individual person. Is it the creative idea person? The person with a knack for identifying which idea among many will be most effective? The person who transforms ideas into concrete realities? Or is it the whole process?

Since the process is repetitive, as in parent-child and husband-wife relationships, is leadership best seen as a person or as a relationship? For us, the successful interplay in the relationship as a whole moves a team of people toward the achievement of their goals.

A Case of Leadership as Relationship at the United Way

Let us illustrate this idea of leadership as relationship in a real-life situation. At the United Way, Pat Brandes, first as a vice president, then as the chief operating officer, staffed the Committee on Investments, which is the organization's main strategic decision-making body. At first glance, we might observe that she generally presented policy, in this case strategic proposals, for the committee's consideration, and then guided them toward a decision. This activity was a leadership transaction, but to see more we want to look at the interactions and contextual factors that held it in place.

In fact, ideas were often generated in staff meetings, in meetings with volunteers, and during encounters with grant recipients, that is, community-based organizations. Pat Brandes says she often didn't know the origins of ideas and that generally she was not the initial author. An idea would strike her, though, and she would ask her staff to conduct some best practice research to further her understanding and her ability to argue for it.

Sarah Alvord tells this story about staff involvement in innovative ideas. Her boss, Mary Chase, a United Way of Massachusetts vice president, taught her a valuable lesson about dealing with leaders. "When we meet with Pat Brandes," Chase would say, "we have to make sure to provide her with all the information she will need when dealing with the Committee on Investments. . . . We have to be clear and concise. Pat doesn't have a lot of time. . . . Not only do we have to give Pat what she has asked for, we have to anticipate what else she needs. . . . There is no room for sloppiness." So Mary Chase and Sarah Alvord would not only conduct the relevant research but rehearse their presentation before seeing Brandes.

Beneath the great practicality of this lesson, there is another, interpersonal message: Pat Brandes is an important person, who will brook no incompetence. She communicated that message not through yelling or punitive actions but through her own passion for the United Way's work. It was contagious. Each meeting thus had a sense of importance and urgency. By the time Alvord approached Brandes's office, she was nervous, excited. Her adrenaline was flowing. It was a little bit like being granted a royal audience, she said.

Brandes would be stunned by this image. She puts on no airs and does not have the appearance or the ringing voice of charisma. But she does work extremely hard, and she wears her values, her compassion, and her urgency on her sleeve. Plus she is very likeable. No one wants to displease her. So she does seem to elicit this kind of response in people. Brandes would say that the key to the moment is a sense of shared goals, and a shared belief in the importance of what they were doing together in the organization's mission of supporting communities. She and Alvord would both be right.

Best practice ideas had to be presented to the Committee on Investments, which consisted of key players in the Boston community, able to help raise money for projects and to pull the political levers that facilitated their implementation. To prepare for this meeting, Brandes would first meet with the committee chair to clarify the idea, to give her time to absorb it and make it her own. Then the two would figure out the best way to frame and introduce it. They, too, would rehearse. Over time, they became very effective partners. The chair would facilitate conversation, taking initiative in the introduction of ideas, then following the ideas of the committee members—always exerting a light guiding hand. The chair's facilitation permitted Brandes to sit somewhat outside the conversation, as a bystander, unless her arguments were necessary. What is more, Brandes generally had one of her staff people present the idea. This highlighted the young staffer, who was excited about the opportunity and usually did an outstanding job. This, too, permitted Brandes to maintain a calmer, more objective-seeming air. As a result, her contributions to conversations carried even more weight.

Volunteer committees are said to lead the United Way, and the decisions of these committees set the organization's policy. By helping facilitate conversation rather than presenting her own ideas, Brandes emphasized the committee's leadership. She was its servant—though, of course, she had framed both the staffer's research and the committee's deliberation. By standing aside—taking the role of bystander—Brandes retained for herself the maximum flexibility. She could enter conversations as initiator, follower, or opposer.

Eventually, the committee would make a decision, often close to what Brandes or Chase and Alvord had worked out, or to what the community organizations that Alvord had consulted had in mind. As Brandes says, by the time an idea is hatched, she doesn't know whose it was in the first place. Throughout this process, Brandes and the committee chair were always in close contact, discussing issues and writing the agenda together; and Brandes met separately with other committee members, who came to think of her as both colleague and friend.

When a decision was made, Brandes would take it and hand it off to other members of her staff for implementation. Before they actually went out into the field, though, Brandes would meet with them, frame the conversation about strategy, facilitate conversation, and, or so it felt to them, get behind *their* decisions about the best way to implement the ideas. As they implemented the plans, they reported to Brandes on what they learned, the results of a careful program evaluation process. Brandes fed this information back into the committee.

All of these closely linked processes represent the DNA of leadership at the United Way of Massachusetts. In every organization there is a ritual or recursive cycle of loosely or closely linked rituals that together constitute the day-to-day operations of leadership. It is the linkage of these rituals that constitutes the everyday process of alignment.

In these rituals, behavioral patterns are reinforced by cognitive and affective patterns. Sarah Alvord's beliefs (cognition) and her excitement (feeling) both about the mission and about Pat Brandes's place in enacting it fueled her efforts (behaviors), which, in turn, enabled Brandes, who enabled the Committee on Investments, whose clarity provided direction to the implementation groups. The hipbone is connected to the thigh bone, as it were, and both are connected to the flashing of neurons in the brain.

Of equal importance, these rituals take place over and over again, with Brandes and with her other staff people, who then adopt the style and practice it with their own reports. Eventually, the style permeates an organization and becomes identified with the organization. This is what organizations like Hewlett Packard proudly call "the HP way." New recruits and visitors hear about this style in such phrases as, "This is how we do it here." In other words, a leadership style, a leadership process, becomes deeply embedded in an organization's culture.

Components of the Leadership Relationship

To go beyond the behavioral aspects of leadership relationships, we will look a little further into those behaviors and add two other components of leadership at its most basic level: thoughts and feelings, or the cognitive and affective level of experience.

Behavioral Patterns. As we suggested earlier, certain behaviors, through repetition, become ritualized and automatic. It is as though they have a life of their own. People don't think about these behaviors, they just act. These automatic behavioral interactions may be said to form the skeleton of leadership relationships. At the United Way, Pat Brandes mined her organization for ideas. This is a type of initiative. Once she settled on a good idea, she charged her direct reports with a research task. They followed Brandes's initiative. They, in turn, assigned the research to others. These middle-level staff people developed a research plan, conducted and analyzed the research, and presented it to Brandes, who presented it to the committee. The committee, facilitated by its chair, with Brandes's occasional guidance, deliberated and came to decisions, which were then implemented by a second group of staffers.

However thoughtful the people at United Way were, however, this simple behavioral pattern provided the structure within which almost all else took place and that stabilized the organization in a profound way.

Cognitive Patterns: Ideas, Beliefs, and Stories. Behavioral patterns are supported—one might even say held in place—by cognitive patterns, that is, ideas and beliefs about what is true and right. These views may or may not be conscious. Pat Brandes might consciously believe in empowering community groups or in being respectful of people. However, she might be surprised to learn the degree to which underlying beliefs control behavioral patterns. For instance, she might be surprised to learn the extent and the intensity of her staff's belief in her wisdom and capability. She might find pleasure where behavioral patterns mirrored her belief in the democracy of ideas—you hardly know their origin, she says—and yet she might have mixed feelings about her staffers' more hierarchical orientation in supporting her ideas. She and her staffers believe it is vital to delegate work and serve volunteer decision makers; still, those decision makers believe, in good measure, that they are serving Brandes and her good work.

Over time, stories grow up about these ritualized methods—about "how we do things here." The stories celebrate when the leadership is successful, and denigrate when it is not. Stories teach. Here is how one relates to the leader, how the leader tends to relate to others. Here is how to be successful with the leader. Here is how to mess up. These stories are passed on to newcomers as a way to induct them into the organizational culture. Even when the ideas are descriptive—here is how we generally do things here—they are also prescriptive—here is how one should do things here.

Often enough, the leader's personal story—perhaps one of rising from poverty—embodies the organization's mission, particularly when the leader is the organization's founder. Rick Little of the International Youth Foundation has a personal story like this. Shiela Moore of Casa Myrna has a story to tell about communities coming together to take care of individuals who, for the time, cannot care for themselves. These stories tend to link the leader's character and activities to the forward progress of their organizations. The story of the leader of a mentoring organization, for example, might tell how important guidance had been to the leader at a crucial moment in her life. The founder of a teen-empowerment program might relate a moment in his life when he realized that only he could help himself, that he had to take charge of his own life.

At Youthbuild, Dorothy Stoneman endlessly repeats how, years ago, members of the East Harlem community insisted she could and should take on more leadership than she thought should could. She did, and it worked, and that's what she preaches to the thousands of teenagers who pass through Youthbuild programs. In those programs, everyone is encouraged to be a leader. This message gets across in team meetings, mentoring meetings, organizational literature, and inspiring speeches. It is as important to staff as to teenage clients. At a certain point, the staff gets it, and that makes them part of the community. At a certain point, teenagers get it, and that says that they are on the way to productive citizenship.

Everything that staff and teenagers do in the programs is guided by stories that we recognize as stories and by other lessons, rules, and organizational legends. When people behave according to the stories, they are aligned with the program. When they do not behave according to the stories, they are not aligned. They will need more education and training.

The behavior of leaders is, itself, the subject of stories and exerts considerable influence over organizations. In something as simple as this, if a leader goes on a diet and visibly loses weight, the example will be set, and the organization will likely shed pounds. If, therefore, one behaves like the leader, that might be fine. If behavior is contrary to the model set by the leader—even if this is not conscious—it may be criticized. And if the behavior looks too imitative, as though one were trying to be the leader, one would be nudged or pushed aside. It is equally true that a range of stories is told about the leader, and when stories align, there is movement. When stories diverge or are contradictory, there is stuck-ness, with each story vying for supremacy.

AFFECTIVE LEVELS

The feelings that people have can become as patterned as ritualized behaviors and fixed ideas. For instance, some people make us feel good, bad, safe, endangered, calm, or anxious. Situations such as deadlines, big presentations, or differences of opinion regularly bring out particular feelings in us. Often enough, the particular situation or the particular behavior of another is not that relevant. With some people, for instance, we have learned to be wary and anxious; even when they are kind, even when their agenda is clear and aboveboard, we have the same reactions as when they are unkind or when we are pretty sure they have hidden agendas. When preparing for a presentation, we might get a little nervous. As the day nears, we may get more nervous. As we approach the room, the anxiety may shoot through the roof. The same events, then, can elicit vastly different responses in people.

So far, we have focused on one person, that is, on the patterning of our internal experience. When two or more people regularly encounter one another, the internal patterns of each person are influenced by the other. Jorge is the executive director of a community organization. Over time, Maria has gotten nervous when he approaches, afraid that he will ask her to do something beyond her capabilities. No amount of reassurance from Jorge—"You're much better than you think," he has said—works for Maria. In fact, the reassurance seems to make it worse because it seems patronizing to her. As Maria's anxiety has increased over several months, Jorge has grown more tentative. Maria experiences Jorge's tentativeness as his wish that he didn't have to deal with her, which intensifies her concern about performing the task Jorge wants done. In response, Jorge has given Maria easier tasks, which confirms Maria's suspicion that Jorge doesn't really think highly of her, which makes Jorge even more tentative.

Entire teams become patterned. Some organizations can be said to be excited, warm, or depressed. Others can be depressive. The president of a board was a kind but pessimistic man who had focused on getting funding from a community funding organization and had been turned down. He blamed the funding organization for his organization's problems, and he would regularly report these failures to the board. They would make suggestion after suggestion for how to approach the situation differently, to which he would say he'd tried that and it doesn't work. After a while, the board fell into a pessimistic lethargy reminiscent of an adolescent whose parents wouldn't give him what he wanted. Like the board president, they had become victims, unable to muster the energy and creativity to solve their problems. In this organization, then, the DNA of leadership was depressed.

In another organization, one that trained leaders of youth-based organizations, the executive director was oddly inarticulate. He would begin to express himself, then hesitate, at a loss for words. Others would fill in the next words and thoughts. When they did, the leader was so affirming and enthusiastic that almost everyone liked to be in his presence. It made them feel smart, appreciated, and understood. Since they tended to attribute their ideas to him—we're just saying what he's thinking, they would say—he felt good, as well. He became known as a leader who brought out the best in others. When he attended meetings, the entire staff wanted to come and to speak up. They took on his habit of responding enthusiastically to other people's ideas, and this habit spiraled, because of the spirit of the organization. In this organization, the DNA of leadership was excited.

In both organizations, we can see that regular behavioral patterns are anchored by patterns of thought and patterns of feeling. One could also say that patterns of feeling are reinforced by patterns of behavior and thinking. The three realms—behavior, cognition, and affect—are inextricably linked. Leadership in these and in all organizations is structured by the interaction of these three realms.

DNA

Organizational results are determined by transactional patterns between leaders and followers that form at the beginning of their relationships and then repeat over time, yet lie beneath the surface of things. Leaders remain ignorant of these patterns—or ignore them—at their peril. Effective leadership is highly correlated with self-awareness, and so becoming more aware of the behavioral, cognitive, and affective strands woven through one's relationship to the organization counts as useful personal work. Optimizing the roles being played in the system—mover, follower, opposer, and bystander—offers a way to reinforce, extend, or disrupt patterns, that is, to enable greater or lesser alignment. The patterns described in this chapter are as powerful in determining outcomes, and as real and fundamental, as DNA.

Reference

Kantor, D., & Lehr, W. (1975). *Inside the family.* San Francisco: Jossey-Bass.

10

The Practice of Alignment

Since alignment is the fundamental act of leadership in organizations, we need to know how leaders achieve it. Those who are most effective do so in numerous small ways. Each interaction during the course of a day is an opportunity to connect people with people, people with strategy, and strategy with effort. Major events such as the hiring of an executive director or the development of a strategic plan also offer alignment opportunities. Whatever the specific content of a leader's activities, she must also be actively engaged in the process of alignment.

Informal Efforts: The Everyday Practice of Alignment

In this section, we will illustrate the constant flow of leadership activities that, together, represent the everyday practice of alignment.

Let's begin with the example of an executive director (ED) engaging her direct reports at a senior management meeting. The team is discussing the progress of an important project, and the ED notes that the project leader is working largely in isolation—unhindered but unsupported by others. Without much fanfare, the ED suggests that the project director work with both the finance officer and the human relations director to determine how to staff the project in the best possible way. As they do so, she wants them to note what support they might also need from other project leaders in the organization. Finally, she wants them to report back to the senior management team a few weeks later on both the project's progress and what they have learned about needs for additional collaboration among other directors.

This alignment of people, departments, and tasks might have been enough, but the ED is not finished. During the course of the conversation about how the three will work together, the ED indicates, in no uncertain terms, what kind of collaboration she would like to see. Among other things, she wants no jockeying to gain position. Each has an important role, she says, and she expects them to treat each other with respect, and for that respect to be obvious. In effect, she wants them to become models that people who report to them will see and imitate. In another context, this almost schoolteacher-like approach might seem out of place, maybe even condescending, but this organization has had a long history of turf battles, and the ED is determined to end them. Of course, she isn't just speaking to the three people to whom she's directing her comments. Everyone else around the table is meant to overhear. The communication is to them as well. She wants their employees to see, feel, and follow their lead, so that a culture of respect will eventually be built.

If we were to follow this ED around, we would see many other teaching opportunities that the ED found during the course of a day. Some arise spontaneously. After the team meeting, for example, she met a program director in the hall. After a few social amenities, the ED asked if the director had read a memo she had sent out with some new ideas about paid and volunteer staffing. What did the program director think about the memo? She mostly liked it but, upon urging, admitted she had some changes she would like to see. The ED thought them more than acceptable and asked the program director to write up the suggestions so they could, under both signatures, send out a revised memo to all the program directors.

The next meeting was with representatives of community groups eager to play a role in the organization's service delivery. The ED had asked the relevant program directors and the director of community affairs to participate in the meeting.

Later in the day, she met with her development director. The development director complained that he was having two kinds of trouble. First, the organization's executives were not making themselves available for fundraising meetings; second, potential financial contributors were suspicious about the organization's ability to come through on its promised services. In response, the ED asked the development director to raise the issue at the next senior management team meeting. She would support him. She also asked the development director to set up a meeting with the potential contributors. She would attend and would bring along program directors to hear what the contributors had to say.

And so it went; day after day, people were aligned with each another. The leader joined with those who were on board with the organization's strategy. Strategy and organization were linked and relinked to the community they served. Feedback loops were built and encouraged.

In a second, somewhat different situation, a finance officer brought an idea about how to reorganize the relationship between marketing and information technology to the ED in a different organization, one which did not have a history of turf battles. The ED had also been thinking about this issue, but saw the problem and the solution differently. After back-and-forth discussion, during which each argued his idea, the ED decided not to decide, wanting to think about it for a few days. With time, he decided that the finance officer's plan was probably good enough, though not exactly what he would choose. What's more, he realized that the financial officer's solution fit better than his own with the organizational culture. It would be more easily accepted and more easily implemented.

Still the difference bothered him and he couldn't yield right away, at least in a graceful and wholehearted way. But the more he thought about what bothered him, the more he realized it wasn't the content or the quality of the finance officer's solution itself. It was his pride and his need to be right. So he decided to use the opportunity to learn to swallow his pride; to nurture the initiative and support of his finance officer—and others—he would have to overcome this character trait. This was an area in which he could and should grow. With this realization, feeling pretty good about himself, he gave the finance officer the go-ahead. Here, then, is a case where the leader aligns himself to the organization, not the other way around—all in the service of organizational effectiveness.

Finally, it may help to recall Shiela Moore and Casa Myrna. In effect, community leadership stimulated the process of change and alignment by funding and staffing a strategic planning process. That is, community demands (objectives) for Casa Myrna's services and a larger culture that now saw the value in such services convinced community foundations to provide resources. A strategic plan, providing a road map of alignment, was created. This, in turn, persuaded a community leader, Carmen Rivera, that Casa Myrna was a good place to invest her resources. It already fit her values and her personal objectives—creating an incubator for minority female leaders. Carmen Rivera's board leadership led to Shiela Moore's appointment as ED. Then, in a thousand little ways, Shiela Moore brought Casa Myrna into alignment so that it could achieve its objectives. She took the strategic plan as its central given and worked with operations to make implementation of that plan possible. She talked, one-on-one, with all of her senior managers, changed the ways people talked with one another, helped Jossie Fossas institute financial and information processes, professionalized the development process, and increased Casa Myrna's links to the communities that supported it and that it served.

What is the meaning of these efforts? Alignment is a series of leadership moves, over time, marked by consistency in style, content, and direction.

HOW THEORIES OF LEADERSHIP LOOK IN PRACTICE

To return to the theories of leadership sketched in Chapter 3 (trait theory, contingency theory, path-goal theory, and so on), we believe that each has its value, that most talented leaders use most or parts of each, and that, together, they help leaders in the process of alignment. Here we want to revisit each of these theories to illustrate its value in the practice of alignment.

The first and most prominent theory concerns traits, those universal qualities that distinguish leaders from others. The great man theory is a subset of this idea. Each of the many leaders we have mentioned is intelligent, forward-looking, and resilient. Each, by virtue of her or his dedication to a cause and a characteristic method of working, attracts people and rallies them to accomplish her or his ends.

Styles vary wildly. Shiela Moore is systematic, and she aligns her organization step by step. Alan Shapiro is highly personal, and he aligns his school through teaching and relationships. Suzin Bartley is passionate, dedicated, and charismatic—people only join her if they are believers, and they become loyal followers.

Situational leadership, the idea that different kinds of leadership are required in different situations, can be represented by the same three examples. Surely, we see Shiela Moore adapting in this way—taking a very personal approach with Jossie Fossas, adopting a consensual decision-making approach with her senior management team, and taking a clear, virtually autocratic approach with those who could or would not get on board with Casa Myrna's new operational mode. Suzin Bartley is also flexible in this way. When morale is low, she is likely to give an inspirational talk. When individuals need some help or a push, she finds a moment for intimate conversation. When a staff member is working effectively, she is on the sidelines as a cheerleader—her appreciation goes a long way toward keeping relatively low-paid staff members aligned with the cause.

Contingency theory, as we described, emphasizes the matching of leadership style to organizational context. We have already seen how presciently Carmen Rivera matched Shiela Moore to Casa Myrna's next developmental steps. Alan Shapiro, son of immigrant parents who lived in an apartment building with scores of relatives, seems to have recreated that extended-family atmosphere at the Community Therapeutic Day School. Before Boston was scandalized by the news of its Catholic priests abusing children, Suzin Bartley had established her organization as a bulwark against such exploitation. When the scandal broke, her fit with her organization and the Children's Trust Fund's fit with Massachusetts's culture and its current needs could not have been more secure.

According to path-goal theory, leaders succeed by structuring tasks that motivate people because they believe they can succeed and will be rewarded. Casa Myrna's transition to a more professional organizational structure, with more defined roles for staff members, brought out the best in staff with particular skills. At the Community Therapeutic Day School, where the children are so troubled and the work is so hard, the teachers feel successful largely because of the supportive environment created by the leaders. The way the teachers are supposed to work and their goals are realistically aligned with their current capabilities, those capabilities are thoroughly supported by senior staff, and parental expectations are firmly managed.

Leader-member exchange theory emphasizes dyadic relationships. Each of the leaders we are describing has a talent for one-to-one relationships. Each motivates, teaches, and learns through these relationships. None stands far above the crowd. Each is accessible.

Each of these leaders has also been psychologically minded. Each is self-aware. Alan Shapiro, for example, quite consciously cedes administration, innovation, and much of organizational development to his partners. Suzin Bartley knows she has a tendency to control every detail of her operation, and so she hired a chief operating officer to manage as her second in command. Shiela Moore could almost be said to have turned Casa Myrna around one relationship at a time, beginning with support for Jossie Fossas. Each of these leaders is a very keen, sophisticated observer of others. They individualize their approaches to their staffs. They have specific developmental plans for each key staff member, based not only on their skills but also on their temperament, their maturity, and their preferences. In the current vernacular, the leaders we have studied have very high emotional intelligence, and they use this form of intelligence over and over again to move their staffs into alignment with their organizations' missions and strategies.

Formal Approaches to Alignment

In addition to the moment-to-moment opportunities for alignment described in the previous chapter, there are major opportunities for alignment that occur as part of what we think of as a natural leadership cycle. Some of these are formal and predictable. Strategic planning provides such a formal, predictable opportunity. Others are less predictable. The departure of an ED, and the need to find another, requires a clarification of the mission, strategies, and culture of the organization to which a new leader must be matched. This is a major opportunity to align an organization.

BOARDS OF DIRECTORS

Boards of directors, in particular, have powerful opportunities and responsibilities to align organizations. These opportunities take place throughout the leadership cycle. When an ED is mostly acceptable, there is the responsibility to provide feedback and hold her accountable. When there is a need to hire a new ED, the board is responsible for managing the organization during the transition, creating and managing a search for a new ED and hiring, contracting, and integrating the new ED into the organization.

Performance Review

Each year, the board has the opportunity to formally ask, is the ED helping the organization meet its objectives? Is the strategic plan correct? Has the ED aligned the organization in the service of its strategy? And is the ED (still) the right person for the job? Do her character, style, values, skills, and personal objectives fit with those of the organization? Each year, through performance reviews, responsible boards get to ask these questions and to act on their conclusions.

Finding a New Executive Director

If the board asks the leader to leave, or if an ED announces her intention to move on, the board has the responsibility to prepare for the search process by reviewing the organization's mission, vision, strategies, culture, and operations. They must write a job description that indicates how the ED will align with the organization. In the contract, they develop indicators that will track how well the ED is aligned and how that relates to success. During interviews, they must screen for the capability to align the organization to achieve strategic ends. Boards cannot look for total compliance, however, for they must also look for creativity, strength, and the ability to disagree. On the other hand, boards should not be looking for an executive director whose mind is fully made up, and who can't adjust to an organization's culture, resources, and strategies.

Interviewing potential leaders is a revealing process. Not only do boards learn about candidates, but their own efforts to articulate what their organization is all about teach them about themselves. Boards and candidates meet in an interactive process. As they imagine how they will fit with different candidates, boards learn about a variety of ways they can align themselves. Each candidate brings out a different side of the organizational personality. Similarly, the candidates, if they are not narrowly focused on impressing the board members, enter a learning process during the interviews. They not only emphasize and de-emphasize aspects of their own personality but, with each interview, see different aspects of the organizational character. After a while, the candidate who is chosen should have developed sufficient ideas and alliances to make the job of alignment a much easier process.

Managing During the Leadership Transition Period

During periods of leadership transition, the board may find itself with considerable operational responsibility. This is less true when competent and highly respected leaders depart on good terms, to retire or take on an exciting challenge elsewhere. In such cases, the current ED continues to manage and, if all goes right, orients the incoming ED. But departures due to firing or medical emergencies require a great deal from boards. In general, they form transition teams. These teams must stabilize their organizations. In cases where the ED had neglected management duties they must rapidly shore up the situation. In cases where the executive director's departure follows a period of extended conflict—between staff and ED, between board and ED, among the staff, or between staff and community members—the board will have to resolve the conflict.

To take on such responsibility, the transition team might hire an interim leader, either drawn from inside the organization or brought in from the outside, or dedicate vast amounts of time themselves. In either case, the board will become much more aware of the organization's strengths, weaknesses, and unexploited opportunities. In particular, they will see and feel in a visceral way how well the organization is aligned. Serving as de facto, collective executive director, the board will be responsible for aligning the organization's operations behind its strategy.

During this transition period, effective boards become introspective and review their own role leading up to the ED's departure, the efficacy of the strategic plan, the quality of the staff, and so forth. If the interim period is prolonged, the board can have a powerful impact on the organization's alignment. Afterward, with a new head hired, boards may be so relieved that they hand the organization over to the new leader peremptorily, or they may let go control only with difficulty. Either way, the development of an effective leadership partnership to align with the organization takes time and effort.

Integrating (or Aligning) a New Executive Director With the Organization

Once a new ED has been selected, it is the board's responsibility to help integrate her into the organization—in effect, to help align the ED to the organization and the organization to her. A good part of this process takes place through a wholehearted welcome, a laying on of hands, introducing the new ED to the staff and community. Done well, this is no small task, no simple gesture. There should be meetings held with staff, with community members, and with financial contributors. At these meetings, the way that the board has chartered the ED—her responsibilities, authority, and challenges—should be explicit.

When integrating the ED, boards pave the way—or fail to pave the way—for her success by helping align her with the people, culture, and values of the organization, and vice versa, aligning the organization to the ED's skills, values, and objectives. There will be some differences. It is partly up to the board to make those areas of misalignment known and begin to chart a course for reconciling major conflicts.

Supporting and Guiding the Executive Director's Development

During less dramatic performance reviews, boards may find themselves concerned or critical but still respectful of the ED's overall achievement or potential. If this is the case, it is their responsibility to hold the ED accountable. "How will you align operations and strategy," they might ask, "and is this the best strategy for this community?" Boards must ask such broad questions to fulfill their own responsibilities.

Then, too, the board might decide that not all of the ED's skills are entirely up to the task. Perhaps her management or financial skills need some improvement. Coaching or coursework might be firmly recommended. Perhaps the ED is not acting on her espoused values—let's say, broad-based decision making—to match the organization's values. She talks about consensus but then acts in autocratic ways. The board may question her awareness of her actions or her commitment to inclusion, then but offer coaching and ask for future feedback from staff to see if espoused and enacted values are in sync.

The Board Must Align Itself

Poor performance by the ED suggests that the board should engage in some introspection of its own. Board members should ask not only whether their selection process has been effective but also whether their management of the ED has been effective. Micromanagement and neglectful management can each present difficulties. Has the board been giving the ED regular and helpful feedback? Have they raised sufficient funds for the ED to succeed? Have they been sufficiently active in the community? In essence, have they formed and maintained a strong leadership partnership with the ED, one that takes into account different roles and different skills and resources, and one that maintains a shared voice—as they articulate the organization's mission and operations in the community?

Then, too, boards must learn to speak with one voice themselves. Within their meetings, differences and dissension are valuable assets leading to richer information and more robust decision-making processes. But once the board makes decisions it must act as one toward the ED. Boards divided within themselves and giving contradictory feedback to EDs make their own jobs, and that of the ED, harder. Clearly, the board and the ED have to be aligned.

EXECUTIVE DIRECTORS

EDs and executive teams also have ample, predictable opportunities to align their organizations.

Strategic Planning

With their boards, for example, EDs lead strategic planning processes. These processes can vary from sketchy to exhaustive. Strategic planning is specifically and powerfully designed to align organizations around a small, focused group of directions. The process has four major phases.

First, an organization designates an individual or small group as administratively responsible for managing the strategic planning process. Depending on the organization's culture, that group can range from small and selective to inclusive. Right from the start, the strategic planning process should be aligned to both the organization's current culture and the one its leaders want to encourage.

Second, the team sets about defining the context in which the organization exists—client/customer and community needs both met and unmet, competing ways to deliver those needs, and the economic or political environment. Then the team defines the organizational *mission*, its *vision* of what the organization would look, feel, and act like if that mission were actualized, and its *objectives*. The objectives are the specific ways in which the mission would be manifest.

There are a variety of ways to develop an understanding of context and elicit ideas about missions, visions, and objectives. They range from small group meetings with outside experts, to small group meetings with various organizational stakeholders, to sequential small group meetings culminating in a synthesis meeting, to a large group event engaging all stakeholder groups in the same room at the same time. Each of these styles reflects the preference of different organizational cultures. Each is also more or less powerful in its emphasis on alignment.

Third, once the team has a sense of the organization's mission, vision, and objectives, it must determine how to achieve them. To do so, it must first examine the *current state* of the organization's affairs. This examination looks at the organization's financial base, its staff and other resources, its market (the people it serves), the way it is structured, the processes by which work is accomplished, and so forth. A common structure for the current state examination is a SWOT analysis (strengths, weaknesses, opportunities, and threats). This SWOT analysis should provide more than information about these individual areas. It should tell you how well current operations are organized to achieve the organization's objectives. This is the principal form of organizational alignment. ·

The fourth step in the planning process is to determine how to close *gaps* between the organization's current state or current capabilities and the abilities required to realize its objectives. To do so, the strategic planning team devises specific tactics. The planning team must ask: What kind of budget, staffing, work processes, communication, and leadership are needed? How should all of these be organized to work most effectively together? How should operations and leadership be aligned to strategy?

This is the gist of strategic planning, which, at its heart, is a process of organizational alignment. It should be reviewed or renewed every three years or so, and during the interim years, alignment to strategic ends—and not just the bottom line—should be measured.

Launching Major Initiatives

Strategies are put into effect through both regular organizational activities and independent initiatives. Major initiatives present major opportunities for alignment. For such projects to succeed, they must be planned with the same eye for fit and coherence as a strategic plan. For example, to give them the proper weight and to clarify both their purpose and their place in the organization, they must be chartered. The charter specifies the initiative's purpose, its responsibility and authority, the resources it will require, the way those resources (staff, materials, money) will be organized, its relation to other initiatives and departments, and its approximate timetable. It designates a champion and a leader. It is the champion's job to clear away obstacles to the initiative's success, represent it to the board, and advocate it to a community or to customers—and to make sure that the initiative is in keeping with the organization's basic strategic directions. The leader is responsible for the initiative's success and is accountable to the project's champion.

The writing of the charter, like the writing of an ED's job description, aligns the initiative with the organization's general strategy, operations, and culture. At the same time, it should be pulling other initiatives and departments more fully into alignment.

From the beginning, it may help to keep organization and community abreast of the initiative's progress, so that everyone feels involved and invested—aligned. This was Shiela Moore's purpose in creating large graphs to chart the progress of Casa Myrna's projects, and in displaying them in a very public place. This is how organizations use newsletters, e-mail listservs, and the like. The idea is simple. Keep people involved; get them on the same page.

The point here is that neither the initial charter, nor the initial planning process, no matter how thorough or inclusive they are, will forever align the organization behind its initiative. The process of alignment is ongoing. The ED who is attuned to this constant need, who thinks of that as her job—her central job—will succeed more than others at moving initiatives forward in the service of the strategic plan.

Ongoing Opportunities

There are many other regular and predictable ways EDs help to bring their organizations into alignment. For example, in the formation and management of executive teams, EDs have, minimally, an opportunity to make sure that everyone is on the same page, coordinating efforts rather than competing for position, supporting one another, and prioritizing activities to serve the strategic plan. Each agenda item presents an opportunity to teach and to insist on alignment.

Just as boards hold EDs accountable to organizational strategy, so EDs have that opportunity in their performance reviews of their staff, and when major staff people are hired. In smaller ways, these actions provide EDs with opportunities comparable to the board's opportunity in hiring a new professional leader. They permit the ED to clarify what she wants from a department, how she wants it to relate to the rest of the organization, its purposes, its processes, and its culture. Like the firing of an important staff person, hiring a new one sends a message to the whole organization—This is the type of person who fits with our future.

The Dangers of Overalignment and the Value of Friction

Having argued throughout the book for the value of alignment, we want to reiterate a very important caveat, namely, there can be too much alignment. Without creative friction, an organization can become mired in complacency, causing a diminishment of conversation and, with it, a desiccation of information and ideas.

If, for example, two people are close to being in sync and have to work on a project together, they must talk. At first, there will be two, not one, sets of ideas on the table, two ways to structure the project, deal with staff, and work with clients and community organizations. By the time the two reach consensus—so long as they both agree that consensus is the goal before springing into action—their plan is likely to be the richer, both for the increased information available at the start and for the dynamic process that led to the final plan.

What is true for two individuals is also true for two groups, departments, or organizations. Even though acquisitions and mergers often fail because two organizations fail to synchronize management styles and organizational cultures, they can also thrive when sufficient time and energy is spent exploring similarities and differences and coming to consensual decisions about what works best for the whole. In the end, leaders must align the two organizations, but the process of getting there is the best way to leverage the resources of both organizations.

When hiring an ED, then, or a senior manager, the opportunity to increase organizational alignment should not bypass the opportunity to begin with a somewhat more dynamic situation. It is important, for example, to hire someone who shares the organization's basic values and its dedication to its mission, and who appreciates its strategic approach, but it can be very productive to hire someone who does not fit entirely. Shiela Moore, for example, believed in the Casa Myrna mission. She approved of its strategic plan—enough that she threw herself fully behind it. But she believed that the Casa Myrna culture should change in order to carry out the organization's mission. She fit well with the culture of minority women, but not with its undifferentiated and process-oriented mores. In the conversation that ensued, Casa Myrna became a much more differentiated organization, with each person having a more clearly defined role, and it became more outcome-oriented. Conversations were briefer. Action plans followed from these briefer conversations. In the process, Shiela Moore gravitated toward consensus-based decision making.

Throughout the life of an organization, changes take place that destabilize it and throw it out of alignment. Economies change. Workforces evolve. Demands for services shift. Staff leaves. These destabilizing processes are not only inevitable, they can be good. They necessitate adaptation and change. Refusing to change and holding on too tightly to the fully aligned system one has built leads to isolation, stagnation, and incompetence. Rather than avoid threats to alignment, leaders need to identify, consider, and make creative adjustments to them. If they did not exist, leaders would have to create these threats.

11

Utilizing States of Organizational Readiness to Achieve Alignment

No matter how versatile and effective, those who try to change others in pursuit of alignment will inevitably encounter resistance. Resistance wears many faces, including outright refusal, denial, skepticism, lethargy, incompetence, pessimism, and helplessness. Sometimes people resist by questioning the competence, credentials, or motives of their leaders. Others lobby in private meetings and in the corridors. Still others become secretive and enter a bunker-like mode until the siege of change passes.

Leaders like to think that good planning and solid management are the keys to successful change; however, the course of change frequently belies this orderly expectation. Even the most experienced and skillful leaders have been confounded and frustrated by the inconsistent outcomes of careful planning.

Many leaders plan and implement change efforts with hardly a thought to the readiness of their employees. Others think about readiness but in ways that do not facilitate change. Some, for instance, equate the need for change—as they perceive it—with real readiness for change as experienced by others. Many leaders think about readiness but lack the patience to identify or to wait for it. They forget that their own past successes and their ability to rally their organizations around a particular strategy have ridden the back of past difficulties and the opportunities those difficulties created. Leaders may assume that persuasion and reason will win the day. Or they insist that alignment and change depend on a motivated workforce. Finally, rather than picking their moments, leaders may try to create a permanent state of readiness for change in a negative way, by declaring that "only the paranoid survive," or in a positive way, by striving to create a "learning organization." In our view these methods and reflexes, on their own, represent failure modes.

Some initiatives work effortlessly—a little advice, a simple instruction, and some just-in-time training are sufficient for success. Yet too often our best efforts, combining our most inspired, time-consuming analysis and shrewdest planning, fall flat or meet unexpected and crippling resistance. What makes the difference? Is it luck? Is it the quality of the people involved in the change project? Is it the leader's delivery? Or is successful change more a function of timing than we have heretofore acknowledged? Is organizational change dependent on organizational *readiness*?

Seeking answers to this conundrum, we have studied successful interventions by asking participants what made the difference (Dym & Hutson, 1997; Dym, 1995). On one level, their answers reveal little. They say they just did it, or they tried hard. They cite relatively minor suggestions and offhand comments that they took for wisdom. They describe being influenced by experiences outside the work situation: the influence of a book they had read, a lesson learned at home, or something a friend said. Even though leaders and consultants had been working steadily and systematically to help facilitate change, credit is given to what seems like peripheral, almost random events. How can we understand this?

The logic beneath these explanations seems unavoidable: People and organizations change—rapidly, strongly, and thoroughly—when ready to change. When ready, they will pick up almost anything from the environment and make use of it. Even the slightest nudge from a manager can act as a powerful catalyst. Conversely, when people are not ready to change, they will ignore or resist the best efforts of others to change them. As anyone who has repeatedly tried to act less defensively or more assertively knows, we resist even our own plans to change.

It appears there are deep, underground currents of readiness that, once tapped, serve as powerful catalysts for change. Although this statement may appear mysterious, in fact it reflects two of the most basic premises of science and systems theory. First, physicists have shown that systems outside their normal constraints, systems far from equilibrium, are vulnerable to change even due to the impact of random experience, just as an avalanche can be triggered by a loud noise. Second, during periods of disequilibrium, there are many potential paths of growth and development—what biologists call bundles of opportunity. Like new sprouts in spring, these bundles are quietly waiting to be watered and fertilized. By supporting these preexisting bundles, we can fuel and guide change.

We believe that readiness takes many forms. Sometimes, for instance, people and organizations are in so much pain that they believe they must change. At other times, systems are so out of kilter, so uncertain, or so disorganized that they can't help but change in their efforts to regain balance. At still other times, people are so open, so curious, and so receptive to the influence of a new leader that they see every new idea or program as pointing the path to successful action. There is much variety but the core principle seems clear: Organizations change when they are ready.

In this chapter, our purpose is to introduce a way to categorize the patterns of readiness—we call them states of readiness—and to describe intervention styles that match these states in order to enhance the potential for successful change.

Need for a New Theory of Readiness and Change

The idea of readiness is not new. The tradition of tribal elders and teachers who wait years before their charges appear ready to receive their wisdom and then offer it at just that moment, when the students either let go of conventional expectations or grow confused and disheartened, is an ancient one. Currently, the importance of intervening when the time is right is pivotal in theories of change across many disciplines. In crisis theory, for example, the urgency of crises is said to create opportunities for change. Developmental psychologists, such as Vigotsky (1978), look for periods of transition from one stage of development to the next; these transitional periods, in individuals, groups, and organizations, not only signal change but provide "windows of opportunity" for outside input. The educational theorist Eleanor Duckworth (1987) has emphasized identifying and capitalizing on "teachable moments." Evolutionary and systems theorists such as Gregory Bateson (1972) and Ervin Laszlo (1987) assert that systems in disequilibrium are vulnerable to change, often random and unpredictable, but, with forethought, open to planned interventions.

Leading organizational change theorists recognize the importance of readiness, to wit, Michael Beer (Beer, Eisenstadt, & Spector, 1990), Richard Beckhard (Beckhard & Harris, 1987), Marvin Weisbord (1987), Robert Schaffer (1988), Warner Burke (1992), Ronald Heifetz (1994), and of course Kurt Lewin (1948). Each, in a different way, has advocated the location of change efforts outside the stable center of organizations and the encouragement of creative processes that thrive when people and ideas interact freely and in unfamiliar ways, before solid plans and strategies are formulated.

Building on these insights as well as our own reflection and research, we have conceived readiness as a pragmatic enabler of organizational alignment. The intent of our theory is to provide leaders with both the ability to recognize readiness and, once recognized, a broad range of approaches to change and alignment. Further, we propose an array of strategies that match well with three different states of readiness.

Readiness is derived from the Greek word *arariskein*, which means "fitting" or "joining" or "being arranged for use." So it is that certain kinds of interventions fit best in particular organizational climates at particular times—and not in others. A system can be entered at any point, for that is the nature of interconnection and interaction that we know as a system. This is the nub of it—when interactions are aligned according to both timing and fit, there is readiness.

Three States of Readiness

Our research identifies readiness as existing in three different states. Each requires its own, specific kinds of interventions. The first of the three states we call *forays*, which are changes in progress that either have not come to fruition or are not sufficiently recognized to exert a strong influence on the whole organization. They are best served in the style of martial arts, by pushing them from behind. In effect, we support and augment forces for alignment that are already in motion. The second type we term *responsive states* of readiness, such as curiosity, receptiveness, and determination. They are best served by information, advice, and guidance—a mentoring kind of leadership. The third type we find is *unstable states of readiness*, like confusion, anxiety, and crisis. They need to be reframed as integral aspects of the change and alignment process and cultivated as seedbeds of creative thought.

This threefold categorization provides options to leaders. Aligning each aspect of the organization—its culture, structure, processes, and strategic direction—may require a different approach. The idea is to have options, to identify whether and how groups are ready for change, and then to design interventions with those states of readiness in mind. If the intervention targeted to one form of readiness shows signs of failure, we can look elsewhere to intervene. This transforms the development of change strategies from guesswork into an empirical process.

FORAYS

No matter how rigidly or bureaucratically organized systems are or may appear, there are always changes afoot—people are always trying to improve things. Leaders and other change agents must learn to see these forays for what they are: tentative, incomplete moves that people and organizations make to improve, and to align, their organization. Their efforts are forays from one way of doing or thinking about things into another.

Individually, forays look like this: An executive director resolves to work with her staff in a collaborative fashion and succeeds for a few days, but then falls back into a more autocratic approach. Without even trying, another new, young executive director finds himself being more assertive than usual with his board of directors, but he can't maintain it in the face of their criticism. With determination, a leader treats her staff with great respect, just as she wants them to treat clients, and in keeping with her organizational mission. She does this repeatedly, week after week—but just as repeatedly she becomes cranky when she observes their mistakes.

Organizationally, forays look like this: Amidst an entire school in which many teachers and departments plod through their days in a bored, lethargic manner, several teachers have come together informally, excited by their challenge and pushing each other to innovative work with children. In an organization slowed by departmental boundaries, three managers regularly and knowingly cross those boundaries and, de facto, work in an interdisciplinary climate, and counsel younger colleagues how to do the same. Creative strategies and new work processes that build strength but then get ignored or voted down are forays. Successful projects and teams whose learning does not spread to the general culture of the corporation—these, too, are forays.

Even sluggish groups have moments of creative energy. Groups that scapegoat one person have moments when compassion for that same person runs high. Managers find that they can motivate certain work groups for a while but never for long. Forays are present in all organizations, all of the time. It is essential for leaders to learn to spot them. If we can learn to identify and support forays, to help them grow, to use the momentum of people's own energies, then we have hold of the most powerful change agent possible.

Capturing Forays

There are at least five ways to capture forays. Often leaders apply these approaches in a sequential way, so that each approach to capturing forays may be considered one step in a sequence of approaches.

1. *Acknowledge the foray.* Simply noticing a foray is the first step. Voicing that observation is next. Simple statements like the following are sometimes sufficient to fuel the foray and give it a better chance for realization:
- "The collaboration among department heads is very encouraging."
- "You seem more assertive lately."
- "The executive team seems all about problem-solving these days—versus the bickering we used to have."
- "We've been talking about teams for years—it's nice to see we've actually begun acting like teams."
- "We seem to be on the same page when we're out in the community. That makes it so much easier to recruit volunteers."

Having noted a foray, it helps to keep noting and commenting on it whenever it arises. The observation can become like a leadership mantra, as though the incantation can bring the change into being—and it can. These verbal frames add life and validity to the foray.

2. *Highlight the foray's direction.* Once the foray is in motion, leaders should highlight its progress:

- "If the collaboration among department heads continues, I can imagine them forming a solid executive committee."
- "Your recent assertiveness seems to have put you in position to take on more important projects."
- "Now that the teams are so effective, I'd like to place more responsibility in their hands."
- "With all these volunteers, I think we can expand our activities in the community."

3. *Engage the foray.* Leaders can provide resources and support for a new or progressive foray. For instance, a leader can identify staff members who understand organizational strategies and reward them with recognition, expanded responsibility, and authority. In addition, leaders can create an evaluation metric for everyone, rewarding those who are productive and "on the bus," and limiting the influence of those who are not.

Often forays require new responses from leaders. Take an executive director who has been trying unsuccessfully to get her executive committee to become more decisive, but they keep deferring to her judgment. When they do make a strong decision, even one she does not entirely agree with, she should support the decision.

4. *Assume the foray is here to stay.* As forays gain strength, treat them as though they are the rule, not the exception. This encourages them to be so. As they say in Alcoholics Anonymous, you often talk the talk before you walk the walk. You act as though an attempt to change were already accomplished or at least in full swing, and this gives you the courage and momentum to change for real. Here is how this approach looks in organizations:

- Several members of a generally apathetic board of directors express concern over the current physical capacity of the organization and interest in a new building. Whereas the former board president had grown cynical about early enthusiasm and a lack of staying power, the new president takes the interest at face value, envisions with them a realistic goal for their efforts, helps the concerned members form a committee, and provides staff support for its efforts.
- An executive director gives free rein to her executive committee—and lets the rest of his company know—before they have developed in all aspects of their collaborative leadership.
- A few staff members begin to deal with domestic violence clients in a way that is congruent with the strategic plan. The program director notes their efforts and reports to the executive director that the new program is a going concern. The executive director funds this program at a higher rate than others.

5. *Support the foray until it can stand on its own.* Few forays flower with one-time support. They may have to be engaged many times. Persistence can

be a pain in the neck to people who are not ready, but persistence in support of forays is much appreciated.

Leaders may not always succeed in identifying and supporting forays, however, or support during stable times may prove inadequate. They may have to wait for unstable times, when patterns of thought and behavior loosen, to push forays into lasting change.

RESPONSIVE STATES OF READINESS

Responsive states include curiosity, receptiveness, urgency, and determination. As they approach the task of alignment, leaders frequently assume responsive states are in play because they are the easiest to manage through information, planning, advice, and guidance. These states are familiar enough, but we would like to review the variations and suggest intervention approaches specific to each.

Curiosity

Early on in planning and change efforts, staff, board members, volunteer workers, and others are often curious. They are willing to take a look at what leaders have in store for them, and to keep an open mind.

Preferred intervention style: When encountering curiosity, leaders should offer information and avoid pushing. They should suggest alternatives and expand the field of vision. Future scenario planning can be ideal for this state of readiness. If a leader tries to sell or persuade, however, or to move to action steps, she is moving too fast and may alienate potentially open-minded people. Alternatively, pushing when others are only curious may precipitate an early control struggle that will doom even the best of projects.

Receptivity

When receptive, people are actively open-minded. They are exploring and not yet locked into a solution. They are prepared to hear proposals for change. This often comes in the form of a request. They have identified a problem but don't yet have a solution, and they are asking to be told what can be done. New leaders who follow on the heels of organizational difficulties are often met with this kind of receptivity; the early days of their tenure are marked by a honeymoon period.

Preferred intervention style: When the organization is receptive, leaders have room to present their own approach to organizational success or, better still, to present two or three approaches that would work. The organization may respond eagerly to the new leader's suggestions. If it is important to the leader that the organization take equal ownership, then having staff choose from more than one approach may be preferable. Organizational receptivity means the leader can move in a strong, positive manner.

Urgency

When there is urgency, there is a strong perceived need to do something and, often enough, a strong perceived need for help. Time is of the essence. Key questions indicate this state of readiness: "Are we too late?" "Can we fix what is clearly broken?" "Will our organization survive?" "Will we let down our clients?" "Will our jobs be preserved?" Urgency can be experienced during a sudden downturn in organizational life—funding is declining or unclear; clients are diminishing; the community does not feel well served and says so; a clear opportunity is missed and a competitor takes it.

Preferred intervention style: During states of urgency, leaders can and should make clear, decisive suggestions. They can emphasize the type of structure, processes, and working methods that will win the day. In other words, leaders are in a position to align the organization in their preferred styles and rally support for immediate successes.

Determination

When determined, people have identified a problem and believe they must solve it. By way of example, a private school has been losing enrollment to another local school and knows that it must fund the construction of a new building in order to compete; or a state agency says it will only fund larger community-based organizations, leading a smaller organization to acquire a merger partner; or a board feels its executive director is taking the organization down the wrong road and it must step in. When events are dramatic and their consequences are well understood, the determination to get on with things closes down the psychological space available for alternative solutions.

Preferred intervention style: For trusted leaders, this form of readiness can be extremely welcome. The will and energy for change are in place. The leader has only to provide a credible way to move forward. Aligning programs, people, financial priorities, and processes at such a time is relatively easy. What leaders must demonstrate at such times, however, is self-confidence and belief in their staffs.

The Limits of Responsive States

There is a limit to responsive states of readiness that is important to note. In general, people and organizations in responsive states do not feel threatened.

This indicates that they do not anticipate radical change, either in the form of a dramatic restructuring or of a paradigm shift in the way the organization's mission, strategies, or operations are conceived. Transformational experiences grow from instability or from small powerful new forces in an organization's life that, with support, have the capacity to pull the organization into entirely new ways of performing their work. Thus the intervention strategies offered for the responsive states are not quite appropriate for radical change situations. When the utilization of responsive states proves either ineffectual or not helpful enough, leaders may turn to unstable states of readiness.

USING INSTABILITY TO GENERATE MOMENTUM AND CREATIVE IDEAS

Physical scientists have demonstrated that systems in disequilibrium are vulnerable to change. This observation is equally true for people and organizations. Individuals, groups, and organizations, when disrupted, can find themselves feeling confused, anxious, sometimes helpless, and ready for relief. When confusion exceeds a group's ability to cope with even ordinary matters, they reach out for almost any way to get oriented—even if what they find is new and unfamiliar. They become alert for people who can help. They pay attention to thoughts, strategies, and feelings that had been buried and forgotten during stable times. Or they take risks and behave in uncharacteristic ways, as when crisis brings out the best in some individuals and organizations. Unstable states provide the soil in which forays grow.

Where, you may ask, do unstable states come from, and do they come frequently enough for impatient planners to make use of them in aligning their organizations and designing interventions? They do. Leadership changes, reorganizations, and challenges from the marketplace, for example, periodically throw people into states of confusion, anxiety, panic, and crisis—and get them wondering if their way of doing business is viable, or even if they are in the right business. During the course of any given three-year period, organizations are likely to question themselves at a basic level.

Like responsive states, unstable states range from mild to very intense, with the appropriateness of the intervention style based as much on the intensity as on the particular character of the state.

Confusion and Disorientation

Leaders and staff become confused and disoriented at work more often than they let on. Rapid growth, for example, may render informal management incompetent. Funding agencies may insist on better financial controls and more sophisticated information systems. As details fall between the cracks, as they often do when grassroots and entrepreneurial organizations grow, staff may lose confidence in themselves and their leaders. They are no longer new and able to get by on enthusiasm, effort, and innovation, but they don't yet know how to reorganize in a more professional way. At such junctures, leaders are often unclear how to lead and staff do not know how or whom to follow. Confusion reigns.

Preferred intervention style: Instead of putting on a brave face, it is often helpful to name and affirm the confusion. Perhaps with the help of an outside consultant or a strong board of directors, leaders can frame the confusion as a natural consequence of organizational change and growth, and note that such confusion can be a source of energy and creativity. Here, then, is the counterintuitive side of leadership: Instead of rapidly resolving the confusion to mollify the anxiety, sustain or amplify it. Get people together and give them permission to wonder out loud what is going on. When clarity is absent, random, potentially creative thoughts emerge—forays that can be noted and supported. Curiosity and urgency may emerge—a responsive state calling for direct responses. There will be a great desire to reestablish order. If the new order can incorporate new, adaptive ideas and if the urge for order helps the organization push toward a new and coherent way to work—a new alignment—then the confusion will have served a great purpose.

Anxiety

Anxiety combines confusion with worry. Organizational problems are personalized and staff members take them home. Problems remain somewhat vague, unfocused. The nature of anxiety is that it lacks a clear object. Anxiety draws people inward, away from colleagues, realistic evaluation, and collaboration.

Preferred intervention style: To get anywhere in an anxious climate, leaders must name, not ignore or deny it. Otherwise, people will be preoccupied, unable to concentrate or commit to thinking, planning, and problem solving. It helps to draw out both the individual and collective elements of the anxiety—what people fear for themselves and for the organization—in order to see the connection. "If we don't bring the community to our doorsteps [or students to our school, or patients to our clinics], our organization will be in trouble, and I'll be fired." Once these anxieties are recognized and vented, people can get down to the productive work that has evaded them during the period of high anxiety. One of the best ways to initiate this kind of process is for the leader to model it, that is, to express her own anxieties—without adding facile explanations for how she resolved them. Her efforts to resolve her own anxieties should come after others have vented theirs, and as part of a collective process of coming to terms.

During times of high anxiety, it is also important to provide structure. First, acknowledge the anxiety and name it. Second, encourage creative management that breaks the rules of business-as-usual. Third, provide an organizational method to work toward a clear definition of the problem and potential solutions. Coming up with a rough version of a new strategic plan, one that people believe will lead them out of their troubles, is among the best ways to alleviate anxiety and, through broad participation, to realign the organization.

Panic and Crisis

There are times in organizational life when people panic, become fearful and frenetic, grow irrational, and lose their capacity for practical problem solving. Panic can be contagious. It can begin with one or two people, or with one team or unit, and spread to others like a grass fire while leaders—if they haven't initiated the panic or been contaminated themselves—look on helplessly. Similarly, organizations can go through an identity crisis. They are changing so rapidly—through growth, change of services, change of location, or change of leadership—that they no longer know who they are, and they cannot utilize their accustomed responses to situations. They feel awkward and inept and, as a result, they act that way.

Preferred intervention style: This is a time for leadership to step forward and normalize the process. It could be said by way of explanation that during any creative enterprise—say the revamping of the organization's service, or the loss of a trusted leader—before they clearly conceptualize and experience what is new, people may feel like swimmers out to sea, may grow fearful, and may panic. The challenge for leadership at such times is to remain calm, and to share both practical and impractical thoughts that can become the seeds of creative solutions. As Andre Gide wrote, "one doesn't discover new lands without consenting to lose sight of the shore for a very long time" (translation quoted in Bridges, 1991, p. 34).

Besides normalizing and stating the potential in such moments, it is essential to contain the panic. An executive director can call an all-day meeting, saying, "We'll stay until we come to a solution, or until we figure out who we are as an organization." Time is also important, since people panic when they think time is running out. Strong leadership is required from someone who is not in a panic, someone who has perspective, someone who has watched groups and organizations enter—and leave—such crises several times before, and come out better for it. Thus organizations can become transformed, because the extreme disorganization created by panic loosens all patterns and opens the door to radical new patterns of experience.

Table 11.1   Recommended Intervention Styles for Alignment Readiness

Alignment Readiness			Rigidity
Forays	Responsive States	Unstable States	
Note	*Curiosity* Offer information	*Confusion and disorientation* Acknowledge and affirm situation	Look for forays
Highlight	*Receptivity* Make recommendations	*Anxiety* Name it and provide structure	Disrupt patterns of thinking
Engage	*Urgency* Insist on a solution	*Panic and crisis* Normalize and seed new ideas	Disrupt patterns of behavior
Support	*Determination* Provide technical support		
Least Intrusive to Present State			**Most Intrusive**

READINESS IN THE SYSTEM

Readiness is not a character trait or a quality that resides in others. A person can be ready to change in one situation or with one particular person and not with others. Context determines readiness as much as any particular quality of determination, urgency, openness, or vulnerability within the context. If two people are joined in their urgency, for instance, they are more likely to move than if one is urgent for change while the other is bored, or if the other feels compelled to defend the status quo.

Leaders must be prepared to meet the readiness of others when and where it emerges. There's no point in asking advice from someone who is prepared only for resistance. There isn't much value in others taking chances to leave familiar shores if their leaders are made nervous by risk, instability, heated discussion, or intimacy. Leaders have to engage and encourage the potential inherent in the readiness of others to change. The intervention styles appropriate to various states of readiness to change are summarized in Table 11.1.

CREATING READINESS

Generally, in any organization at any given time, at least one of the three states of readiness is present, but this is not always the case. Even in the absence of these states of readiness, opportunity to change remains. The patterns that hold a system in place and make it resistant to change can be disrupted. By disrupting ingrained patterns, states of readiness can be generated.

For example, leaders can disrupt patterns of thinking. They can demand new levels of performance and they can challenge assumptions. Similarly, dialogue groups and T-groups frustrate easy, rational modes of thought and push participants, first toward confusion (unstable states), and then toward more creative modes of thinking (forays). A similar experience occasionally takes place with particularly compelling speakers or inspiring leaders, who first connect with their audiences through shared ideas and experiences and, once the audience is rapt, lead them to entirely unexpected conclusions.

Further, leaders can disrupt the behavioral field. Asking a group of employees to rotate through each other's roles, for example, will frequently confuse them (unstable states) as much as it will broaden their appreciation of each other's activities; and the confusion sets the stage for creative thinking about roles and collaboration. In some firms, the process is called "walking a mile" (in someone else's shoes). When leaders restructure teams, committees, departments, and work processes, old patterns of behavior and cognition are similarly disrupted.

Leaders may change the way people feel about their work. When, for example, a leader says to a complacent group that the competition is becoming such a threat that jobs are at stake, she may create unstable states and a seedbed for forays.

A Decision Sequence

Just as there are many types of readiness, there are many roads to alignment. We have developed a decision tree to guide leaders as they decide which form of readiness seems most appropriate for their interventions. The order is based on two principles: (a) moving from the least to the most intrusive and (b) emphasizing change that is invited or native to a system we intend to change.

STEP 1: IDENTIFY AND SUPPORT FORAYS

Forays are the initiators of change most natural to the people and systems leaders must influence to achieve alignment, so they offer the best chance of long-term success. If, for some reason, you can't find forays to support or your support doesn't bring about substantial change, turn to responsive states.

STEP 2: ADDRESS RESPONSIVE STATES

The interventions here are straightforward and simple: Provide information and guidance. Because people are curious or receptive in responsive states, you have been invited to intervene; there is little to lose. If worst comes to worst, you will be ineffective. Don't push. Pushing will create resentment and control struggles. Instead, if your approach to responsive states fails, look again for forays.

STEP 3: SUSTAIN UNSTABLE STATES

Remember, you don't have to create crises. The natural ups and downs of organizational life regularly create small and large experiences of instability and confusion.

STEP 4: DISRUPT PATTERNS OF THOUGHT,
BEHAVIOR, AND FEELINGS THAT INHIBIT CHANGE

The purpose of such disruption is not to force change—you can't impose beliefs or behaviors—but to open gaps in patterns that permit people to learn and grow.

Changing Ourselves to Facilitate
Organizational Change and Alignment

Aligning organizations always requires changing the people who work in them. For leaders, this generally means changing people with whom they already have relationships. This also means that leaders, like others who have spent time in an organization, have become integral parts of its stable patterns of thought, behavior, and feelings. Being part of the patterns presents both a challenge and an opportunity. The challenge is in the difficulty of personal change—gaining the perspective to see one's own patterned behavior, and having the will to utilize that perspective to change one's place in the pattern.

Changing oneself represents one of the most powerful tools available to the leader as agent of organizational change. Leaders are obviously important in organizations. Everyone observes their activities. When the leader's action is a little out of character or a little unusual, people try to interpret it. The interpretation goes on internally—"What does this mean for me?"—and externally. People talk in corridors, at lunch, in meetings. Many if not most people make adjustments to perceived changes in their leaders.

This means that when leaders change, there is often a ripple effect. One person changes, and that influences yet another and another. Observing these changes, the leader may adjust again. In our words, the leader's initial change represents a foray. When others change in response and new patterns are built, then the foray has pulled the organizational system into a significant change.

Let's illustrate this process. Suppose that a manager exhorts her staff to work harder, but they do not. Upon closer examination, she discovers a pattern: The harder she pushes, the more they resist; the more they resist, the harder she pushes. This is a pattern that needs to be broken. The easiest way for the leader to break it is for her to change her own behavior. Imagine, for instance, that she waits for a moment when she is expected to push, and she doesn't. At first, the team is bemused and a little confused, but as she continues not to push, they become disoriented—entering an unstable state of readiness—and one of the members calls for help. The initiative in this instance is a foray that she can identify, highlight, and support through acknowledgment and praise. If she persists in this way, she will alter the course of her employees' behavior.

Let's imagine that this leader had two reasons for wanting her staff to intensify their work: first, to increase productivity, and second, to model a type of behavior the organization wants to encourage among their teenage clients. The leader is trying to align the organization. She wants its stated goals—engaging adolescents to rise above negative peer influence regarding hard work—aligned with its own behavior. The teenagers had also been exhorted to work harder, without success. The chain of events that begins with the leader's efforts to change herself leads to greater alignment in her organization.

Whenever leaders find themselves at an impasse with their staffs, changing their own behavior can set in motion such chains of events. A leader's changes tend to destabilize the culture and processes of work, unfreezing stuck patterns and making reorganization possible. At the point where the organization grows unstable, each of the interventions we have discussed in this chapter becomes workable. Forays can be supported. Curiosity, receptivity, and even determination to change will emerge, presenting opportunities for leaders to introduce or reinforce the strategic directions around which alignment is built.

Leveraging Forays: A Case Study

Because our thinking is so greatly influenced by the efficacy of forays, we now turn to a case to further illustrate the effective use of these natural seeds of change.

Whole Health, Inc (WHI)—for reasons of confidentiality, a composite of several medium-sized health care organizations—is a three-state, $150 million system, still run a bit like an entrepreneurial "mom and pop" operation, with virtually all direction provided by a brilliant, mercurial CEO, Hale Marston. Driven by an ambition to expand WHI and operate it on the basis of the latest management practices, Marston has navigated WHI through several periods of rapid expansion and organizational change. Mergers and acquisitions have been a regular part of WHI life. At the same time, Marston has been given to bouts of immense fiscal anxiety, during which he would abruptly trim the WHI budget, reorganize departments, and cut staff. These cycles of change were so constant that employees often said they "didn't know which way was up." To combat what they felt to be constant, erratic change and drift, and what seemed like a disregard for their opinions and interests, employees at all levels often hunkered down and grew secretive, self-protective, and unmotivated. As a result, the financial trends have flattened out or declined during the last few years.

Barry was asked to help develop a more measured and inclusive decision-making process, one that would motivate the many skilled people throughout the organization and place corporate resources more squarely behind clinical operations, the basis of WHI's financial health. Together they developed an elaborate plan to broaden and rationalize decision making both at corporate headquarters and at clinics. The plan included, among other things, the development of cross-functional teams at the executive level and in the management of the clinics.

As they began to implement these plans, Barry remained alert to developments at WHI—forays—that would enhance progress. That was fortunate because the CEO, at first, and despite explicitly leading in this direction, had great difficulty delegating management and decision-making capacities to the newly forming teams. Much of the progress eventually emerged through the leveraging of small changes, somewhat outside of his main concerns, and these eventually helped solidify their original plans.

A FORAY IN THE FINANCE DEPARTMENT

Change picked up steam in what seemed an unlikely area. The chief financial officer (CFO), Doug James, had created a cross-functional team to reengineer a few of the key processes in the finance department: procurement, collection of receivables, and, eventually, patient admissions. The last, initiated to rationalize the financial contracting process, overlapped with the clinical organization and represented a migrating foray, that is, a change process whose influence spread from one department to another. Note that the reengineering began in a domain that was far from the CEO's expertise, an area Marston wanted to improve but did not personally and closely manage in the way that he managed clinical and human resources or even corporate communications.

The reengineering process went well, streamlining and improving the procurement and collection processes. It demonstrated a bottom-line value, saving money. In addition, the efficiency and effectiveness of the reengineering process itself had become noticeable to others at WHI through reports to the executive committee and by members of the cross-functional reengineering team to their own departments, which included clinical services and human resources.

Throughout its 14-year history, WHI had operated in a helter-skelter, entrepreneurial manner. The reengineering process introduced a basic change in the way business was conducted. Decisions had been made either by the CEO alone or by senior managers, in consultation with the CEO. They tended to be rapid, impetuous, sometimes brilliant, and often disruptive to organizational processes and culture as well as to the individual lives of employees. Reengineering emphasized careful, lengthy analysis of data and processes, and elicited the opinions of many middle-level managers from several departments. The foray into reengineering finance department processes represented a paradigm shift from an entrepreneurial to a professional management style, with a cross-functional, team-oriented approach.

Enthusiasm among those who participated in the reengineering process grew steadily, as its success became clear and its sturdy, respectful method provided relief to workers accustomed to the old style. As word got out to others at WHI, the enthusiasm of the reengineering team grew and became contagious and its influence began to spread.

Barry saw the reengineering effort as a notable foray, and advised that it be extended. The executive committee decided to adapt it to several other areas, namely, the reorganization of the clinical services, product development, and internal communications departments.

The CFO and the new HR chief, who was a member of the reengineering team, agreed to provide training sessions for other departmental teams. Then the executive committee highlighted the method of the ongoing and new reengineering teams at the annual, three-state meeting of WHI senior managers. This was meant both to teach and to pique the interest of well-placed people throughout WHI, many of whom had expressed a desire for better information about corporate activities and, in general, for more orderly management practices.

In addition to spreading its influence by training others and by building a cadre of enthusiastic, well-placed supporters, the original reengineering team began to spread the range of its activities into clinical services by examining the patient admissions process. Thinking ahead, the reengineering team imagined that successful reorganization of patient admissions would lead to an improvement in the information systems process, which begins with the admissions process. The process of change, begun with a simple effort to improve procurement, had gained a powerful, perhaps relentless, momentum by that time.

A FORAY IN AN OUTPATIENT CLINIC

Another consultant was hired to work with an important and troubled clinical management team whose disorganization had led to a loss of patient census, a high turnover rate among employees, and a general sense of malaise in the outpatient clinics. After a few months of work, the consultant reported that the multidisciplinary team had begun to improve its operations in several ways. They were individually taking responsibility for their actions, learning from mistakes, and building on successes. They were beginning to introduce a more collaborative and deliberate decision-making process based on the collection and analysis of information. Accountability—or the lack of it—had been a big problem, and began to improve as more people and information were included in the decision-making process.

The team leader, Anne Frost, who had been timid in her leadership and even more timid in dealing with corporate managers and executives, had begun to take much stronger, clearer positions. This was noticeable in the meetings of senior clinical managers, who said that Frost was a "different person," and it also came to the attention of a few executives. When, for instance, a corporate executive simply made a decision about Frost's team and began to implement that decision without either consulting with or notifying Frost, she, with the consultant's encouragement, confronted the corporate executive, who later apologized. More important, he promised to collaborate with her on all decisions bearing on her clinic.

This foray was similar to the one in the finance department, with its emphasis on careful planning and decision making. Its emphasis on accountability was an important addition to the shift signaled by the reengineering process; and Frost's insistence that the chain of command not be violated, that decisions not be made for people, or that decisions be made by or at least in consultation with those who would carry them out, would be a particularly important change at WHI. This foray represented the emerging view of the new executive committee, and it received an increasingly receptive audience in the corporate offices, reinforcing the partial shift from entrepreneurial and charismatic leadership to professional management.

How was this foray, this small change in a single clinical team, leveraged across the organization? First, Barry brought it to the attention of the VP for clinical services, Mark Sharpton, and helped him see how this would help the general reorganization of his department. At first, Sharpton had been a little threatened by the consultant, but he gradually realized that the work of the clinical team was very much in keeping with his own plans. He realized it would both further his own ends and show him in a good light. In his communications throughout WHI, Sharpton began to highlight the clinical team's advances and to use them as an example of future directions. Barry also brought the foray to the attention of the entire executive committee, and pointed to the similarities it bore to the reengineering processes initiated by the CFO. The CEO and the VP of clinical services agreed to hire the same consultant to help replicate the process in one or two more, key, clinical teams. Then they agreed to publish both the clinical and reengineering changes in the WHI newsletter, with the idea of communicating that change was afoot throughout the organization—and indicating the shape of that change.

Then both clinical teams were encouraged to "pull" different, more reasonable and collaborative responses from corporate offices, and so meetings were arranged to develop more rational bases of decision making, communication, and resource allocation. The systemwide group of clinical managers that observed the growing prestige of Frost's team asked her to describe how she did it, how she got the corporate officers to deal with her on a more collaborative basis. She proudly shared her experience, and others set out to try something similar.

A FORAY IN CORPORATE MANAGEMENT

At this same time, a new executive committee—mostly new members with a new emphasis on teamwork—had begun to stabilize. They met regularly, made decisions collectively—increasingly on the basis of analysis and shared opinions, and sometimes when the CEO was not present. The better this team operated, the more responsive they could be to the forays that were developing in individual departments, particularly as the professional management style began to define their own operations. The executive committee understood that its own processes would need to remain different than separate departments and the clinics because it included the CEO, who operated in a more entrepreneurial, impetuous, and creative style than was the emerging norm. The CEO himself was vividly aware that his attention had now, by necessity, migrated to the larger world of mergers, acquisitions, and general strategic positioning.

The CEO needed the executive committee to work in a largely autonomous way. To do so, their credibility and visibility—and by extension the credibility and visibility of the new managerial style—had to be increased. So the executive committee barnstormed throughout the three-state area of their clinics, establishing their individual and collective identity and their responsiveness to the field (they had been accused of not being responsive). Then, at a systemwide meeting of WHI's top 200 managers, the executive committee reported on the reengineering process and asked advice on many subjects critical to their work, including how to continue to spread collaborative management.

In summary, two forays were originally identified—reengineering in finance and the management intervention in Anne Frost's clinic—and these generated another—the development of the executive team. As these were sustained and extended, the work style represented by the forays became the norm at WHI. As a final note, the excitement that grows from this bottom-up method, as small changes begin to build, is undoubtedly a key element in the successful leveraging of forays.

Summary

In this chapter, we have taken on a practical and immensely important yet generally neglected issue—readiness for change. We have described how leaders can navigate around the shoals of lethargy, resistance, denial, and other obstacles to change in the process of aligning their organizations, and how they can identify the times and places in both individuals and organizational systems when change is most likely to take place. We have illustrated the decision process with a case study. The work of alignment requires designing interventions that match well with specific states of readiness.

References

Bateson, G. (1972). *Steps to an ecology of mind.* New York: Ballantine.

Beckhard, R., & Harris, R. T. (1987). *Organizational transitions: Managing complex change.* Reading, MA: Addison-Wesley.

Beer, M., Eisenstadt, R. A., & Spector, B. (1990). *The critical path to corporate renewal.* Boston: Harvard Business School Press.

Bridges, W. (1991). *Managing transitions: Making the most of change.* Reading, MA: Addison-Wesley.

Burke, W. (1992). *Organization development: A process of learning and changing.* Reading, MA: Addison-Wesley.

Duckworth, E. (1987). *The having of wonderful ideas and other essays on teaching and learning.* New York: Teachers College Press.

Dym, B. (1995). *Readiness and change in couple therapy.* New York: Basic Books.

Dym, B., & Hutson, H. (1997). Utilizing states of organizational readiness. *OD Practitioner, 29*(2), 32–43.

Heifetz, R. A. (1994). *Leadership without easy answers.* Cambridge, MA: Harvard University Press.

Laszlo, E. (1987). *Evolution: The grand synthesis.* Boston: New Science Library.

Lewin, K. (1948). *Resolving social conflicts.* New York: Harper.

Schaffer, R. H. (1988). *The breakthrough strategy: Using short-term successes to build high performance organizations.* New York: Harper Business.

Vigotsky, L. S. (1978). *Mind in society: The development of higher psychological processes.* Cambridge, MA: Harvard University Press.

Weisbord, M. R. (1987). *Productive workplaces: Organizing and managing for dignity, meaning and community.* San Francisco: Jossey-Bass.

12

The Alignment Exercise

To integrate themes in the book, in this chapter we offer an exercise that leaders can implement in their organizations in order to assess and achieve alignment.

To initiate and champion this exercise, we have two types of leaders in mind. First there are the executive directors and chief executive officers on whom we have focused throughout the book. They direct the organization's operations and, in general, articulate the mission, vision, and strategies that guide operations. Second are the heads of boards of directors. Early in the life of organizations, boards and their presidents tend to support executive directors, so much so that they are considered "rubber-stamp boards." As they mature, however, boards take their roles in policy making, fiduciary responsibility, and performance review for the executive director increasingly seriously. It is their job to hold the executive director accountable for aligning the organization in the service of its mission.

Boards of directors generally come into their own when their organizations outgrow the spirit and methods of their grassroots origins. At such times, executive directors often strain to stretch their skill to meet the expanded challenges. What had seemed freewheeling, exuberant, experimental, and nail-bitingly exciting now seems random. Work plans and financial records fall between the cracks. The very existence of the organization may seem in jeopardy. As a result, many executive directors are replaced or, if finances will permit, complemented with a more managerial second in command—often called a chief operations officer.

This is a time that calls for alignment or realignment. The same may be said for most leadership transitions. The transition may arise when a long-standing leader decides to retire or move on. In such cases the transition is generally orderly. But if the leader had been beloved and charismatic—often true of founders—then the ability of a new leader to find acceptance and room for her or his own style is limited. There is all the more reason, then, for the organization to prepare itself through an alignment exercise that clarifies who they are and what kind of leader is best for them at that particular time. This possibility of conscious choice helps with the new leader's entry and the old staff's acceptance.

When leaders are forced out or leave abruptly, an Alignment Exercise may be even more important. It provides the organization an opportunity to pause and take stock before selecting a new leader. Generally, organizations are impatient and anxious at such times and rush to find a new leader before clarifying who they are and what led to the previous leader's abrupt departure. Although the results of a full strategic planning effort would be wonderful in such a situation, few boards and few organizations have the patience or resources to launch such an effort during a leadership transition crisis. The Alignment Exercise provides a comparable idea about the organization's strategic and operational directions, one more appropriate to the need for rapid and decisive action.

More important, the Alignment Exercise can be utilized as a regular, systematic—perhaps annual—way to permit organizations and their leaders to identify the challenges ahead.

The Alignment Exercise is really a sequence of exercises designed to accomplish several goals:

- Assess organizational alignment.
- Assess an organization's readiness to change, that is, its ability to realign itself.
- Construct and implement a realignment plan.
- Evaluate the impact and effectiveness of the plan, and then redesign the plan in light of new information.

After we have described the Alignment Exercise, we will present a composite case of how it goes in practice.

The Alignment Exercise

PHASE 1: ASSESSMENT

Convener: The board of directors

First participant group: The Alignment Exercise begins as a conversation among representatives of the three stakeholder groups: leadership, organization, and community or market—specifically, the executive director; one or more mid- to senior-level managers, chosen for their perspective and insight; and one or more clients, chosen for their close relationships with and knowledge of the organization.

At this point in the exercise, three stakeholder participants are chosen for the following reasons. First, we want each of the main constituencies represented. Second, we want to shine different lights on the question of alignment. The different angles of vision will permit us a more complex, three-dimensional view of how and when the organization is aligned and how it is not. Third, we want to generate some creative friction. The introduction of multiple views will highlight both gaps in alignment and potential for new alliances, programs, and strategies.

Substitutes: As readers will see, the knowledge, preparation, and stamina demanded of this threesome will be considerable. To ease the burden, we suggest that there be a "substitute" assigned for each of the three. At any moment in the exercises, the substitutes can sit in.

Second participant group: There is a second, larger, participant group made up of all the significant stakeholders in the organization, that is, representatives of all the groups who have an impact on the organization's effectiveness and who are affected by the organization. Stakeholders include those who work for the organization—the senior management team, for example, or a representative group of staff members. In a school system, it might include principals, representatives of teachers, and administrators. There are also external stakeholders, including community groups, funders, venders, and parent associations, and representatives of these groups should be included whenever possible.

Articulating Multiple Views on Alignment

Each of the three participants in the first group will describe how well aligned the other two constituencies are, from the perspective of whether they make her or his own constituency effective. For example, the executive director will discuss how organizational structures, processes, culture, and strategies either facilitate or derail her or his ability to lead. She or he will also discuss how well the organization is aligned with the market and community that it serves. The mid- to senior-level manager will discuss the executive director and the market. The client will discuss the leader and the organization. This is not a debate. Each person will speak freely while the other two listen. Ideally, a third-party facilitator will moderate the presentations and subsequent dialogue.

After each has spoken, each will reflect on what he or she has learned from the other two. The executive director, for example, will summarize what the manager and client have indicated about her or his ability to align all parties and, additionally, personal alignment and misalignment with them. The other two will then follow suit. Again, this is not a debate. Each person will be asked to listen respectfully to the others and, to the extent possible, to respond in the second part in a nondefensive manner.

Expanded Views on Alignment

The three-way conversation takes place in a "fishbowl." That is, it takes place with others watching. These are the stakeholders, the second participant group. They are asked, first, to silently take in the three-way conversation, and then, to comment. They can comment on specific issues raised or omitted by the threesome and they can comment on the process among the three participants. For instance, did they seem open to each other's ideas. Were their ideas complementary—different but adding value to the others? Were they aligned in spirit and values, if not in method? Again, this is not a debate. Each stakeholder is encouraged to have a say, then to listen to others.

When the stakeholders have finished with their comments, the original three are asked to articulate something they have learned about the need for better alignment or to ask questions of the stakeholders. Stakeholders are then asked to clarify or elaborate their points or to add some new commentary.

Recording Views on Alignment. During both conversations, views of alignment will be recorded on newsprint that lines the four walls of the conference room.

Digesting the Complexity of Alignment and Misalignment. After the two initial conversations, all participants are given a full half hour to examine what has been recorded on the newsprint-lined walls. All participants are asked to identify the five most important areas for alignment work. Importance is defined in two ways: areas that have received considerable attention during the presentations; and areas in which alignment would have the greatest, leveraged, impact on the organization's effectiveness.

Achieving Focus. Participants return to the fishbowl format. Now the threesome is asked to work as a team, focusing on the major areas of organizational life in need of increased alignment—using the newsprint priorities and discussing their meaning, particularly how well or poorly each fits with the organization's strategic plan. After a time, they are asked to articulate their conclusions—as a team.

The stakeholder group is then asked to comment on the threesome's focus. Have they got it right? Does it really fit well with the strategic plan? Does the organization have the resources to carry it out?

The threesome makes a final formulation.

PHASE 2: PLANNING

Assessing Readiness for Change

Phase 2 begins much as Phase 1 began, with each of the three key participants assessing how ready the organization is to move itself into alignment behind its strategic plan. For each of the major changes required to move the organization into alignment, they will ask the following questions:

- Are the relevant people curious, receptive, or determined? Imagine, for example, that the major programs in a domestic violence organization emphasized care-taking and nurturance but the organization's philosophy emphasized independence and self-care. Alignment requires that the programs revamp themselves to fit with the philosophy. The threesome must ask itself, then, whether the program director and staff are open to new training and instruction about such changes.
- Are their already forays within the programs? Individual staff members, for instance, who are already insisting that clients come up with plans for themselves, or subprograms that are more in keeping with the organizational philosophy, should be identified. These are directions and strengths that can be built upon.
- Are there areas of confusion and disorganization—negative states of readiness—that make it easy, with a strong hand, to reorganize in a more aligned way?
- Where concrete resources are required—staff time, money, consulting—will they be available? If, for instance, the organization is growing rapidly, now housed in multiple sites and dealing with multiple government agencies and private funders, and needs a serious upgrade in information systems in order to bring the organization into alignment, will there be funding to improve the systems?

After the threesome discusses readiness, they will receive feedback from the stakeholder group.

Designing the Alignment Plan

Alignment cannot be achieved all at once. The threesome is asked to construct plans for the focused alignment opportunities that were identified during the assessment phase. For each opportunity, a rough project outline will be developed during the Alignment Exercise. Suppose there were four key opportunities as follows:

- Bring central programs into alignment with organization philosophy.
- Provide management training for the executive director and a few other senior managers so that their skills match the challenges ahead.
- Develop outreach centers in designated neighborhoods, staffed by neighborhood residents (again, the idea of people taking charge of their lives).
- Update information systems to help manage the expansion and decentralization of the organizational programs.

For each of these initiatives, a committee, drawn from both the threesome and the stakeholder group, would be formed. Each committee would work separately for a few hours to build a project plan for one of the initiatives. Then each committee would report to the whole group for feedback and conversation and to charter the alignment plans.

This plan would then be sent to the board of directors for approval and to the senior management team for implementation.

PHASE 3: CHARTERING

In its leadership capacity, the board of directors is responsible for hiring, firing, and performance review for executive directors, and for setting the organization's strategic direction. Since so much of leadership concerns the alignment of organizations, the board must insist that leaders do so. In that sense, boards, while avoiding the intrusiveness and control of micromanagement, must, at a high level, make certain that alignment has been achieved.

So, much as boards must guide and approve of strategic plans, so they must charter alignment plans. This means that they designate a champion, generally the executive director, and, with the executive director, a project leader for the implementation of the plan. They assign a budget, a timeline, and markers by which to evaluate the progress of the implementation, and establish reporting requirements.

PHASE 4: IMPLEMENTATION

Senior Management Team Convenes. During the week following the Phase 2 planning, the senior management team (SMT) meets to discuss the implementation of the alignment plan. For each of the alignment projects, the SMT assigns a champion from among its ranks and a manager, either from its ranks or from the next level of managers. In addition, the SMT proposes a rough timeline for each team and for the collective alignment process.

Alignment Management Team Convenes. A second meeting is called, including both the SMT and the four managers of the alignment projects to make sure that the projects are coordinated—that is, aligned with one another. At this first meeting, the team leaders are asked to come back within, say, a month with a refined project plan, including methods, budget, timeline, and indicators of success and trouble. This alignment management team will then meet regularly to monitor the progress of the projects.

Alignment Exercise Group Reconvenes. After a reasonable period—to be determined during the initial assessment and planning process—the original group, both the three key participants and the larger stakeholder group, reconvenes. The purpose is twofold: first, to learn how their plans have progressed; and second, to give feedback, each from her or his own perspective, on the impact of the alignment plan and its execution.

PHASE 5: EVALUATION AND RENEWAL

Approximately one year later, the Alignment Exercise participants again reconvene to review the progress and impact of last year's plans, to learn about changes in the leader, the organization, the community, and the market, and to prioritize new alignment projects. The structure of the exercise is the same, with its alternation of the threesome and the stakeholder group, the handoff to the senior management team, and review by the Alignment Exercise participants.

Case Study: Safe Harbor

We have designed the Alignment Exercise to fit our theory of effective leadership and to embed our ideas in practice. Understanding that exercises can be difficult to comprehend without being able to visualize them, we have constructed some case materials to illustrate the exercise at work. The organization described is a composite of a few with which we are familiar.

We'll call the organization Safe Harbor. It is a nonprofit organization, with a staff of 170 people (full-time employees, or FTEs), that manages group homes for people who have spent considerable time in psychiatric hospitals and who have suffered severe and debilitating mental disorders. Safe Harbor, whose annual budget has grown over 20 years to its current annual mark of $15 million, is funded by a variety of government agencies, but primarily from the state's department of mental health. Over the years, the management of group homes has required Safe Harbor to purchase a considerable amount of real estate; in response, it has developed considerable skill in the acquisition and management of real estate, perhaps equal to its skill in working with the residents of the homes. In effect, there are two closely related but very different "businesses."

There are two strong pressures on Safe Harbor that require it to assess and realign itself in the near future. First, its founding executive director (ED) will almost certainly be leaving. Under her recent stewardship, the chief financial officer has embezzled a considerable amount of money. This might have been enough to question her leadership, but it is also taken as indicative of a very loose management style, which, with the continued growth of Safe Harbor—and the increasing scrutiny of state funding agencies—is certainly not appropriate and can no longer fly under the radar. Nor can she be rescued as easily as she has in the past by grateful board members—those with family members in group homes. While still loyal, these board members are growing a little uneasy; the sums of money required to cover inefficient management is growing large. Second, state funding agencies want Safe Harbor to either merge with or acquire another, somewhat smaller organization in the near future. State oversight is easier and more cost-effective, they believe, with large service providers.

The clinical and real estate programs are managed by a pair of very competent women, one very orderly and calm, the other passionate, brilliant, and a little frazzled. Together, they have made a very good, complementary team. They also keep themselves continually accessible to all of Safe Harbor's employees, work inordinate hours, and are showing signs of burnout: occasional decisions that lack their normal thoughtfulness and thoroughness, outbursts at house managers, and a dispirited attitude toward problems.

Most employees are young, in their twenties. Except for the house managers and district directors, they have learned clinical skills on the job. This is also true for several ex-patients who are now employees and who have taken it upon themselves to represent the residents' point of view. For almost half, Safe Harbor is a transient commitment. It is work to do while they figure out what they want to do with their lives and an outlet for their idealism. This group contributes to high staff turnover and the need for continual recruitment and training activities at Safe Harbor. Those who stay have mixed feelings about this transient youth cadre; without careful management by the house leaders, there is always a threat of divisiveness, which may take the form of philosophical differences over the treatment of residents but looks at least as much like a town-and-gown type of class conflict.

PHASE 1: ASSESSMENT

Convener: The board of directors. The Alignment Exercise is jointly organized by the executive director and the board of directors, but it is specifically sponsored by the board. The board of directors had grown alarmed about the executive director's loose management style and by signals from state funding agencies and decided they needed to realign Safe Harbor in order to move effectively and aggressively into the future. Their decision to take a strong stand and direct action was itself new for the board, which had pretty much rubber-stamped almost everything the ED had brought before it.

First participant group: Representatives of the three stakeholder groups. This core group consists of the ED, representing Safe Harbor's professional leadership; the director of residential treatment and director of real estate, representing the operational side of the organization; and a board member with a relative in a Safe Harbor treatment home, who is otherwise the managing partner in a large law firm, representing the community and market for Safe Harbor's services.

Second participant group: Stakeholders in Safe Harbor. This group includes the entire senior management team and the three district directors for homes; the executive committee of the board of directors; the director of a patients' rights organization; two bankers who have helped finance the group homes; two key members of state agencies; and the director of a mental health hospital, whose patients move on to Safe Harbor homes.

Conversation Among First Group

The ED began the conversation with a nostalgic summary of Safe Harbor's history, emphasizing its growth during her 20 years of stewardship, its ability to overcome downturns in the economy, its ability to take advantage of the deinstitutionalization of mental health services, and its reputation for careful and respectful attention to its residents. She thought that, in spite of the financial glitch, as she called the embezzlement, Safe Harbor was still well managed; for this, she praised the clinical and real estate directors. However, she indicated again that she was ready to leave—once Safe Harbor was again on strong footing—and that she may well have lost the passion she once had for management. She had grandchildren now, and a book she wanted to write.

Next the clinical director spoke. She had a long, mostly respectful and successful history with the ED, had, in fact, been mentored by the ED, but felt strongly that the ED's heart was no longer in the work and that the ED's attachment to old ways of working was now interfering with her own efforts to keep clinical services at the cutting edge. Among other things, she believed the homes were too isolated from the community; despite the complications of more community interaction, she believed this was in the best interest of residents and of Safe Harbor, if it wanted to retain its reputation for superior clinical work. If this didn't take courage, her next statement did: Why, she wondered, hadn't the board of directors held the ED accountable? Better governance would be necessary for Safe Harbor to move ahead responsibly. Here, the clinical director not only took on her boss but the board, which would select the next ED—and she dearly wanted that position.

The director of real estate began by noting that their current financial stability owed more to the purchase and management of the homes than what was going on within them, which, she was careful to add, was excellent. However, she wondered if Safe Harbor shouldn't emphasize real estate more, make it primary, and use it as a platform for housing a greater variety of social service activities. This would represent a basic strategic shift, but she thought it made sense. She also thought that the clinical director was fully capable of managing the new strategic directions, either in her current role or as the future ED. She, too, wanted Safe Harbor to pay more attention to the communities in which they resided, particularly asking what services the communities most wanted from them. Of course, this would mean significantly upgrading the operational capabilities of the real estate area. As she finished this statement, she looked over at the board and pointedly declared that they would have to take a stronger hand in Safe Harbor's strategy.

Finally, the board member took his turn. He did not think it was a good idea to spread Safe Harbor's work beyond what it did so well. He wanted them to stay focused on group homes. He, too, had a long history with the ED and was deeply grateful for the way she had "held" his sister for all these years. He was, therefore, not pleased to see her go. She had been the visionary. Couldn't she imagine staying on if she had more managerial and administrative support? he asked. He thought the board had done well to support Safe Harbor in the fulfillment of its mission.

Reflection

Now each of the core group members reflected on what was heard. The ED, for example, thanked the board member for his loyalty and affection, but sided with her own managers. "It's time to move on. They understand and appreciate the future better than we do," she insisted. But if they do move toward an expanded service concept and increased community activity, she warned, they had better make sure that all the hospitals and state agencies that had supported Safe Harbor over the years were on board. "And our banking partners, as well," she cautioned. Then she wondered if her senior managers were implying that she should leave even earlier than she had planned and said that she did not want to, that she wanted to make sure everything was well organized before she left. Her words were moderate and gently spoken, but nevertheless contained a warning that her managers could not help but hear.

This time, the board member jumped in next. Trying to stay in the spirit of the exercise, he backtracked a little and said that the clinical and real estate directors had done an excellent job and had made some interesting proposals. Although he had thought it the board's job to support the ED, he could see that the future would require it to take on a larger role in Safe Harbor's governance. But he still wanted Safe Harbor to stay with what he now called its core competence.

Each of the senior managers then took a turn at reflection. Each, for example, affirmed the ED's historical rendering and expressed gratitude for her support of their management effectiveness and for the strategic directions they had proposed. The real estate director, who had no aspirations for the ED position, backtracked a bit on the timing of the leadership transition, indicating that she would be happy to see the ED lead the move to the future, and to have that as her legacy. The clinical director, feeling a little isolated and, perhaps, a little defensive, wondered if the ED really wanted to put in the long, hard hours required to make the changes required. Having raised the red flag, she then backed off a bit, saying that the ED's inspirational ways, reputation, and contacts might, in fact, move Safe Harbor more quickly and securely along in new strategic directions. She was trying to act out her own leadership style, trying to be gracious and decisive at the same time, and trying to position herself for the future, even if the transition was to be a little more protracted than she had wished.

Expanded Views on Alignment

Having observed this conversation, which took about an hour, the larger stakeholder group reversed roles. That is, they entered the center of the room for a conversation, while the core group took seats around the room's periphery. Their conversation was long and complex; we will only note a few of its highlights.

One of the bankers began. He said that he had appreciated Safe Harbor's pioneering history and accomplishments—and, perhaps, the strategic ideas that senior managers had expressed about the future—but the embezzlement and general looseness about financial accountability had not been mentioned. And if accountability had been lacking in the financial area, he asked, might management also be a little lax in other areas? Before shifting strategies, he said, Safe Harbor had to make sure its house was in order. Maybe the next leader should be less a visionary and more a businessman, he averred. There was little bite to this suggestion, though, because he had, in fact, respected the ED. But he had raised the issue of the right fit for the next leader.

Then one of the district directors joined in. She said that she had nothing to add to the discussion about strategic directions—though they seemed exciting, she did think that some of the group home staff would object to adding new activities—but she did have something important to say. In her opinion, there was too much turnover among home staff, which made the group homes less stable environments for residents. If Safe Harbor were going to expand its activities, she thought they should increase the pay for residential home directors, so they could solidify the old business. Maybe that would allow the central office people to expand without worrying about eroding the heart of Safe Harbor. This might also help answer the banker's concern for accountability and solidity.

The head of the board's finance committee joined next. She, too, chided the senior managers for giving such short shrift to Safe Harbor's lax management during the last few years—and, she added, the board's lax oversight of the ED. That said, it seemed clear to her that government trends pointed to the need for larger and more versatile organizations, and she praised the clinical director's proposed directions. But, ignoring what she knew to be the clinical director's aspirations, she proposed that such directions might require leadership characterized by both entrepreneurial daring and financial savvy. Was there that type of leadership within the organization? she wondered aloud. Was there a combination of internal executives who might lead the way, or should they look outside?

Finally, a second district director stepped into the fray. She focused on staffing questions. What kind of staff would be best, she asked, for an increased range of social services? Is the current management capable of training and supervising them? Do the leaders understand enough about these new areas to be as effective as they have been, or should there be new types of leaders?

Core Group Reflection

The ED and both senior managers each admitted that they had glossed over past difficulties. The director of real estate operations then wondered if, in spite of all of their experience and expertise, the Safe Harbor senior management wasn't in need of a very savvy financial/operations person, someone who could translate their future hopes into better defined systems, and who could deal on equal footing with bankers. This suggestion took both the ED and the clinical director by surprise. It felt disloyal. Each said that, in general, they had managed Safe Harbor and its partnerships in state government and financial institutions pretty darn well.

The board member/lawyer jumped in at this point to diffuse the contentiousness and to make a suggestion. Maybe Safe Harbor needed a much upgraded financial officer. This was a bit heretical, since the current officer had been with the organization a long time, worked harder than anyone, and was much beloved. Still, the lawyer insisted, the current officer was essentially a bookkeeper and knew very little about structuring financial deals in the way that might be necessary if Safe Harbor were to expand its service offerings through acquisitions. After several moments of silence, the ED spoke up. She said that she hated the idea but thought it correct. It would enable her to move more effectively into a transition period, and, if the clinical director was ever to become executive director—the possibility was now out on the table for the first time—she would definitely need a financial and operations chief to balance her own skills.

The real estate director immediately supported this statement, seeing it as an opportunity to advance her own projects and to support her friend and colleague, the clinical director. While the conversation was supposedly limited to this small group, all of them could see heads nodding from the stakeholder group around the room. It seemed that a kind of consensus was building.

Stakeholder Group Reflection

Instead of relying on the appearance of agreement, the stakeholder group was asked to return to the fishbowl. There, they rapidly affirmed the main directions the core group had taken: its strategic directions, the type of leadership required, and the slower, one to two years of leadership transition that the ED had wanted. They also emphasized the district director's point that the leaders should not assume that the current organization at the local level (residential homes and community) was the right one for the future. Accordingly, future leadership must have an appetite for organizational change and innovation.

In fact, they wondered if Safe Harbor might have to become more centralized during the upcoming growth period.

PHASE 2: PLANNING

Assessing Readiness for Change

Judging from the fairly rapid movement toward consensus, Safe Harbor exhibits a considerable readiness for change. Recall that there are three types of readiness: positive states, like determination and receptiveness; negative states, like disorganization or confusion; and forays.

The ED is determined to have her legacy and to leave the organization well aligned. The director of clinical services is determined to drive a new strategy, that is, to assume leadership, and others are quick to see the merit in this. They are receptive. The director of real estate operations seems equally pleased with the new strategy and lends her support to a variety of leadership options.

The upcoming leadership transition lends just enough sense of uncertainty to create urgency to the planning and alignment efforts.

There are forays, as well. The director of clinical services has already experimented with expanded services. In one community, for example, she has added outpatient therapy, recreation activities for both residents and other community members, and a housing assistance fund available to nonresidents. Anticipating potential changes, the director of real estate operations has explored the purchase of larger buildings that could serve as both residences and community service centers.

Reflections

All of this is noted by the core group—with the help of a professional facilitator and the concurrence of the larger stakeholder group. In fact, it is the stakeholder group, with its several board members particularly engaged by the conversation's direction, that seems most ready for change. They seem excited by the need to step up to their role in governance, or lay leadership, and excited to take a role in refining the Safe Harbor strategy that has been sketched during the Alignment Exercise. In fact, one, somewhat unintended, outcome of the Alignment Exercise will be to align lay leadership more actively to Safe Harbor's strategy and operations.

Designing the Alignment Plan

The core group is not required, nor would it be able, to design a full set of plans to implement the vision that emerged in the first sessions, but it can set in motion processes that will lead to such plans. Here's what they can do at this first day of meetings.

Design Task 1: Sketch the Alignment Needs. First, they sketch the main areas of alignment work, which looks essentially like this:

- The need for new strategy to fit the changing face of state requirements and community needs. These include expansion and increased variety of services.
- The need to determine what kind of services the communities served by Safe Harbor need and want, and what services state agencies will support Safe Harbor providing.
- The need for leadership that combines firm management with entrepreneurial risk taking.
- The need for a clearly articulated leadership transition plan.
- The need to determine what kind of staffing, staff training, staff recruitment, and operational organization will support both rapid growth and increased variety of services.
- The need to determine what kind of salary structure will support and stabilized the increasingly complex work of middle-level management in the execution of the new strategy.
- The need for a development, or finance, strategy, in order to fund the expansion.

Design Task 2: Establishing Task Forces to Design an Alignment Plan. Second, the core group would propose task forces to take on the research and design in each of the above areas. Ideally, these committees would be jointly led by a board member and a staff member, whose knowledge and portfolios best coincide with the area to be explored. Later, they would then expand committee membership, according to need and preference.

Design Task 3: Developing a Rudimentary Plan for Alignment. Now the task forces go to work in breakout areas of the conference space. They will work for two hours to build a rudimentary project plan to bring their area into alignment with the plan. During this period, both the ED and, if one is employed, the organization development consultant, will roam among the task groups as resources, supplying information—this is feasible; this is the rough cost of such a plan; these are the resources required to execute such a plan—and problem-solving support.

Design Task 4: Task Groups Report to the Whole Group. Each group reported their findings and ideas. The ED decided she wanted to assume leadership for this exercise. With the consultant facilitating, she continued to hone each idea as it was reported. The more the ideas poured in and the longer the exercise went, the more her former malaise seemed to drop away, and the more energized she seemed. To those who knew her, she looked increasingly like the leader they had known a decade ago: clear, decisive, and funny. For years now, it had seemed she was forever telling people how their new ideas wouldn't work—"We tried that some years ago," she would say, "and it didn't really work." Now she took each person's ideas, built on them, and related them to the others. For everyone except the director of clinical services, the experience was exciting. And the ED's leadership seemed in such sync with the moment. The clinical director, on the other hand, was nervous. What if the experience was so good for everyone that the ED decided to stay? This was a question that remained unarticulated and unanswered but cropped up in more than one person's mind during the hour or so of the reporting exercise and during the following weeks.

Design Task 5: Reporting to the Full Board of Directors. According to Alignment Exercise instructions, the core group takes on the task of bringing together and refining the reports, but in this case the executive director was so energized by the process that she volunteered for this task. At first, everyone concurred. But then the director of real estate said that these plans pertained to the future, a future first put forth by the director of clinical services, who might well be Safe Harbor's future leader. Instead of the ED making the presentation alone, the real estate director proposed that she do so in partnership with the clinical director and the board president, who also seemed quite energized by the day's events. Deflated by the suggestion, the ED began to object but stopped herself. "Hold on," she said. "Let me contact that better self we all knew and loved. Yup, she says it's a good suggestion. We'll do this as a threesome." That brought the house down, as applause rang through the old, pea-green-colored conference room, seeming to turn it brighter. "All in favor," said the board president. "Aye," said everyone present.

PHASE 3: CHARTERING

The threesome reported their rough plan at the next board meeting. Since the board's executive committee had fully participated in the Alignment Exercise, the board was already aware of its basic ideas. Perhaps more important, the executive committee had communicated their commitment and their excitement, a form of lobbying, no doubt, and very successful, at that. To an extent, then, the chartering meeting was somewhat of a formality, made more so because of the presentation that the threesome made. They had listened carefully to the criticism about their loose management style and came in with a dazzling PowerPoint presentation, which described the alignment needs and the implementation process—budget, timeline, evaluation criteria, and so forth—in precise detail. In effect, the Alignment Exercise had already begun to act as a change agent.

PHASE 4: IMPLEMENTATION

Senior Management Team Convenes. Two weeks after the board chartered the alignment plan, Safe Harbor's senior management team met to discuss how to implement it. They had attended the Alignment Exercise. They had heard the criticism. They knew that a leadership transition was not too far off. They knew that the board of directors was now more watchful. And they were determined to do a bang-up job on the implementation.

They would champion the plan collectively, they decided. They would do so in a way that kept the organization's values at the forefront. Change was important but so was continuity, particularly as represented by the humane values that had always animated Safe Harbor.

For each item—strategy, market research, and restructuring the local organizations—they assigned an individual champion from among their ranks. Then they decided who among the staff should lead each project. Since the plan was clearly future oriented, they selected project leaders who could and would operate effectively in the organization as they envisioned it two and three years from now—and who exemplified the Safe Harbor culture and values at their best. This meant, at least informally, promoting some of their younger staff, while asking some of the old hands to manage the current, day-to-day operations. Everyone would notice. Some anxieties would be aroused. Feelings would be hurt. But the senior management team was determined to implement the plan effectively and with brio. In keeping with their values, they would attend to the anxiety and hurt feelings but also keep them in a perspective that placed service to their clients first.

As with the whole plan, the senior management team assigned a rough budget, timeline, and evaluation criteria. Each team was then asked to come back to the senior management team with refined plans, which would be discussed and, with revisions, approved.

Projects Established

Those placed in charge of these projects were often a little surprised, not so much about the task itself but at the crispness of the assignment and about the insistence and explicitness of the requirement that all work be in the spirit of Safe Harbor's values. Most Safe Harbor staff had grown accustomed to a good deal of autonomy. Project leaders said they couldn't tell if these assignments, which carried important responsibilities but would be so closely watched, meant more of the same or more supervision. All in all, they were a little nervous but also excited about the responsibility and about the clear empowerment to do their work. To a person, they felt grateful that the senior team thought them worthy and thought them keepers of the Safe Harbor culture.

Alignment Management Team Convenes. Four weeks later, the senior management team met with project leaders. The purpose was twofold: to make sure the refined projects were in keeping with plans, and to make sure the projects were aligned with one another. This group of people then continued to meet monthly for the following year. The camaraderie built at these meetings, even with the tussling to make sure each person's project got its due, became a hallmark of the "new" Safe Harbor.

Alignment Exercise Group Reconvenes. At the end of the first Alignment Exercise day, the board president, with the agreement of everyone present, decided to reconvene the entire group—the core and the stakeholder groups—to monitor progress and make course corrections. They chose a four-month interval, believing that progress could be made in such a period and that waiting longer would diminish the pressure or urgency that they believed useful. Project leaders who had not been included in the first meeting were included in the second.

The second meeting began as the first had. The core group entered a fishbowl; each member analyzed movement toward alignment from his or her own perspective. Again, the ED began. She noted that all the task groups had moved ahead with spirit and efficiency. The new strategy was taking shape. Funding strategies had already been put in place. Reorganization at the local level had begun, though staff reaction and departures had made day-to-day operations temporarily difficult.

Leaving leadership transition for the last, the ED, taking a deep breath, said that a plan had been put in place. With help from the board, a profile of the next leader had been drawn—and it was not her. The profile called for a hard-driving managerial type, who was familiar with a broad array of social services. So she had agreed to step down earlier than she had originally wished and earlier than the first Alignment Exercise meeting had called for. But it seemed right, she said—right for Safe Harbor, into which she had poured so much of her life's energies. And the accelerated letting go had been sweetened: She would be retained as a mentor and consultant for a period of one year. After all, she had so much knowledge and know-how to pass on. No one knew the levers to push in state and local governments the way she did. No one knew how to motivate the Safe Harbor staff as she did.

Stepping in for the original board representative in the core group, the board president, himself newly energized, talked next. A leadership transition committee, composed of board members and the ED, had already begun to interview search firms, he said. The director of clinical services was still in the running. Since the Alignment Exercise day and its acceptance of her strategic suggestions, she had been reenergized. She noted to anyone who would listen that her third and youngest child had just left for college; her time was her own, and she was ready for a big project. The transition committee had charged her with learning as much as she could about service expansion possibilities. For this, they asked her to reduce her day-to-day managerial load for a year to half-time. This served two purposes. First, it would arm her with knowledge and contacts. Second, it would give her time to groom her successor as director of clinical services. Both activities would put her in a wonderful position to be selected the new executive director.

When it came her turn to speak, the clinical director spoke knowledgeably and passionately about what she had learned during the intervening months. All those who knew her understood that, without saying so, she was making her case for leadership. She had the knowledge, the energy, and, as she had demonstrated over a number of years, the ability to manage a large staff.

At this point the board president jumped back in. He emphasized that the clinical director's promotion was not guaranteed. The board wanted to continue asserting its own leadership, not recede into its rubber-stamp past, believing that the alignment of Safe Harbor with its new strategy required a strong dose of community and business-oriented board leadership. Consequently, they were going to follow the leadership search process by the book.

When the core group completed their reports, the stakeholder group again moved into the fishbowl. They basically concurred with the reports but raised important additional issues. Staffing at the community level was still a problem, they said. State agencies were pretty set in their ways. It was not clear to them how Safe Harbor would reinvent itself and persuade state agencies to fund them in new areas. Why wasn't there more progress in finding a financial officer more in line with the rapid growth envisioned by the Safe Harbor plans?

And so the discussion went. It was a working session. The process of bringing this diverse group together was still new, though it now felt familiar. They felt they were on to something—not just for themselves but for Safe Harbor and those it served. Toward the end of the meeting, two of the board members confided that they had been talking up the Alignment Exercise to other boards on which they sat, and these boards had agreed to try the process. As with the end of the first day of meetings, this announcement brought on applause—a little more restrained, but enthusiastic, nonetheless.

13

Inner Alignment and the Experience of Flow in Leadership

The literature on leadership focuses almost exclusively on what leaders do, and not on their internal experience, what they feel. Along with values and rewards, feelings are what motivate leaders to do what they do. The literature that does address feelings tends to do so in a largely analytical and negative form, much as psychodynamic diagnoses consider the neurotic origins of motivation.

For many, if not most, leaders, the boundaries between themselves and their organizations are slim and porous. Their individual identities tend to be entwined with the group's. In fact, leaders are commonly "overidentified" with their organizations. Their moods and sense of well-being go up and down with organizational oscillations. Founding leaders, in particular, have so stamped their organizations with their personalities that staff, board members, and the marketplace often experience them as one with their creations. They are said to "embody" their organizations; their personal history is at the core of organizational history, culture, and mission. They hire those who fit and fire those who don't. They focus their organizations on goals that are aligned with their own. They foster values and cultures that fit their own and implement structures and processes that feel compatible.

Consequently, when organizations are aligned, leaders tend to feel good—engaged, excited, and at one with themselves—and when organizations are not aligned, leaders tend to be ill at ease, out of sorts, fragmented, and unable to rest. They are unable to rest, that is, until they move their organizations onto the alignment track. Without exaggeration, one might say that many leaders don't feel like themselves until their organizations are at least moving toward alignment with their own values, skills, character, and objectives.

When out of sorts and fragmented within, moreover, leaders frequently move through their organization in disruptive ways. Much as their efforts to realign their organizations, when met with positive responses from their stakeholders, can initiate a virtuous cycle—the more one improves, the more the other improves—the opposite is also true. Disoriented leaders can be gruff and abrupt and impulsive, which can generate a vicious cycle—leader and organization reinforce each other in a negative and descending spiral.

This chapter describes the inner experience of leadership at its best. In particular, we call out the experience of leadership in aligned organizations. We began this book saying that organizations in alignment bring out the best in people, and most of all in their leaders. In this chapter, we want to describe what that best feels like.

There are two sections. In the first, we describe three general ways that leaders experience themselves: in an everyday, matter-of-fact way; in hot pursuit of an urgent goal; and in an intentional, almost calculating—some might say strategic—pursuit of victory. These are broad categories and most leaders combine all of them in various proportions. The second section describes the experience of leadership in its optimal form, following Mihaly Csikszentmihalyi's (1990) general description of optimal experience as "flow." Although our description is too broad to perfectly fit any single leader, we believe it comes close to capturing the internal experience of leaders in aligned organizations.

Varieties of Effective Leadership Experience

It would hardly make sense in this book to suggest that there is only one kind of leadership experience, after emphasizing variety as much as we have. We make no such suggestion. We are emphasizing the general experience of successful leaders. Three types of experience have repeatedly surfaced in our research and experience.

EVERYDAY, MATTER-OF-FACT LEADERSHIP

When asked to describe their experience of leadership, most people look puzzled. "Do you mean, what do I do?" they ask. Then they often go blank. Being people who like to succeed, they prod the interviewer to ask questions so they can respond more intelligently. Their response, far from being inadequate, represents an important aspect of leadership experience. They don't imagine themselves as leaders; without that conceptual vessel, they don't readily recognize feelings they have in the course of leadership as a leadership experience.

Many, perhaps the majority, say they never tried to be leaders, and still don't. Gerry Martinson, director of the Big Sisters Association of Massachusetts, put it this way: "I'm a leader because I raised my hand. . . . I didn't decide to be a leader. . . . I raised my hand and I was chosen."

A sizable minority, even after years of being in leadership positions, is surprised to find themselves there. Peter Karoff, founder and past president of The Philanthropic Initiative recalled an early leadership experience that, 40 years later, retains its authenticity: "The first time I realized I was functioning in a leadership role—and it was a huge surprise—it was in Roxbury, following the death of Martin Luther King. That period was such a big part of my life—raising money for social justice and Black power, going to people's kitchens to raise money. . . . It turned out I was leading the group. . . . It just happened and it surprised me. . . . I felt unprepared." Karoff is not alone; many leaders recall similar moments.

When pressed about assuming leadership roles, they say they are ordinary people with an extraordinary sense of duty and efficacy. Here is the gist of their experience of themselves: "I see something that needs doing and I do it. No big deal. I've always been that way. I'm only surprised when others don't behave this way."

These everyday leaders have a powerful sense of duty. Many more than expected are women. In our culture, leadership images are primarily those of men; women leaders often act in an imagistic vacuum and, as they frequently say, invent themselves from scratch. The duty they feel seems to come from traditional aspects of their upbringing. Many women were raised to take care of things—people and situations. They watched their mothers do so. The extension of this behavior in organizations really doesn't feel like a big deal to them. When just doing what must be done in repetitive and competent ways eventually places them in leadership roles, they almost don't think about it. When they do, and when they are made aware of their prominence and effectiveness, they may be proud but also nervous. Someone may criticize them for assuming a role that is not theirs; someone may take it away from them. Returning to a matter-of-fact approach is safer.

For some, taking leadership can be less than ordinary. It can be a step backward. Think of doctors, lawyers, engineers, and many others who develop their craft, develop close relationships with patients and clients, and feel in right relation to their worlds. Often enough, talent and hard work bring success, success brings recognition, and recognition brings offers of promotion. But promotion is in the eyes of the beholder. Many wonderful solo practitioners who are not suited by skill, training, or temperament for management or leadership will nevertheless make the move because they are asked, because they are told they can add even more value to their organization or profession, or because it is the only apparent road to increased recognition. Some may find these management skills within themselves once in their new milieu; many will not.

Alan Shapiro, who loved teaching children, reflects the experience of many people who love what they are doing. At the Children's Therapeutic Day School

(CTDS), the need for his leadership simply arose. Nancy Fuller, then the administrative leader of CTDS, was pregnant and about to go on maternity leave. Shapiro hated the idea of leaving the classroom, where he loved to teach and loved to be with the children. He had long hated leaders, whom he associated with autocracy and abuse of power—how could he, in good conscience, become one of them? Thus he was reluctant to assume the job and let go of his anger and his image of leadership and bureaucracy. But, as he says, it took them nine years to create CTDS, nine years of loving attention, and he couldn't allow an outsider who didn't know and believe in the CTDS way to take the helm. "I couldn't let people trample on it," he said. So he accepted leadership, and almost instantly the job was a good fit because he just continued to do what he did in the classroom. He listened, he held people, he taught. Surprisingly, it was "no big deal."

When asked what he felt, internally, in leadership, Shapiro was confused, a little dismayed. He wanted to come up with a good answer, but none came. He talked about trying his best and accomplishing that. He talked about getting others to try their best, and accomplishing that. That felt good. But when pressed to describe what "good" feels like, he said, "That's what you're supposed to be doing." He named it, the feeling of being in sync and doing what you're supposed to be doing.

There's another way that leadership has an everyday quality for some. It is a discipline: doing the right thing, refusing to be lazy or petty, taking the high ground, and doing it over and over until it is done right. Call this the Zen of leadership. Csikszentmihalyi describes this state as "autotelic," where the goal of the activity is just to do it and do it well, and there is no other reason.

Zen Buddhism preaches an everyday outlook that captures the mindset of these everyday leaders. Instead of seeking far-off goals—fame or enlightenment—Zen asks you to give your full attention to everything you are doing, in the moment, and to do it well. Charlotte Beck's (1989) idea of "everyday Zen" is not far from the leadership practice of a Gerry Martinson. Zen is not alone this way. Maimonides, the medieval Jewish philosopher, is said to have more or less abandoned most of his theological and religious practices toward the end of his life and turned to his medical practice to do good as an end in itself, in small rather than large ways. Abraham Heschel, the twentieth-century philosopher who walked arm-in-arm with Martin Luther King in Southern freedom marches, is said to have increasingly turned away from theology and preaching and toward an everyday discipline of *tsdakah*, which means charity, which, in the Jewish tradition, literally means changing the world.

The simplicity of these three models—living a life, one act at a time, aligned with good, kind, ethical principles, and clear in its practical impact—is very much the experience of everyday leadership.

A Burning Goal

There are people who are so focused on achieving certain goals that there is no experience they call leadership. They are not self-conscious. That is, they are not conscious of themselves as leaders. They are only conscious of achieving or not achieving their goals. Suzin Bartley, executive director of the Children's Trust Fund of Massachusetts, is such a person. She is a person of great immediacy and compassion. In fact, compassion doesn't go far enough in describing how she relates to the suffering of others, particularly children. As she puts it, "I can't screen pain. . . . I can't tolerate pain in others." She has almost no boundaries, and others' pain becomes "unacceptable." She is bursting with a raw, terrible energy. "I have to do something about it." Helping others is one and the same with relieving her pain. Everything else that follows—program development, lobbying, putting together an organization, sponsoring research on childhood sexual abuse—are efforts to relieve the pain, theirs and hers. People like Suzin Bartley and Gerry Martinson lead because they must, because they can't tolerate the world as it is and the pain or guilt they feel inside. It is personal with them. They set out on a course and people follow. They don't try to lead. They exhort others because they can't imagine that others don't feel the same pain they do. They think it entirely reasonable that others follow—what else can one do? They can't conceive that others are following *them*—others are joining a cause that must be joined. Lindalyn Kakadelis, in Charlotte, North Carolina, is like that. Those who joined her fight for poor children did so because they trusted her, but her experience had little to do with that. For her it was a feeling of alignment in common struggle. She thinks of herself as someone doing the right thing and helping others do the same—not as a leader.

Intentional Leadership

Some leaders—Shiela Moore is one—are very intentional. They think through where they want to go and rehearse conversations with stakeholders before launching into them. At the extreme, these tendencies can be manipulative; in moderation, they can be strategic. As highly intentional leaders very consciously set about their tasks, the experience they have can be one of total concentration, much as a scientist or a chess player concentrates. And, when things are working well, they can virtually lose sight of everything except the object of their focus. During these moments of concentration, the world narrows and time stops.

At such times, these leaders are like athletes who are "in the zone." When people are "in the zone," nothing can go wrong. Baskets are "as big as the ocean." You feel, you believe, you can run faster, jump higher, and last longer than the competition. In the case of leaders, everything you say or do brings people on board, motivates them, brings out the best in them, or gets them to join together where once they were at odds. Even decisions that had been hard, that had caused pain, and that had found you waffling, now come easily. You are clear, definitive, and bold. Shiela Moore describes times like this and the joy at the end of an effective meeting when she virtually wakes up and sees that her strategy has worked. But Moore is not as unselfconscious as some. She has the experience of being both fully inside the engagement with her staff and outside, as if observing her interactions in a movie. She is at once conscious and unconscious—trusting fully in her instincts. At the end, when things have worked out well, she sometimes says to herself, "Damn, I'm good."

FLOW

For more than 30 years, Mihaly Csikszentmihalyi, a leader in the "positive psychology" movement, has studied people who like what they're doing, who are motivated to do what they do for the shear joy of it, and who seem to know how to live. The results of his work suggest that there is a universal, positive mental state—he calls it "flow" experience—that is like being carried by the flow of a river: effortless, not requiring exertion or control, and spontaneous, even though the context may be challenging or even dangerous. His book *Flow: The Psychology of Optimal Experience* is well-known. For us, it describes many of the internal experiences leaders feel when they and their organizations are aligned.

Csikszentmihalyi (1990, p. 71) describes the conditions that are conducive to the experience of flow, or optimal experience, again supported by a considerable amount of research:

1. A sense that one's skills are adequate to cope with the challenges at hand.

2. A goal-directed, rule-bound action system that provides clear clues as to how well one is performing.

3. Concentration is so intense that there is no attention left over to think about anything irrelevant, or to worry about problems. Self-consciousness disappears, and the sense of time becomes distorted.

4. An activity that produces such experience is so gratifying that people are willing to do it for its own sake, with little concern for what they will get out of it, even when it is difficult or dangerous.

In his description of optimal experience, Csikszentmihalyi develops a number of themes that we believe are equally applicable to the experience of leadership.

A Sense of Mastery

As we have seen, leaders sometimes have that feeling of being on their game, or in the zone, that sense that they are in control of things no matter the obstacles placed in their path. Csikszentmihalyi calls this a sense of mastery, an infrequent but near-universal experience. "Yet we have all experienced times when, instead of being buffeted by anonymous forces, we do feel in control of our actions, masters of our own fate" (Csikszentmihalyi, 1990, p. 3).

Peter Karoff experienced that when he shifted from his insurance business, during which he dedicated a good deal of time to community work, to a full-time engagement with social justice and charitable giving. He founded The Philanthropic Initiative. "I gave my business life a 50% effort," he says. "TPI got 110%." At TPI, he goes on, there was a "magnificent alignment between my skills and what I was passionate about." There were times when the whole organization was aligned in this way, and they were able to help clients realize their goals. "When that happens, with lots of people doing it, it's really amazing."

Josh Elkin, executive director of the Partnership for Excellence in Jewish Education, both an organization and a national movement, talks about mastery this way. When work is going well, it "feels very good, very positive. . . . The hard work has paid off. I have a good feeling about the sound use of human resources." He has figured out how to find synergies. When he has helped others to work at their best, Elkin himself feels "a sense of empowerment." He believes—not just hopes—that he "can accomplish the next challenge, and the next." He is filled with optimism, not just for himself but for his mission. He and his organization will realize it together.

What Can Be Done Should Be Done

At times the possibility of achievement or mastery was almost enough in itself. Some leaders talk about seeing not only what should be done but what can be done. Call it a sense of possibility, a second sense, or a sense of what is imminent. Peter Karoff, for example, says the one thing that best defines his leadership may be this quality. It "drives" him. "It's always been a visceral sense of what can be done. I have had an instinct of what could be done and what needs to be done. I've always been drawn to it." Often, he can only articulate the goal itself, not the method, and hands it over to others. When they do it, he is often surprised, he says, and pleased. But the next time, the process will be the same; and he will trust that instinct, even without a clear picture of whether what he imagines is possible.

Of equal importance, his staff trusts that instinct. Peter tells stories about others taking his rudimentary ideas and returning months later with completed projects. He's not sure whether they saw the details more clearly than he, right from the start, or, more likely, had faith in him and his foresight. This unstated trust in his initial vision and faith that it can be realized is the bond between him and his organization, the basis of his leadership, and a form of alignment that yields achievement beyond what was thought possible.

Consciousness

Alignment is conscious and not a trancelike rhythm. Csikszentmihalyi (1990, p. 26) defines consciousness this way: "Certain specific conscious events (sensation, feeling, thoughts, and intentions) are occurring, and . . . we are able to direct their course." Consciousness is more that the ability to direct mental energies, moreover, for it includes the ability to observe oneself doing so. One is actor and observer in the same moment. It is an experience common to successful athletes. The night after a game, while reviewing their moves, they can see themselves, as though from the outside, as though they were watching a movie. This is what Shiela Moore describes when maneuvering people and situations to meet the strategic needs of Casa Myrna. Suzin Barley describes similar experiences during legislative battles to preserve the Children's Trust Fund.

One Is Stretched to the Limit

According to Csikszentmihalyi (1990, p. 3), "The best moments usually occur when a person's body or mind is stretched to its limits in a voluntary effort to accomplish something difficult and worthwhile. Optimal experience is thus something we make happen."

Csikszentmihalyi (2000, p. 391) writes elsewhere that in activities that support flow "there is a one-to-one ratio between challenges and personal skills." When the ratio is off, there is relaxation, apathy, or anxiety. Thus, "When a person is at or above his or her mean level of both challenges and skills, the optimal condition of flow is reported" (Csikszentmihalyi, 2000).

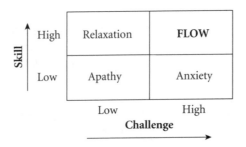

During the course of our research and as we reflect on our years of experience, it has struck us that when leaders are aligned internally and externally there is no talk of vacation (relaxation), boredom or disinterest (apathy), or fear (anxiety). There is only the higher calling of flow, the language of optimal experience.

Bartley talks about situations that have stretched her to the limit—when the funding for the Children's Trust Fund was threatened by Governor Romney and she worked, nonstop, for three weeks to mobilize every resource conceivable to bring CTF back to life; and when she served on the state task force to look into child abuse in the Catholic Church, which "was the hardest thing I've ever done, it pulled me back to childhood; I had to struggle with my own demons even as I struggled with the church hierarchy." She was no rookie, though. She had been in these extreme situations before and knew that if she gave her all, if she totally concentrated her energies, she had a chance to win, and that the combination of effort and winning would yield an indescribably wonderful experience. Those who know and admire her might say that Bartley is a bit of a junkie for these types of experiences, much as those who love extreme sports are compelled to return time and time again to situations that others would find too dangerous, too terrifying.

Exhilaration

Stretching oneself to the limit creates a concentration that is pure and devoid of distractions. During that time, body and mind are oddly quiet. And when concentration, effort, and quiet lead to the goals, the experience is extraordinary. Again Csikszentmihalyi (1990, p. 3): "On the rare occasion when [we do feel that sense of mastery], we feel a sense of exhilaration, a deep sense of enjoyment."

Here's how Bartley puts it: "It's almost physical . . . recognizing that you've been able to effect change on behalf of kids, kids who will never really know you. I get a sense of calm, almost like an internal sense of affirmation. 'Oh gee, this is it, I was right.' When it hits, there's an intense feeling of satisfaction: 'By God, I did it.' At least for a moment, I feel self-congratulatory. I literally jump up and down." She continues: "When I've given as much as I've gotten in life, it's like a spiritual high, a physical high. It's luxuriant in its nature."

A Sense of Internal Order

"The lack of inner order is the subjective condition that some call ontological anxiety, or existential dread," writes Csikszentmihalyi (1990, p. 12). "Basically, it is a fear of being, a feeling that there is no meaning to life and that existence is not worth going on with." For many, the struggles of leadership grow out of a rage against disorder and alienation. Alan Shapiro describes his disappointments during his early work at Head Start. The chaotic and autocratic culture "drove me crazy," he says. "I felt like I could die or kill someone if I continued like that. I needed to do something about it."

On the other hand, Csikszentmihalyi (1990, p. 16) continues, "The optimal state of inner experience is one in which there is order in consciousness." The struggle against anxiety and disorder impels people to take action—an external experience that leads to an internal relaxation and order.

In speaking about a teacher revolt to reform an early 1970s Head Start program, Shapiro says that they worked and planned and worked and planned again—all of which was exciting and energizing—until they had accomplished their mission. "Then it (the program) was aligned. It's like you're balanced, like in Tai Chi. It's a wonderful feeling, very calm, but it's also like nothing. The goal seems less important than the process, the relationships, all of us working together."

A Calling

In private moments, leaders talk about their work as a calling, very much in a religious idiom. It is not something they chose, that is, not entirely. It is as though they were called. And this idea of being called is deeply rooted in Western religious traditions, epitomized by what Abraham Heschel (1955) calls "God's search for man." These leaders hear the call. In fact, some define their leadership in precisely this way: They hear the call to service louder than others. It is not that they are special, or more talented than others, but that they are more intense, more driven, and they cannot rest while they hear the call. They must do the work they are doing. Their cause is just. If they didn't do their work, they could not live with themselves.

Suzin Bartley: "If you have a goal, and make progress, you're feeling, not quite above the fray, it's reaffirming . . . the path you're on is a righteous one . . . about being a good person. . . . It goes back to my Catholic values. . . . We're meant to do for others. . . . Those are the magical moments. . . . I have been part of something that has changed people's lives for the good. It's a gift to me. The gift reaffirms and recharges."

Josh Elkin echoes Bartley's sentiment: "When things are humming . . . after hard work, when we can see the impact of our work, when we can feel competent in our ability to solve problems, I can step back, and it's very validating." He feels validated as a person, a leader, and a member of a movement. They are, at the moment, one and the same.

It is in this spirit that nonprofit leaders appeal to others, to staff, and to funders. They do so unapologetically, as though they were sharing a gift. They feel the work, the ability to spend each day in the service of something they believe in deeply, to be a gift to themselves, and can't conceive that others—at least those with values and feelings—would feel differently. So recruiting and rallying others is responding to the call.

Trusting Oneself

When they are at their best, when they are aligned with their organizational purpose, leaders trust themselves implicitly. Peter Karoff: "I felt best about being a leader when the people around me have taken responsibility and performed at a high level. I didn't realize this until I stepped down from TPI. They told me how much they liked about how I empowered them, though I didn't try. A leader is like an editor or artistic director. He has a well defined sense of what is excellent, what will produce results. He knows when he's been handed something that is really strong. I know. . . . I just feel it. . . . It's instinct . . . a time when I trust myself."

So deep and instinctual is the trust, and so far beneath the level of consciousness, so inarticulate, that leaders surprise themselves with their own certainty and adamancy. And after such moments, they are sometimes startled, as though emerging from a trance.

Overcoming Disorder

Generally, consciousness and order are achievements, as people move from a period of disorder to order. "Whenever information disrupts consciousness by threatening its goals, we have a condition of inner disorder, or psychic entropy, a disorganization of the self that impairs its effectiveness" (Csikszentmihalyi, 1990, p. 37).

This is the psychic or intrapersonal equivalent of nonalignment. Something happens in the environment that disrupts our way of understanding, behaving, and feeling. We struggle to find a new internal alignment. In fact, we cannot rest until we do. In the case of leaders, they cannot rest until their organizations are aligned. In many ways, their internal alignment is dependent on external, or organizational, alignment. And in some ways that is what defines leaders as leaders.

"When the information that keeps coming into awareness is congruent with goals, psychic energy flows effortlessly" (Csikszentmihalyi, 1990, p. 37). Leaders we have spoken to have talked about a sense of internal order—everything being in the right place, like an athletic moment when the whole body seems to work together. They also talk of the internal order being part of an external order. Other people—their staff, other stakeholders—at least for a moment, all fall into place. It is as though everyone's efforts have been choreographed.

Alan Shapiro began to meet with a friend, to plan an insurrection, and to remake the Head Start program in a way that really served the children and their families. The more he planned and the more others joined, the calmer he felt. There was a sense of order and well-being inside. That, he says, is as close as he comes to a defining experience of leadership.

Engagement

During the experience of flow, leaders are fully engaged, single-minded in their efforts, and focused on their goals. These times contrast with others that do not fully engage their attention and abilities. Peter Karoff puts it this way: "I gave my business life a 50-percent effort. The Philanthropic Initiative got 110 percent. At TPI, there was such a magnificent alignment between my skills and what I was passionate about. There were times when the whole organization was aligned in this way . . . when we're working with a complicated client situation. . . . Based on our ability to teach, we help realize this goal. When that happens, with lots of people doing it, it's really amazing" how "effortless" it felt "and how productive we were."

Connection

Not only does the proximate world seem and feel orderly, matching the internal sense of order, but the leader feels connected to it. The experience of connection is as varied as there are leaders and organizations.

Suzin Bartley began by discussing the bonding experience of hard work, comparing it first to war: You've been in the trenches together, fearing pain, fearing defeat; when you win, you feel so close to your team. But closeness, she says, doesn't quite capture the feeling. "There is something about the collective mind, the collective good. Having others with you makes the winning more special. I compare it to the way people have when they have spiritual connection."

Peter Karoff puts it this way: "When people are doing the good work, I love them, I feel immensely proud, I glow—even more than the actual success."

Relation of Internal and External Order

"There are situations in which attention can be freely invested to achieve a person's goals, because there is no disorder to straighten out, no threat for the self to defend against. We have called this state the flow experience" (Csikszentmihalyi, 1990, p. 40). This state leads to connection and to order: "Flow helps to integrate the self because in that state of deep concentration, consciousness is usually well ordered" (Csikszentmihalyi, 1990, p. 41).

Leaders say that during these moments they feel very calm and quiet. There seems to be little to no extraneous noise or activity around them. They feel at peace with the world even during apparently tense moments of negotiation or conflict resolution. Suzin Bartley described this peace: "It's almost physical. Recognizing that you've been able to effect change on behalf of kids, kids who will never really know you. I get a sense of calm, almost like an internal sense of affirmation."

When people are in a state of flow, they are almost entirely in the moment. They are totally focused on what they are trying to accomplish. They lose sight of time. They are not thinking about past failures or about other things they need to do in the future.

A Pattern of Meaning

Csikszentmihalyi (1990, p. 7) describes a common phenomenon: "People manage to join all experience into a meaningful pattern."

Suzin Bartley: "It goes back to my Catholic values. . . . We're meant to do for others. . . . I have been part of something that has changed people's life for the good."

For Alan Shapiro, the CTDS provided a "tremendous sense of mutuality" that "affirmed a vision I have of how people want to live their lives. You're not just going to work, you're going to live, really live. There's meaning."

Affirmation and Reaffirmation of Self

The achievement of goals is immensely personal to leaders, particularly nonprofit leaders. It brings together their values, their need for achievement, their rage at injustice, and their desire to defeat enemies. It confirms that they have taken the right path, something they sometimes doubt during hard times and painful struggles. They put their whole selves into the battle. They feel they must win.

And when they do win, they feel their life is worthwhile. They feel they are good people. They can like themselves. As Bartley says, "it affirms" her very existence. "It makes you feel good about the work you're doing, validates you, and makes you keep going. . . . It makes me feel that all the work I've been doing. . . ." She tears up as she talks about the personal meaning of these accomplishments. She continues: "This is that moment when you realize that there will be thousands of kids who will know better when a pedophile touches them." Since she so deeply identifies with those children, her work is also a way of saving herself.

Refueling

These landmark experiences help people to hold on during all the hard times, the times when little progress is made, when they are feeling out of sorts, when their organizations are out of alignment. Suzin Bartley: "The gift of achieving something great reaffirms me and recharges me for the hard times ahead."

Several leaders have observed that the high that they experience in victory and in common struggle does not last for very long. This is very much like alignment, which is a constant goal, not a constant reality.

Alignment, Inside and Out

We end with a brief portrait of one leader, Pat Brandes, formerly the chief operating officer of the United Way of Massachusetts and currently associate director of the Barr Foundation. We introduced her in Chapter 9. Her description of the internal experience of leadership brings together our themes.

When asked about her internal experience of leadership, Pat says she has two types. One has to do with excitement. "There's an adrenaline rush. . . . The endorphins are pumping. . . . It's like when you're running and you've just gotten past the hard part. So there's a gliding aspect to it. . . . There is also a high. And when you're in [this state] you want to do more. You want to keep going and keep going. . . . Not alone . . . you want to share with others. . . . You're motivated and you want to motivate others." This kind of experience, Pat says, is lots of fun, and she seeks it out. However, it also seems a little tainted because, as she admits, "it is driven by ego." Because it is ego-driven, it can turn downward; in fact, it is likely to cycle downward, and it is hard to recover, and hard to bring your team back up with you.

The second kind of experience begins with "a kind of consciousness of the whole." She can sense or feel the way that everything is working around her. It is exactly as though "the stars are aligned." At such times, there is a pervasive "consciousness of how the world is working together, in harmony." In fact, the world feels harmonious.

Creating or communicating that harmony is "the task of the leader—to tap into that place and help others tap into it." She is aware of her own actions, but they don't feel exactly like her own. "When you're acting, it's not as though you're acting in isolation. The center of the universe is not you. . . . It's more like you're in a ballet. You may be the prima ballerina, but everything is happening because everyone is doing what they're doing." In other words, you are participating in a drama that is larger than you. It's not even a matter of being close to other people. "It's being part of a larger something that is taking place."

And you are not in control of that drama. "You're not really in charge." There is a way to lead when you're in charge but that's exhausting. You are pushing and pulling, and you get very little back. "There's another way where you're unburdened," doing what you must, very focused, very clear, and participating in the right—or the only—way. When this happens, you are given to all the time. Every encounter with another is a gift, which leads to "a sense of well-being." You're being given to all the time. "This is a gift," Brandes says. "I happen to be in this place and everything is falling into place. It's not a burden. It's not up to you. Everything is right. The way it's meant to be."

This is clearly not an everyday experience. "I go in and out of this, but once you have had the experience, you can tap into it." In a phrase reminiscent of Bartley's evocation of the experience, Brandes says that she returns to it over and over again, for herself and for others. "Once you have had this experience," moreover, "nothing else quite satisfies." You must be able to return to it regularly. "So you try to figure out what are the practices and settings that lead to it. For example, stepping back and reflecting on the action is a way to become conscious. It's so much better than just getting caught up in the action. So you have to build your schedule to make room for reflection." This, she says, is one small practice among many.

Then there are the settings that make all the difference in the world. Fit is of paramount importance. Above all things, says Brandes, settings are made up of people. There are "certain kinds of people that inspire that space. . . . If you get involved with people who are into politics—I mean small-'p' politics—they take you down. . . . You can't help it. No matter how strong you are or how hard you try. . . . But if you find settings with people who are capable of beneficence, they help you to see the good . . . they bring you up." They help you sustain this experience.

References

Beck, C. J. (1989). *Everyday Zen: Love and work.* New York: Harper Collins.

Csikszentmihalyi, M. (1990). *Flow: The psychology of optimal experience.* New York: Harper Perennial.

Csikszentmihalyi, M. (2000). The contribution of flow to positive psychology. In J. E. Gillham (Ed.), *The science of optimism and hope: Research essays in honor of Martin E. P. Seligman* (pp. 387–395). Philadelphia: Templeton Foundation Press.

Heschel, A. (1955). *God in search of man: A philosophy of Judaism.* New York: Farrar, Straus, and Cudahy.

Bibliography

Abrahams, N. (1996, December). Negotiating power, identity, family, and community: Women's community participation. *Gender & Society, 10,* 768–796.

Adams, C., & Perlmutter, F. D. (1995). Leadership in hard times: Are nonprofits well-served? *Nonprofit and Voluntary Sector Quarterly, 24*(3), 253–262.

Alexander, L. (1997). The civic entrepreneur: Fixing American giving. *National Civic Review, 86*(4), 287–290.

Alger, H. (1990). *Ragged Dick or, street life in New York with the boot-blacks.* New York: Signet Classics.

Antler, J. (2001). Activists and organizers: Jewish women and American politics. In L. S. Maisel & I. N. Forman (Eds.), *Jews in American politics* (pp. 232–249). New York: Rowman & Littlefield.

Arrien, A. (1993). *The four-fold way: Walking the paths of the warrior, teacher, healer, and visionary.* San Francisco: HarperSanFrancisco.

Ashcraft, R. F., & Yoshioka, C. F. (1997, Fall). Leadership practices of Association for Volunteer Administration members. *The Journal of Volunteer Administration,* 20–27.

Astin, H. S., & Leland, C. (1991). *Women of influence, women of vision: A cross-generational study of leaders and social change.* San Francisco: Jossey-Bass.

Barnett, B. M. (1993). Invisible Southern black women leaders in the civil rights movement: The triple constraints of gender, race, and class. *Gender & Society, 7*(2), 162–182.

Bass, L. (2000, March 29). African-American women pioneers: What makes them tick? *Washington Informer,* pp. 17–43.

Bateson, G. (1972). *Steps to an ecology of mind.* New York: Ballantine.

Beck, C. J. (1989). *Everyday Zen: Love and work.* New York: HarperCollins.

Beckhard, R., & Harris, R. T. (1987). *Organizational transitions: Managing complex change.* Reading, MA: Addison-Wesley.

Beer, M., Eisenstadt, R. A., & Spector, B. (1990). *The critical path to corporate renewal.* Boston: Harvard Business School Press.

Benitez, M. (2001). Hispanic women in the United States. In *The American woman, 1999–2000* (pp. 133–150). New York: Norton.

Bennis, W. (1990). *On becoming a leader.* New York: Random House.

Bennis, W. G., & Nanus, B. (1985). *Leaders: The strategies for taking charge.* New York: Harper & Row.

Berne, E. (1961). *Transactional analysis in psychotherapy.* New York: Grove.

Block, P. (1993). *Stewardship: Choosing service over self-interest.* San Francisco: Barrett-Kohler.

Blumen-Lipman, J. (1996). *The connective edge: Leading in an interdependent world.* San Francisco: Jossey-Bass.

Bookman, A., & Morgen, S. (Eds.). (1988). *Women and the politics of empowerment.* Philadelphia: Temple University Press.

Bowen, W. G. (1994). *Inside the boardroom: Governance by directors and trustees.* New York: Wiley.

Bowen, W. G. (1994, September–October). When a business leader joins a nonprofit board. *Harvard Business Review, 72*(5), 38–44.

Bryman, A. (1992). *Charisma and leadership in organizations.* London: Sage.

Burke, W. (1992). *Organization development: A process of learning and changing.* Reading, MA: Addison-Wesley.

Burns, J. M. (1978). *Leadership.* New York: Harper & Row.

Burroughs, T. (1994, January). Ida B. Wells: A founder who never knew her place. *The Crisis, 101*(1), 43.

Cannon, K. G. (1985). The emergence of black feminist consciousness. In L. M. Russell (Ed.), *Feminist interpretation of the Bible* (pp. 30–40). Philadelphia: Westminster.

Champoux, J. E. (1997). Leadership and the self-renewing organization. In T. D. Connors (Ed.), *The nonprofit handbook* (2nd ed., pp. 374–381). New York: Wiley.

Coles, R. (1993). *The call of service.* Boston: Houghton Mifflin.

Collins, J. C., & Porras, J. I. (1994). *Built to last: Successful habits of visionary companies.* New York: HarperCollins.

Conger, J. A. (1990, Autumn). The dark side of leadership. *Organizational Dynamics, 19*(2), 44–55.

Cortes, M. (1998, December). Counting Latino nonprofits: A new strategy for finding data. *Nonprofit and Voluntary Sector Quarterly, 27*(4), 437–458.

Crawford, V. (2001). African American women in the twenty-first century. In *The American woman, 1999–2000* (pp. 107–132). New York: Norton.

Csikszentmihalyi, M. (1990). *Flow: The psychology of optimal experience.* New York: Harper Perennial.

Cyert, R. M. (1990, Fall). Defining leadership and explicating the process. *Nonprofit Management and Leadership, 1*(1), 29–38.

Dansereau, F., Graen, G. G., & Haga, W. (1975). A vertical dyad linkage approach to leadership in formal organizations. *Organizational Behavior and Human Performance, 13,* 46–78.

Davis, M. (1997, Fall). Latino leadership development: Beginning on campus. *National Civic Review, 86*(3), 227–233.

Deal, T. E., & Kennedy, A. A. (1982). *Corporate cultures: The rites and rituals of corporate life.* Reading, MA: Addison-Wesley.

Delgado Bernal, D. (1998, May–August). Grassroots leadership reconceptualized: Chicana oral histories and the 1968 East Los Angeles school blowouts. *Frontiers, 19*(2), 113–142.

Derrida, J. (1982). *Margins of philosophy* (A. Bass, Trans.). Chicago: University of Chicago Press.

Drucker, P. F. (1989, September–October). What business can learn from nonprofits. *Harvard Business Review, 67*(4), 88–93.

Drucker, P. F. (1990). Lessons for successful nonprofit governance. *Nonprofit Management and Leadership, 1*(1), 7–13.

Drucker, P. F. (1990). *Managing the nonprofit organization.* New York: Harper Collins.

Duckworth, E. (1987). *The having of wonderful ideas and other essays on teaching and learning.* New York: Teachers College Press.

Duhl, L. J. (1997, Spring). Leadership in American communities. *National Civic Review, 86*(1), 75–80.

Dym, B. (1995). *Readiness and change in couple therapy.* New York: Basic Books.

Dym, B. (1998, September). Forays: The power of small changes. *The Systems Thinker, 9,* 7.

Dym, B. (1999). Resistance in organizations: How to recognize, understand, and manage it. *The OD Practitioner, 3*(1), 5–19.

Dym, B. (2001, May). Integrating entrepreneurship with professional leadership. *The Systems Thinker, 12,* 4.

Dym, B. (2003). *Leadership transition in a Jewish day school: A guide to managing the transition to a new head of school* [Monograph]. Boston: Partnership for Excellence in Jewish Education.

Dym, B. (2003, October). *Organizational transitions: From grassroots to professional management.* Boston: Partnership for Excellence in Jewish Education.

Dym, B. (2003). *School development and community integration.* Unpublished research paper. Boston: Partnership for Excellence in Jewish Education.

Dym, B., & Glenn, M. (1993). *Couples: Exploring and understanding the cycles of intimate relationships.* New York: HarperCollins.

Dym, B., & Hutson, H. (1997). Utilizing states of organizational readiness. *OD Practitioner, 29*(2), 32–43.

Eagly, A., Karau, S., & Makhijani, M. (1995). Gender and the effectiveness of leaders: A meta analysis. *Psychological Bulletin, 111,* 3–22.

Egri, C. P., & Herman, S. (2000, August). Leadership in the North American environmental sector: Values, leadership styles, and contexts of environmental leaders and their organizations. *Academy of Management Journal, 43*(4), 571–604.

Eisenberg, P. (1997, Winter). A crisis in the nonprofit sector. *National Civic Review, 86*(4), 331–341.

Elazer, D. J. (1995). *Community and polity: The organizational dynamics of American Jewry.* Philadelphia: The Jewish Publication Society.

Elliot, A. (1996). Ella Baker: Free agent in the civil rights movement. *Journal of Black Studies, 26*(5), 593–603.

Erikson, E. H. (1969). *Gandhi's truth: The origins of militant nonviolence.* New York: Norton.

Erikson, K. (1966). *Wayward Puritans: A study in the sociology of deviance.* Hoboken, NJ: Wiley.

Faderman, L. (1999). *To believe in women: What lesbians have done for America.* Boston: Houghton Mifflin.

Feeney, S. C. (1998, Summer). Humanistic leadership in the 1990s: Heart, soul, and head. *Nonprofit Management and Leadership, 8*(4), 473–486.

Fiedler, F. E. (1967). *A theory of leadership effectiveness.* New York: McGraw-Hill.

Foster, R. (2000, Spring). Leadership in the twenty-first century: Working to build a civil society. *National Civic Review, 89*(1), 87–93.

Foucault, M. (1972). *Power-knowledge: Selected interviews and other writings, 1972–1977.* New York: Pantheon Books.

Friedrich, C. J. (Ed.). (1954). *The philosophy of Hegel.* New York: The Modern Library.

Gardner, H. (1983). *Frames of mind: The theory of multiple intelligences.* New York: Basic Books.

Gardner, H. (1995). *Leading minds: An anatomy of leadership*. New York: Basic Books.

Gardner, J. W. (1990). *On leadership*. New York: Free Press.

Gillham, J. E. (Ed.). (2000). *The science of optimism and hope: Research essays in honor of Martin E. P. Seligman*. Philadelphia: Templeton Foundation Press.

Gilliam, D. (1986, September 22). Black women's blueprint for action. *Washington Post*, p. D3.

Gilliam, D. (1995, February 18). NAACP needs this woman's touch. *Washington Post*, p. B1.

Gilligan, C. (1982). *In a different voice: Psychological theory and women's development*. Cambridge, MA: Harvard University Press.

Ginsberg, B. (2001). Identity and politics: Dilemmas of Jewish leadership in America. In L. S. Maisel & I. N. Forman (Eds.), *Jews in American Politics* (pp. 3–27). New York: Rowman & Littlefield.

Glenn, G. (1997, March 6). Following the leaders: The establishment of leadership development centers in historically black colleges and universities. *Black Issues in Higher Education, 14*(1), 49–63.

Goldman, A. L. (1990, July 29). Black women's bumpy path to church leadership. *New York Times*, p. A1.

Goldman, S., & Kahnweiler, W. M. (2000, Summer). A collaborator profile for executives of nonprofit organizations. *Nonprofit Management and Leadership, 10*(4), 435–447.

Goleman, D. P., Boyatzis, R. E., & McKee, A. (2002). *Primal leadership: Realizing the power of emotional intelligence*. Boston: Harvard Business School Press.

Greenleaf, R. K. (1977). *Servant leadership: A journey into the nature of legitimate power and greatness*. Ramsey, NJ: Paulist Press.

Grogan, P. (2000). *Comeback cities: A blueprint for urban neighborhood revival*. Boulder, CO: Westview.

Gyant, L. (1996). Passing the torch: African American women in the civil rights movement. *Journal of Black Studies, 26*(5), 629–647.

Haley, S. (1996). Nannie Helen Burroughs: The black goddess of liberty. *The Journal of Negro History, 81*(1–4), 62.

Hall, P. D. (1994) Historil perspectives on nonprofit organizations. In R.D. Herman (Ed.), *The Jossey-Bass handbook of nonprofit leadership and management* (pp. 3–44). San Francisco: Jossey-Bass.

Heifetz, R. A. (1994). *Leadership without easy answers*. Cambridge, MA: Harvard University Press.

Height, D., & Trescott, J. (1994, February). Remembering Mary McLeod Bethune. *Essence, 24*(10), 102.

Heimovics, R. D., & Herman, R. D. (1989). Critical events in the management of nonprofit organizations. *Nonprofit and Voluntary Sector Quarterly, 18*(2), 119–132.

Heimovics, R. D., Herman, R. D., & Jurkiewicz, C. L. (1993). Executive leadership and resource dependence in nonprofit organizations: A frame analysis. *Public Administration Review, 53*(5), 419–427.

Heimovics, R. D., Herman, R. D., & Jurkiewicz, C. L. (1995, Spring). The political dimension of effective nonprofit executive leadership. *Nonprofit Management and Leadership, 5*, 233–248.

Helgesen, S. (1995). *The female advantage: Women's ways of leadership*. New York: Doubleday/Currency.

Henton, D., Melville, J., & Walesh, K. (1997, Summer). The age of the civic entrepreneur: Restoring civil society and building economic community. *National Civic Review, 86*(2), 149–157.

Henton, D., Melville, J., & Walesh, K. (1997). *Grassroots leaders for a new economy.* San Francisco: Jossey Bass.

Herman, R. D. (Ed.). (1994). *The Jossey-Bass handbook of nonprofit leadership and management.* San Francisco: Jossey-Bass.

Herman, R. D., & Heimovics, R. D. (1987). The effective nonprofit executive: Leader of the board. *Nonprofit Management and Leadership, 1*(2), 167–180.

Herman, R. D., & Heimovics, R. D. (1990, June). An investigation of leadership skill differences in chief executives of nonprofit organizations. *American Review of Public Administration, 20*(2), 107–125.

Herman, R. D., & Heimovics, R. D. (1994). Executive leadership. In R. D. Herman (Ed.), *The Jossey-Bass handbook of nonprofit leadership and management* (pp. 137–153). San Francisco: Jossey-Bass.

Herscher, E., & Tuller, D. (1990, November 9). S.F. lesbians at top of gay leadership: New supervisors to turn to women's issues. *San Francisco Chronicle,* p. A6.

Heschel, A. (1955). *God in search of man: A philosophy of Judaism.* New York: Farrar, Straus, and Cudahy.

Hesselbein, F. (2002). *Hesselbein on leadership.* San Francisco: Jossey-Bass.

Hill-Davidson, L. (1987). Black women's leadership: Challenges and strategies. Report on the symposium held at the University of North Carolina, Chapel Hill, Spring 1986. *Signs: Journal of Women in Culture and Society, 12*(2), 381.

House, R. J. (1971). A path-goal theory of leader effectiveness. *Administrative Science Quarterly, 16,* 321–328.

Iacocca, L. (1984). *Iacocca: An autobiography.* New York: Bantam.

Jaffe, E. D. (1987). The crisis in Jewish philanthropy. *Tikkun Magazine, 2*(4), 27–31, 90–92.

Jeavons, T. H. (1992, Summer). When the management is the message: Relating values to management practice in nonprofit organizations. *Nonprofit Management and Leadership, 2*(4), 403–417.

Jeavons, T. H. (1993). The role of values: Management in religious organizations. In D. R. Young, R. M. Hollister, & V. A. Hodgkinson (Eds.), *Governing, leading, and managing nonprofit organizations: New insights from research and practice* (pp. 52–76). San Francisco: Jossey-Bass.

Jeavons, T. H. (1994, Summer). Stewardship revisited: Secular and sacred views of governance and management. *Nonprofit and Voluntary Sector Quarterly, 23*(2), 107–122.

Jurkiewicz, C., & Massey, T. (1998, Winter). The influence of ethical reasoning on leader effectiveness: An empirical study of nonprofit executives. *Nonprofit Management and Leadership, 9*(2), 173–186.

Kanter, R. M. (1977). *Men and women of the corporation.* New York: Basic Books.

Kanter, R. M. (1983). *The change masters.* New York: Simon & Schuster.

Kantor, D., & Lehr, W. (1975). *Inside the family.* San Francisco: Jossey-Bass.

Karoff, P. (2004). Saturday morning—A reflection on the golden age of philanthropy. In *Just money—A critique of contemporary American philanthropy.* Boston: TPI Editions.

Keddy, J. (2001, Summer). Human dignity and grassroots leadership development. *Social Policy, 31*(4), 48.

Kerfoot, K. (1997, May–June). Leadership: Believing in followers. *Nursing Economics, 15*(3), 151–153.

Kets de Vries, M. (1983). *The irrational executive*. New York: International University Press.

Knauft, E. B., Berger, R. A., & Gray, S. T. (1991). *Profiles of excellence: Achieving success in the nonprofit sector*. San Francisco: Jossey-Bass.

Kotter, J. P. (1990). *A force for change: How leadership differs from management*. New York: Free Press.

Kotter, J. P. (1996). *Leading change*. Boston: Harvard Business School Press.

Kotter, J. P., & Heskett, J. L. (1992). *Corporate culture and performance*. New York: Macmillan.

Kouzes, J. M., & Posner, B. Z. (1987). *The leadership challenge*. San Francisco: Jossey-Bass.

Lane, F. S. (1990, Fall). The problem of leadership. *Nonprofit Management and Leadership, 1*(1), 75–78.

Laszlo, E. (1987). *Evolution: The grand synthesis*. Boston: New Science Library.

Legoretta, J., & Young, D. R. (1986). Why organizations turn nonprofit: Lessons from case studies. In S. Rose-Ackerman (Ed.), *The economics of nonprofit institutions: Studies in structure and policy* (pp. 196–204). New York: Oxford University Press.

Leibovich, M. (2002). *The new imperialists: How five restless kids grew up to virtually rule your world*. New York: Prentice Hall Press.

Lerner, R. (2002). *Handbook of psychology*. New York: Wiley.

Letts, C. W., Ryan, W. P., & Grossman, A. (1999). *High performance nonprofit organizations: Managing upstream for greater impact*. New York: Wiley.

Levinson, D., Darrow, D., Klein, E., & Mckee, B. (1978). *The seasons of a man's life*. New York: Ballantine.

Lewin, K. (1948). *Resolving social conflicts*. New York: Harper.

Light, P. (1998). *Sustaining innovation: Creating nonprofit and government organizations that innovate naturally*. San Francisco: Jossey-Bass.

Lipman-Blumen, J. (1996). *The connective edge: Leading in an independent world*. San Francisco: Jossey-Bass.

Medding, P. (1997). Patterns of political organization and leadership in modern Jewish communities and their contemporaries. In D. J. Elazar (Ed.), *Kinship and consent* (pp. 371–402). Washington, DC: University Press of America.

Minkoff, D. C. (1993, June). The organization of survival: Women's and racial-ethnic voluntarist and activist organizations, 1955–1985. *Social Forces, 71*(4), 887–908.

Nadler, D. A., & Tushman, M. L. (1989). *What makes for magic leadership?* Boulder, CO: Westview.

Nanus, B., & Dobbs, S. M. (1999). *Leaders who make a difference: Essential strategies for meeting the nonprofit challenge*. San Francisco: Jossey-Bass.

Naples, N. (1992, September). Activist mothering: Cross-generational continuity in the community work of women from low-income urban neighborhoods. *Gender & Society, 6*(3), 441–463.

Naples, N. (1998). *Community activism and feminist politics*. New York: Routledge.

Naples, N. (1998). *Grassroots warriors: Activist mothering, community work, and the war on poverty*. New York: Routledge.

Nordlinger, P. (2001, March). In their own words: Women of color talk about leadership. *Working Woman, 26*(3), 18.

Northouse, P. G. (2001). *Leadership: Theory and practice* (2nd ed.). Thousand Oaks, CA: Sage.

Nygren, D. J., Ukeritis, M. D., McClelland, D. C., & Hickman, J. L. (1994, Summer). Outstanding leadership in nonprofit organizations: Leadership competencies in Roman Catholic religious orders. *Nonprofit Management and Leadership, 4*(4), 147–154.

Odendahl, T., & O'Neill, M. (Eds.). (1994). *Women and power in the nonprofit sector.* San Francisco: Jossey-Bass.

O'Hanlon, A. (1993, April 18). Grass roots and glass ceilings: Women carry civil rights groups but aren't allowed to lead. *Washington Post,* p. C5.

O'Neill, M. (1989). *The third America: The emergence of the nonprofit sector in the United States.* San Francisco: Jossey-Bass.

O'Neill, M. (1992, Winter). Ethical dimensions of nonprofit administration. *Nonprofit Management and Leadership, 3*(2), 199–213.

O'Neill, M., & Young, D. R. (1988). *Educating managers of nonprofit organizations.* New York: Praeger.

Parker, P. S. (2001, August). African American women executives' leadership communication within dominant-culture organizations. *Management Communication Quarterly, 15*(1), 42–82.

Pauley, G. E. (2000, January). W. E. B. DuBois on women suffrage: A critical analysis of his crisis writings. *Journal of Black Studies, 30*(3), 383–410.

Perkins, L. M. (1996). Lucy Diggs Slowe: Champion of the self-determination of African-American women in higher education. *The Journal of Negro History, 81*(1–4), 89.

Peters, T. J., & Austin, N. (1985). *A passion for excellence: The leadership difference.* New York: Random House.

Peters, T. J., & Waterman, R. H. (1982). *In search of excellence.* New York: Harper & Row.

Plummer, D. (1995, June–July). "I'm Si Kahn and I'm an organizer." *Canadian Dimension, 29*(3), 31–34.

Poster, W. R. (1995, December). The challenges and promises of class and racial diversity in the women's movement: A study of two women's organizations. *Gender & Society, 9*(6), 659–679.

Prigogine, I., & Stengers, I. (1984). *Order out of chaos: Man's new dialogue with nature.* New York: Bantam Books.

Reid-Merritt, P. (1996). *Sister power: How phenomenal black women are rising to the top.* New York: Wiley.

Ridge, P. S. (2000, January 6). Nonprofit managers may teach a thing or two to corporate counterparts. *Wall Street Journal,* p. A1, col. 4.

Riesman, D. (2001). *The lonely crowd: A study of the changing American character.* New Haven, CT: Yale University Press.

Robnett, B. (1996, May). African-American women in the civil rights movement, 1954–1965: Gender, leadership, and micromobilization. *American Journal of Sociology, 101*(6), 1661–1693.

Rodriguez, J. (1999, January). Toward an understanding of spirituality in U.S. Latina leadership. *Frontiers, 20*(1), 137.

Romirowsky, R. L. (1999). Leadership styles of Jewish family service executives and organizational effectiveness. *Journal of Jewish Communal Service, 75*(4), 282–290.

Rosen, R. H. (1996). *Leading people: The 8 principles for success in business.* New York: Penguin Books.

Rost, J. C. (1991). *Leadership for the twenty-first century.* Westport, CT: Praeger.

Ruhl, O. (1943). *Karl Marx—His life and work.* New York: The New Home Library.

Ryan, W. P. (1999, January–February). The new landscape for nonprofits. *Harvard Business Review, 77*(1), 127–136.

Salamon, L. M. (1999). *America's nonprofit sector: A primer.* Washington, DC: The Foundation Center.

Schaffer, R. H. (1988). *The breakthrough strategy: Using short-term successes to build high performance organizations.* New York: Harper Business.

Schein, E. H. (1992). *Organizational culture and leadership.* San Francisco: Jossey-Bass.

Schorr, L. B. (1997). *Common purpose: Strengthening families and neighborhoods to rebuild America.* New York: Doubleday.

Schriesheim, C. A., & Keider, L. L. (1996). Path-goal leadership theory: The long and winding road. *Leadership Quarterly, 7*(3), 317–321.

Senge, P. (1990). *The fifth discipline: The art and practice of the learning organization.* New York: Doubleday/Currency.

Sirianni, C., & Friedland, L. (2001). *Civic innovation in America: Community empowerment, public policy, and the movement for civic renewal.* Berkeley: University of California Press.

Stapelton, D. H. (1995, Summer). Pursuit of mission: The rise and fall of elite nonprofit leadership. *Nonprofit Management and Leadership, 5*(4), 236–257.

Steckel, R., & Lehman, J. (1997). *In search of America's best nonprofits.* San Francisco: Jossey-Bass.

Stogdill, R. M. (1948). *Handbook of leadership: A survey of theory and research.* New York: Free Press.

Stone, M. M., & Crittenden, W. (1993, Winter). A guide to journal articles on strategic management in nonprofit organizations, 1977–1992. *Nonprofit Management and Leadership, 4*(2), 193–205.

Turner, F. J. (1985). *The frontier in American history.* Melbourne, FL: Krieger.

Vigotsky, L. S. (1978). *Mind in society: The development of higher psychological processes.* Cambridge, MA: Harvard University Press.

Walters, R. W., & Johnson, C. (2000). *Bibliography of African American leadership: An annotated guide.* Westport, CT: Greenwood Press.

Watson, R. A., & Brown, B. (2001). *The most effective organization in the U.S.: Leadership secrets of the Salvation Army.* New York: Crown Business.

Weiner, A. (1998). Women in Jewish communal service: Can the goal of increasing women in leadership roles become a reality? *Journal of Jewish Communal Service, 74*(2–3), 159–166.

Weisbord, M. R. (1987). *Productive workplaces: Organizing and managing for dignity, meaning and community.* San Francisco: Jossey-Bass.

White, J. (1990). *Black leadership in America: From Booker T. Washington to Jesse Jackson.* London: Longman Group.

Williams, L. E. (1996). Fannie Lou Hamer, the voice of a servant-leader. In L. E. Williams (Ed.), *Servants of the people: The 1960s legacy of African-American leadership* (pp. 141–159). New York: St. Martin's Press.

Woocher, J. S. (1991). The changing character of American Jewish leadership: Some policy implications. *Jewish Political Studies Review, 3*(1–2), 103–114.

Woocher, J. S. (1991). The democratization of the American Jewish polity. In D. J. Elazar (Ed.), *Authority, power, and leadership in the Jewish polity: Cases and issues* (pp. 167–185). Lanham, MD: University Press of America.

Woodson, R. (1994, July 6). For real black leadership, look to grass roots. *Wall Street Journal,* p. 27.

Young, D. R. (1986). Entrepreneurship and the behavior of nonprofit organizations: Elements of a theory. In S. Rose-Ackerman (Ed.), *The economics of nonprofit institutions: Studies in structure and policy* (pp. 161–184). New York: Oxford University Press.

Young, D. R. (1987). Executive leadership in nonprofit organizations. In W. W. Powell (Ed.), *The nonprofit sector: A research handbook* (pp. 324–342). New Haven, CT: Yale University Press.

Young, D. R. (1997, Winter). The first seven years of nonprofit management and leadership. *Nonprofit Management and Leadership, 8*(2), 193–201.

Young, D. R., Hollister, R. M., Hodgkinson, V. A., & Associates. (1993). *Governing, leading, and managing nonprofit organizations.* San Francisco: Jossey-Bass.

Zaleznik, A. (1992, March–April). Managers and leaders: Are they different? *Harvard Business Review, 70*(2), 126–135.

Zander, A. (1993). *Making boards effective: The dynamics of nonprofit governance.* San Francisco: Jossey-Bass.

Zimmerman, J. (1993, Fall). Foundation report: Corporate civic action neglects major social problems. *National Civic Review, 82*(4), 404–406.

Index

effectiveness formulas and, 5
fit concept and, 1-2, 8, 9
holistic leadership
    alignment, 44-45
homogenizing process and, 2-3
minorities and, 7
personal values, 95-97
phenomenology of, 12-13
skill sets in, 97-98
styles of, 37-38, 94-95
types of, 2, 67-68
women's leadership patterns, 6-7
See also Alignment;
    Corporate leadership;
    Cultural narrative of
    leadership; Entrepreneurial
    leadership; Nonprofit leadership;
    Theoretical alignment
Leadership flow, 199-200, 204
autotelic state and, 202
calling, response to, 208-209
case example of, 212-213
connection experience and, 210
consciousness of experience/
    perception and, 206
disorder, triumph over, 209-210
engagement and, 210
everyday/matter-of-fact
    leadership and, 200-202
exhilaration and, 207
goal-focused work and, 203
intentional leadership and, 203-204
internal-external order,
    relation of, 210-211
internal order and, 207-208
mastery, sense of, 205
meaning, patterns of, 211
possibility, appreciation of, 205-206
refueling function and, 211-212
self-affirmation/
    reaffirmation and, 211
self-trust and, 209
stretch to meet
    challenge and, 206-207
Leadership patterns, 135
affective patterning and, 146-147
behavioral patterns, 144
cognitive patterns, 145-146

DNA metaphor and, 135, 147-148
leader-follower interactivity
    and, 137-139
leader-organization relationship
    and, 135-137
leadership system roles and, 139-142
United Way example of, 142-144
See also Alignment practices
Learning organizations, 102, 110
Lehr, W., 102
Lerner, R., 69
Letts, C. W., 55, 57
Lewin, K., 113, 163
Light, P., 51
Literature review, 6-7
Little, R., 56, 57, 82, 145
Living systems model, 109-113

Management. See Professional
    management
Marginalization, 5
hegemonic corporate canon and, 53-
    55
See also African-American leadership
Market forces, 63-64, 83, 106-107
Martinson, G., 119, 200, 202, 203
Massachusetts Family Centers, 79
Melting pot concept, 5
Melville, J., 56
Minority leadership, 7, 54, 68
cultural/community context
    and, 75-76
See also African-American leadership;
    Jewish leadership
Modernization process, 3-4
Moore, S., 15-16, 25-32,
    99, 151, 203, 204
Moral leadership, 96-97
Multiculturalism, 8
hegemonic corporate
    canon and, 53-55
See also Diversity issues
Multiple intelligences, 67

Nadler, D. A., 36
Nanus, B., 36
Naples, N., 76
Nativist ideology, 5

About the Authors

Barry Dym is an organization development consultant, executive coach, psychotherapist, and entrepreneur. His clients range from small nonprofits, high-tech start-up companies, and both public and private school systems to large corporations, such as State Street Corporation, The Boston Globe, Honeywell, and Massachusetts Financial Services.

He was the cofounder of the Family Institute of Cambridge (1975) and the founder and director of both the Boston Center for Family Health (1985) and WorkWise Research and Consulting (1997). For 14 years he served as a lecturer at the Harvard Medical School.

He has written three previous books, *Leadership Transitions, Couples,* and *Readiness and Change in Couple Therapy;* has cofounded a professional journal, *Families, Systems, and Health,* and newsletter, *Collaborative Family Health Care;* and has also written many articles, including "Utilizing States of Organizational Readiness" (with Harry Hutson), winner of the Larry Porter Prize as the best article on organizational development, 1998–1999, "Resistance in Organizations: How to Recognize, Understand and Respond to It," "Integrating Entrepreneurship With Professional Leadership," and "Forays: The Power of Small Changes."

Harry Hutson is a leadership and organization consultant whose practice focuses on the human side of strategic change. He designs and leads systemwide planning events, results-focused workshops, and team-building exercises. In addition, he provides individual coaching for executives.

He performed in senior human resources roles for more than 20 years at three multinational corporations—Cummins Engine, Avery Dennison, and Global Knowledge Network. A former secondary school teacher in Moorestown, NJ, his doctoral research explored relationships between the views of influential people in a local community and what was being taught in the public schools. He has served for many years on the board of directors of the New England Center for Children, a school for autism and other disabilities, where he is the vice chairman.

His publications include articles on team-building methods, continuing education, community building, readiness for change, and the relevance of hope for organizational renewal. He has presented workshops at professional meetings sponsored by organizations such as Training Magazine, Organizational Development Network, New England Human Resources Association, Learning Conference (UK and US), Association for Quality and Participation, and Pegasus/Systems Thinking.